the mating trade

the mating trade

JOHN GODWIN

1973

Doubleday & Company, Inc., Garden City, New York

ISBN: 0-385-02367-7
LIBRARY OF CONGRESS CATALOG CARD NUMBER 72–84913
COPYRIGHT © 1973 BY JOHN GODWIN
PRINTED IN THE UNITED STATES OF AMERICA
FIRST EDITION

1722988

I owe a special debt of gratitute to the four persons who dated on my behalf, in the interest of research and sometimes against their own inclinations.

I also wish to thank the following people for their valuable and often time-consuming help:

Phyllis Guest, Jim Breese, Caren Rubio, Carmel Berman, Bruce Elliot, Pam Melton, Dr. Norman Howland, Sandra Rogers, Police Lieutenant P. Craig, Sergeant L. Fosetti, Edith Libby, Dr. F. R. Hilger, Sarah Malkon, Anna Peirce, Dr. Hugh Whisler, Vicky Grossfeld, Margaret Eastman, Paul Solomon, Richard L. Newton, and the Reverend Clifford R. Whipple.

Finally, at my publishers, I must thank Lawrence P. Ashmead for supplying me with several important leads above and beyond his call of duty.

contents

introduction

This book is a personal report on one of the most rapidly expanding enterprises in America. A business which, quite probably, should not exist at all. The mating trade is founded on loneliness and thrives on isolation in every sense of the word. Over the past two decades it has grown from an obscure fringe operation to a billion-dollar industry functioning within our social mainstream.

In the course of my inquiry I joined a total of fifty computer matching outfits, lonely-hearts clubs, singles organizations, dating societies, swingers circles, escort agencies, matrimonial bureaus, encounter groups, game rooms and correspondence services—aside from a score of singles weekends, seminars, conferences, lectures, public meetings and discussions on the subject.

I also interviewed over two hundred men and women connected with the industry, either as entrepreneurs, employees or clients. Some of these talks are quoted verbatim from the tapes and may startle readers by their unvarnished frankness. A few startled *me*. They bear out the conclusion reached by John Barter, a leading British pollster, who deals with a supposedly more reserved populace:

"People don't mind being interviewed about their sex lives, religious beliefs or toilet paper preferences. But they are reticent when questioned about their income. This is the only subject that people object to being interviewed about."

I can add that most of the persons I quizzed were not only ready but eager to discuss their experiences, including searingly painful, traumatic and sordid episodes. Sometimes their self-exposures had overtones of desperation. As one seemingly very cool California lady remarked in parting: "I've probably talked too much— but where else can you find anyone who actually *listens?* I used to think my analyst did, but now I'm not sure about him either. He's got his own divorce coming up."

The late John Steinbeck put it epigrammatically: "Since Thoreau's time, desperation has grown noisier."

Because of the intimate nature of these disclosures, I had to devise a formula that would protect certain of my informants without detracting from the documentary pattern of this book. This was necessary not merely to spare them embarrassment but—in a few cases—legal consequences. The rule I have followed, therefore, is to give the full and correct names of the people and business firms concerned whenever possible. But when only first names or nicknames are used, I've made sure that they are never the real ones or even phonetically similar. On a few particularly drastic occasions I have also changed the locality.

Portions of this book were researched under false pretenses, so to speak. Meaning that I posed as a client or participant in order to obtain firsthand insights. Sometimes the difference between what the management told me and what actually went on was glaring enough to make any connection appear coincidental.

If the *hows* of the mating trade were fairly simple to fathom, the *whys* proved exceedingly difficult. For the real questions here concern the industry's fundamental reasons for existence. Why, in an age and country of unsurpassed communications, do we have a vast, intricate and costly system of enterprises just to get men and women in touch with each other? And why does this system keep growing almost as fast as our expressways?

The people directly engaged in the industry were the least able to clear up these points. They hadn't given them a thought. Sociologists and psychologists supplied only partial answers, mostly founded on personal pet theories and sometimes on an appalling ignorance of the situation. The most revealing replies invariably came from the rank and file—the paying customers. Their views, however, suffered from narrowness of vision. They saw only their own little problem areas and were largely unaware of the general picture.

The answers I assembled will be found under the relevant chapter headings. Together they add up to a strange and frightening malaise that is peculiar to America in the second half of the twentieth century and for which no name has yet been coined. You could call it Jet Age Isolation.

It springs from cities with decaying centers, whose streets lie deserted at night while millions sit alone at home, watching life flicker past on television screens. From towns that are places only on the map, but in reality freeway systems bearing houses as peripheral afterthoughts. From traffic lights so timed that only the quickest pedestrians can scuttle across before the street once more belongs to its true masters on wheels.

It is spawned in the hundreds of semirural communities for whom the trains have ceased running and the airlines never started, leaving them cut off except for autos. In the fear that pervades the entire land when darkness falls, rendering the heart of Philadelphia as lonely and shadow-haunted as a suburban bus stop. The fear that has ended evening strolls, that has emptied the parks, that forces men and women into their private rolling fortresses where they are safe as long as they keep moving. And where they can't meet each other.

The mating trade is a by-product of this mysterious ailment; its growth reflects the progress of the malady. It could be called a symptom or a palliative, according to choice. It certainly is no remedy.

John Godwin

the mating trade

one

ENROLL AND ENJOY

In the fall of 1970, the "Singles King" of Washington, D.C., retired from business. He was thirty years old and—reputedly—a millionaire. To roughly 50,000 youthful Washingtonians his name still suggests visions of joy that now seem as passé as the "Ask not what your country . . ." glory of Camelot.

Mike O'Harro possessed the rare knack of knowing when to get into a scene and when to exit. For five years he and his partner ran what was probably the finest get-together operation in the United States. Then, just as the action began to go sour, he departed. Leaving behind an untarnished image and a glow of nostalgic memories.

Their enterprise was born in 1964, when O'Harro and his friend Jim Desmond were Navy ensigns stationed in the capital. Washington and vicinity bulged with young unmarrieds who had poured in during the Kennedy administration. Most of them were still semistrangers in town, avid for social contacts. The two ensigns had a house in Arlington, Virginia, where they threw weekend parties. The gatherings grew so huge that the hosts were forced to rent larger premises, charging each male guest a dollar to cover expenses. As O'Harro remembered: "When we figured everything up the next day, we couldn't believe it. We had actually made money!" The result of this discovery was the formation of JOPA (Junior Officers and Professional Association), a ghastly title for a delightful outfit. JOPA began strictly as a party-arranging venture, but in due course its founders added several singles bars to their armory. One of them, the Beowulf, is still owned by Desmond.

In its heyday JOPA had a membership scroll of 50,000 names, and on party nights it seemed as if every member was present, having paid three dollars a head for the privilege. According to quite unverifiable estimates, these bashes brought about more than 500 marriages.

Yet at no time did members have the feeling of participating in activities designed for profit. *That* was the essence of the magic wrought by the entrepreneurs. One former habitué summed it up for me: "You forgot all about the door charge the moment you got inside. Mike and Jim were there, circulating and flirting, and we considered ourselves private guests at an outsized house party. There was something about those guys—like they were friends of ours. They *belonged.* They were the kind of fellows we'd have invited home to meet our sisters, if you know what I mean."

O'Harro felt much the same way about his clientele. He had planned to expand JOPA to include singles apartments, nightclubs and a travel service. But although he was coining money, he abandoned his gold mine the moment the vibrations went bad. That was when a different influx began to show up. Conventioneers—married and out for a one-night stand before returning to respectability—transistorized teen-agers, amateur hookers . . . what Washingtonians call the Fourteenth Street crowd.

JOPA was dissolved and O'Harro sold his interest in the bars. But he had started a trend that is booming from coast to coast.

The trend is organized, packaged, money-at-the-door sociability, designed to enable unattached men and women to mingle in more or less congenial surroundings. These affairs differ from the traditional balls and dances by not admitting couples. They are—officially, at least—reserved for single patrons, and their rapid spread arose out of a profound national need. What propelled them—and the entire commercialized meeting syndrome—into their current prominence was a shift in demographic patterns that has affected the greater part of our population.

According to the U. S. Census of 1970, the largest number of Americans today are neither urban nor rural dwellers, but suburbanites. Since the early 1950s, when the outward migration began to gather steam, the number of suburban residents leaped from thirty-five million to seventy-six million, which amounts to the greatest population movement in the annals of this country. (Contrary to a widespread idea, Americans have never, at any time, been a nation of city slickers. Until a few decades ago they were predominantly small-towners. The real urbanites of the world are the English and the Australians—whose popular image is the exact opposite.)

The swing to exurbia deeply disturbed our prevailing courting and marriage habits. Hitherto these were largely governed by what sociologists term "residential propinquity"—meaning the closeness of the partners' homes. In big cities as well as small towns about a quarter of all marriages involved people living within five blocks of one another. Nearly half of all married couples had grown up inside the same three-mile radius. Their families knew each other, at least by sight or reputation. They were not, in other words, marrying absolute strangers.

Any uprooting process would have upset this pattern. But an additional factor turned it into something like a state of mass disorientation. Sociologist Dr. David Koban described it as "the breakdown of our mechanisms for convergence." By which he meant the withering away of places where the sexes can meet.

Most suburbs today are no longer "dormitories with shrubs." Since between 40 and 60 percent of the people living in suburbs also work in them, these erstwhile bedroom tracts are now dotted with industrial plants, towering office blocks, shopping complexes, sports stadiums, schools and medical centers. In daylight they seem supremely self-contained, requiring nothing from the focal cities that spawned them. But when night falls they turn into oddly checkered graveyards—vast expanses of darkness interspersed with glaringly lit, totally deserted business slabs, as inviting as glass and concrete mausoleums.

Given our freeway system and degree of motorization, this wouldn't have mattered unduly if the cities—the actual *urbs*—had continued their roles as centers of social activity. As it happened, however, they fell victims to an ailment known as urban decay. There is an interrelation between the flight to the suburbs and the decaying blight of the cities: One constantly stimulates the other, though which came first appears as insoluble as the question of the chicken and the egg.

The prime manifestation of the rot was the physical danger of the streets. Today the central sections of New York, Detroit, Washington, D.C., Philadelphia, Cleveland and Los Angeles are considerably more perilous than the Ituri Forest of the Congo.

As these conditions tended to keep people at home after dark, they also triggered the wholesale decimation of popular entertainment spots. Those great traditional mingling barns, the downtown ballrooms, were virtually wiped out. The same fate befell another American institution—the hotel cocktail dance—which has almost gone the way of the buffalo.

The newer discotheques provided no substitute for either. There are, for a start, only a handful of them, entirely confined to half a dozen of the largest cities. They are also too noisy for conversation anywhere below shrieking pitch. And to round matters off, a good proportion of them have opted against single patrons by imposing a strict "couples only" rule.

For some fairly unfathomable reasons, America never developed the two splendid meeting places of the Old World: the English neighborhood pub and the European street café. Despite lukewarm beer and lunatic liquor laws, the Englishman's—and woman's— "public house" functions almost as an extension of their living rooms. It has neither a sexual nor an age bias, and there isn't the slightest stigma on a single lass of any vintage dropping in for a snort of something or other. Just how well the pub plays its part was shown by a recent poll conducted in England. It turned out that over 19 percent of the married couples questioned had first met each other at their local "watering hole."

The café functions even better, chiefly because it keeps longer hours and serves anything from champagne to hot chocolate. Émile Zola went so far as to call it "the greatest man-made contribution to human happiness ever conceived," and he may have a definite point there.

The café is the meeting ground *par excellence*, regardless whether you are meeting for the first or five-hundredth time. It caters equally to the married, the casuals, and the would-be daters of all sexes (quite apart from those who come to do their school homework, write their memoirs, nibble hard-boiled eggs, solve crossword puzzles, found a political party, or drink themselves into oblivion). It's a ready-made slice of social life served up daily at bargain prices. And it has never been successfully transplanted to the United States.

Although cafés have been springing up here since the 1920s, they somehow failed to strike roots. Either they remained empty and died of malnutrition, or they were thronged and eventually priced themselves into the luxury bracket. The popular ones often adopted the odious custom of assigning patrons to their seats, so as to cram in the maximum number. This led to the segregation of solo guests at dispersed single tables and killed impromptu socializing stone dead.

A minute sprinkling—a few dozen in the entire country—did retain their original café concept. But over the past five years the urban blight finished off at least a quarter of them. I personally witnessed the demise of one of the best—the Café Figaro in New York's Greenwich Village—and a melancholy spectacle it was. The premises were taken over by a snack-bar chain, which provides about as much conviviality as a bus terminal. Last time I went there the walls were propped up by rows of muddy-eyed, ashen-faced kids, so obviously "zonked out" that they looked like extras from a documentary on the great American dope opera.

The U.S. equivalents of the cafés, the bars, hardly rate as meeting spots. Being lineal descendants of the old-time corner saloons, they have retained much of their acrid masculine air, despite the disappearance of cuspidors and sawdust. The onus on "unescorted females" still lingers over them powerfully enough to keep the ratio between the sexes at around ten to one.

Even if the numerical balance were better it would hardly improve things. For the average Stateside bar might have been built by a confirmed misogynist for the express purpose of keeping the genders apart. It is a drinking machine, pure and simple, with seating arrangements that make it difficult to view the other patrons and enable you to talk comfortably to only one person: the bartender. Stygian darkness prevents you from recognizing any but the nearest faces, as well as from reading a newspaper (no room to spread it, anyway). So you sit, gazing straight ahead, either at a television screen or at a cascading technicolor landscape advertising beer.

True, we have the so-called "singles bars" (which I shall discuss in a later chapter), where conditions are more congenial. But these are so highly concentrated in a few sophisticated city areas that their effect on the general situation is negligible.

Thus at precisely the time when millions of Americans were shifting into the alien environment of the suburbs, they also lost a large proportion of their get-together facilities. Combined with a steep decline in movie-theater attendance (another once-popular mingling scene) this created an immense social gap.

Into this void moved the professional matchmakers. Commerce, as much as nature, abhors a vacuum.

I use the word "matchmaker" here in a very loose sense. Most of the outfits concerned merely bring together swarms of allegedly-compatible people, the "match" being only a gleam on the horizon. But the demand for the social mechanism they provide is such that these groups multiply faster than a researcher can follow (a fairly complete list I drew up in April was already outdated by September). They may number a few dozen members or several thousand, earn large profits or barely break even, rent entire buildings or meet in someone's front lounge; their basic purpose is always identical: to bring the sexes together.

Some of these groups prescribe a certain homogeneity of membership. There are the Stratoliners, Tip-Toppers, Skyscrapers and Peakers for men and women around the six-foot mark; the Alumni for college graduates, the Co-opers for members of co-op stores, the Walnuts for vegetarians, and the Balkaneers for folk dancers. There are groups for single hikers, single nudists, single bridge players, single linguists, single dog and cat owners and single occultists; quite apart from specifically political and religious formations intended for single Catholics, Protestants, Jews, Democrats, Republicans or Socialists. There are Confederate Singles and Agnostic Singles, globetrotters and city boosters. There was even one short-lived body composed entirely of unmarried burglary victims.

The vast majority, however, impose no limitations of any kind. Even the essential attribute of singleness isn't checked out. If an applicant puts it down on the application form, the organizers are happy to take his or her word for it. The reason, of course, is that these are profit-making ventures. The idea is to fill the available premises with paying participants—let them sort out the personal details among themselves.

Unlike the dating clubs, these enterprises do not effect introductions or attempt matchings. They merely provide a setting and leave whoever chooses to enter to their own resources. Which, by and large, makes them good hunting grounds for the socially aggressive and purgatories for the timid.

The heavyweight in that league at the moment is Saki's Ltd. of New York, which in an average year sponsors around 250 affairs drawing over 100,000 people. Its cofounders and directors are a remarkable pair, whose names make them sound like an adagio team: Saki Grigorovich and John Juliano.

Miss Grigorovich, a very intense lady in her early thirties, was born in the Ukraine, spent a nightmarish childhood in a Nazi internment camp, and arrived with her parents in the United States in 1952. She not only graduated from Jersey State Teachers College and gained her Masters at New York University, but also became an accomplished murals painter.

She met her partner John Juliano at N.Y.U., and together they formed Saki's around a formidable nucleus of personal friends. "Or rather they were Saki's friends," Juliano put in. "She had about a million of them."

Juliano stands in complete contrast to his codirector. New York-born and -bred, he served in the Navy, trained as a physiotherapist, and worked as manager for several pharmaceutical companies. Tall, curly-haired and soft-spoken, the father of three sons, he seems to spend most of his working hours attached to a telephone receiver, answering an endless stream of inquiries—relevant and inane—with smiling unflappability.

He is capable of taking calls in the midst of a narration, discuss several unrelated subjects and return to his theme without losing the thread. You get the feeling that he would have made an excellent personnel chief. You also get the feeling that he could use a competent secretary.

"Our main problem is finding suitable premises for our functions. I scout around all the time, looking for them." He ran his hand over his wavy mane. "They have to have—*meetability*, if there is such a word. They must be large enough so they don't get too packed. People must be able to circulate without using their elbows. But they shouldn't be so vast that people feel lost in them. Also—there should be nooks to retire to. That's important—a bit of privacy."

He smiled, settled another telephonic emergency, and continued: "Then you have to make sure the atmosphere is right. I mingle with patrons all the time, listen in to their complaints, and we adjust the settings accordingly. It's a constant hassle. Nightclub proprietors have this mania about dimming lights—part of their mystique, I guess. I keep saying 'No, turn them up. People want to *see* who they're meeting.' And then . . . excuse me—" He was back on the telephone. Briefly, this time.

"And then there's the music. Bands are inclined to get too loud —they drown out everything else. I try to make them keep the sound down to conversational pitch. People want to hear them-selves talk. Well, some of them, anyway. So we compromise. Turn the volume way up for the kids—they don't care much about talking. And tone it down when we have the older set . . . excuse me."

When I left he was once more smiling unflappably into the telephone.

Saki's organizes between four and six events a week. The settings vary from midtown Manhattan ballrooms, Upper Eastside bars and town-house flats to chartered excursion boats on the Hudson River. Usually the patrons are divided into Younger Set (20–30) and Older Set (27–49), though no one is asked to produce a birth certificate. Members get special admission rates—mostly two dollars, compared to three dollars for outsiders.

As I surveyed the locales, I had to admire Juliano's selections. Size, layout, lighting, music and air conditioning were invariably just *right*, security effective without being obtrusive. Even the sex ratio averaged the ideal fifty-fifty. He couldn't help the abrasive grittiness of the atmosphere, the peculiar mixture of bumptiousness and desperation that hangs over every New York gathering.

Saki's is strong on dress; its brochures feature the slogan, "Dress Well and You'll Be Treated Well." Consequently, its patrons are the most stylish in the entire singles scene. There is a total absence of hairy male forearms protruding from short sleeves. The girls wear cocktail dresses, pants suits or hot pants beneath coifs that look as if they had been poured over their heads with icing sugar.

One of Saki's events can serve as a fair sample. It was held at *La Martinique*, a huge nitery capable of absorbing a thousand or so guests, with two bands playing in relays, an immense dance floor and enough secluded corners to accommodate half the crowd.

The first impression was of a kind of rotation milling, like an ant heap being stirred clockwise by an invisible spoon. But very soon a definite pattern became discernible, a minuet of encounters that lasted throughout the evening.

There was an inner ring, the circular bar, occupied chiefly by men, and an outer ring, consisting of tables, dominated by females. Between these two circles lay a neutral belt, reserved for amblers and leaners of both sexes. The meetings that occurred inside this

zone had a cursory ships-passing-in-the-night air, leading—perhaps
—to an exchange of blink signals, but little else.

The purposeful movement was embodied by men strolling round
and round the outer ring of tables, peering at the faces of the
seated ladies—sometimes stopping to stare with the feral intensity
that comes from myopia. If what they saw pleased them, they
asked for a dance. The acid test, so to speak, took place on the
dance floor; the result becoming apparent after the music stopped.
Either the male would deposit his partner back at her table and
leave her there to resume his prowling. Or he would squeeze in
beside her and order drinks for both. The table, apparently,
symbolized at least a temporary commitment. I never saw a girl
ushered from the dance floor to the bar.

Both sides excelled in the abominable manners with which New
Yorkers manage to make life just a little more depressing for
each other, their daily dress rehearsal for the apocalypse.

I watched a small, balding man approach an angular redhead for
a dance, asking once, twice, three times in a voice growing pro-
gressively squeakier. Having gazed straight through him twice, the
flame-haired lady waved her thumb westward and replied: "Go on,
take a walk, shorty."

Turning to me, she added indignantly: "The noive of some
people!"

I agreed with her.

A few minutes later I saw her counterpart in action. A husky
young man, wearing sideburns and a canary-yellow jacket, who
leaned over a table with two girls and threw a dance offer in their
general direction. One of the girls arose, which caused him to bellow:
"Shit, not *you*—HER!"

His choice duly followed him to the floor.

I took the opportunity to get into conversation with the reject.
She looked like a plump little mouse and appeared singularly un-
crushed by the experience. Her name, I discovered, was Shirley. She
lived in Brooklyn, where her father owned a prosperous stamp
shop. Her father, it turned out, was largely responsible for Shirley
attending every singles function within subway distance. She was

too nervous to drive. Anybody, she explained, would become nervous living with *her* father.

"Once he signed me up with one of those matrimonial bureaus," she related. "But without telling me. So all of a sudden these men start ringing me. They all claimed they knew a distant cousin of mine, or someone. And they came to visit. But they never flirted with *me*. All they wanted to do was talk to my father. 'How's the stamp business going these days? Very good, I hear.' That's how it went all the time. My father tried to switch them over to me. Sometimes he'd try and sneak out of the room and leave us alone. But they weren't having any of that. 'Oh, please, do stay. You're not disturbing us at all.' Then back to stamps it was."

Shirley sighed, mouselike. "Oh, one of 'em did take me out. For a cup of coffee. On account he had blood pressure and wasn't allowed to drink. We talked for a while."

"What about?" I asked.

"What about? About my father and his goddamn stamp business!"

Shirley belonged to Saki's "Old Guard," the stalwarts who rally to every occasion, including the theater parties and singles weekends thrown by the organization. Next summer she was planning to participate in Saki's vacation program (five days in Acapulco for $219). She was one of the thousands of people whose entire social life consists of such activities. To her a party meant a gathering that charged admission. She couldn't recall having been to one of the "other kind" for years. She wasn't even sure that they existed any more . . . "I never seem to hear of them," she mused. "You mean on birthdays and like that?"

I met her male equivalent in the washroom. He was inhaling something from a phial stuffed up his nostrils to relieve a sinus condition. A rotund gentleman in his forties, who talked with a postnasal drip. His baby-blue sweater, sprinkled with zodiac signs, didn't mash with his pudgy, *angst*-creased accountant's face.

"Sure, I know a lot of the people here. You get the same bunch turning up week after week. A lotta drags. This whole scene's a drag, if you ask me."

"Then, why bother to come?"

He switched nostrils and sniffed deeply before replying. "I'll tell you. I'm divorced. I pay alimony and child support. My ex-wife sits on her arse and gets half my salary. And half of that goes to her scientology classes. Mfffff." He gave a final sniff and pocketed the phial.

"So I can't afford to get hooked again, you understand. You get a steady girl friend and before you know it she's talking marriage. I can't afford it. So I come here and play the field.

"The thing is," he said, "to latch on to the newcomers. All the regulars do that."

"And how's the response?"

He wagged his hand, *Fiddler on the Roof* fashion. "So-so. If they live way out somewhere and you've got a car, you do pretty well. Once you've driven them home they *have* to ask you inside, more or less. Till then, you gotta play it cool. Otherwise they get scared. This is a scary town, you know. Everybody's scared. I'm scared too. We're all scared." His face brightened. "Listen, are you a doctor by any chance? Is there anything in this about sinus being psychosomatic?"

I told him I wasn't a doctor. After that, his interest in me weakened. He said, "See ya around," and went off to catch newcomers.

I kept my eyes open for the particular aspect he had mentioned and saw that he was right. The regulars tended to pass each other with casual nods, rather like fraternity members exchanging recognition signs. But they pounced on the fresh meat, the greenhorns, arriving with dew on their brows and unsullied hopes in their hearts. Both male and female veterans became fellows of the chase, using the same opening gambit: "This your first time here?"

The physical scene, I found, was almost identical at these events throughout the nation. Same setting, same music, same territorial divisions, whether you joined the Singles II in Washington, Servetus in Portland, the Sunshine Club in Miami, the Ambassadors in Chicago, the Stardusters in Houston, the Mixers in Cincinnati, the Executives in San Francisco or the Round Table in Los Angeles. What differed was the atmosphere. It grew more relaxed, less overtly predatory the further west I went. The undercurrents remained, but the veneer of jollity didn't crack so fast.

Management had nothing to do with it. Nor had liquor consumption. One of the most slapdash and simultaneously moistest affairs I attended was also the least tension-plagued. This was the annual Bachelor Rally in New Salem, North Dakota, which rather resembled a Grand Ole Opry production of *Li'l Abner*.

New Salem is a prairie town of fewer than one thousand inhabitants, set in the ranch country near Bismarck. It has three motels and what appears to be a ratio of one bar per ten adults. The Bachelor Rally began as a hoax in 1967, when an anonymous letter writer sent out notes to various cities announcing that the town housed fifty bachelors, each with a ranch worth $100,000, just a'rarin' to get wed. This resulted in an invasion of eligible females, which filled every available accommodation inch in town. The unwed rancheros turned out to be fictitious, but such a good time was had by all that New Salem decided to formalize the stampede.

Four days each June are turned over to the Bachelor Rally, when the local population triples under the impact of eligibles and the backdrop becomes a cross between carnival and rodeo, with slight bacchanalian overtones. Every person on Main Street seemed to clutch a beer can, at least half wore cowboy hats and spectacles. The average age of the gathered bachelors and 'ettes was around fifty. No one introduced anybody. They met, they talked, and frequently walked off arm in arm. The only discordant sounds came from the loudspeaker, which suffered from adenoidal valves.

The folks who met in New Salem were nearly all small-towners with severely limited social opportunities. Their aim was to find marriage partners, which they achieved at an amazing rate and often within forty-eight hours.

It was this basic identity of aims that gave the prairie Rally its friction-free character. Every other singles event I witnessed was rent in twain by the same hoary dichotomy: the women seeking some form of durable liaison, the men instant and noncommittal sex.

Women's Liberationists may object to the above statement. They could argue that the female sex drive has been proven at least as strong—probably stronger—than the male's; that women are merely *conditioned*—by custom, propaganda and economic inequality—to search for permanence. This may well be true. But it is a truth that has not, as yet, percolated down into the broader strata of American femininity. Even in the most casual dating situations, girls tend to weigh the long-term potentials of their partners—if only as a mental exercise. Women who deliberately set out to catch themselves a bedmate for that particular night are still somewhat scarce.

They do exist, of course, and sometimes in bewilderingly unlikely guises. I met several of the breed while researching this book, and none of them even remotely resembled the popular conception of a nymphomaniac.

One of the most memorable was a tiny New England schoolteacher, with curly hair, a rosy infant's face and an awe-inspiring I.Q. She talked in a thin, dead-level voice, never smiled, and could easily have passed as one of her own pupils.

We were discussing Boston's colonial architecture, when I saw her toss a casual wave to a man passing our table. I asked whether she knew him.

"Slightly. Fucked him last week. He wasn't much good, though. Conked out after ten minutes." She pondered gravely for a moment and added: "I think his name is David."

That evening I was lucky enough to meet not only David, but another of the teaching lady's discards. Their accounts tallied in every respect. She had approached them, danced with them, taken them home, slept with them, and finally turned them out in dawn's early light. At subsequent events she had ignored them. We watched her depart, towing yet another stud, destined—no doubt —for a like fate.

A second case was a middle-aged receptionist in San Diego; stout, russet-colored and excruciatingly arch. She crooked her little finger when raising a glass, said "oops, pardon *me*" when hiccuping, and "heck" when she meant hell. A curiously rococo air surrounded her. She used lavender scent and tortoise-shell haircombs, habitually wore white gloves and referred to male visitors as "gentleman callers." She even had the genteel gluttony of the bloomer period, consuming Gargantuan meals in ladylike mouthfuls, exclaiming—between mastication—about the deliciousness of whatever she was putting away.

After a few drinks, however, her conversation became anatomically detailed. She produced a string of chatty anecdotes about the one or two dozen gentlemen she had met at singles balls, each of whom was "perfectly daaarling" and—somehow—ended up in her bed. Occasionally there were mishaps:

"He was a daaarling person, really, a psychologist. Big bush of white hair and those striking brown eyes. Brown eyes turn me on like anything, did you know that? Blue eyes do, too. Yes, well, it didn't work out so good, unfortunately. I was already undressed—staaark naked, you know—and I think I must have excited him too much. He came—you know, ejaculated—all over the sheets. Well, it just crushed him. Nothing I could say did any good. He left shortly afterwards. Poor daaarling—he was so terribly ashamed."

In her other cited instances the action went according to plan. She had a better memory for occupations than for names. The string included an insurance promoter, a driving instructor, the owner of an obedience school for dogs, an engineer and one gentleman of undetermined background called Albert.

She provided a striking example of the ease with which sexual roles can be reversed. The only requisite is a slight adjustment of attitude. From what I gathered, she had gone through one bout of wedlock and harbored no desire for repetition. Nor did she seem to attach much value to binding relationships. Hers was the true hunting spirit—each strike signified a conquest as well as a source of retrospective amusement.

What she lacked in youthful appeal she compensated by flattery, another tested male recipe. She laid it on with a trowel, using verbal frills only those totally devoid of humor have the courage to utter. The line has worked on women for centuries (read Casanova's *Memoirs* for some of the choicest blossoms), and apparently goes over equally well with men.

The trait shared by these two dissimilar ladies was their eagerness to talk about their experiences, even with an almost total stranger. If this proved anything, it was the absence of any real stigma attached to their behavior. On the contrary, some of their revelations sounded suspiciously like boasting.

But, as stated earlier, their attitude was exceptional. The great majority of women join singles organizations in the hope of finding what the majority of male members just aren't willing to provide.

Thus an element of barely suppressed belligerence permeates these assemblies, sometimes so strongly that the sexes seem to be circling each other in a sparring crouch. Not a stance conducive to romance.

The degree of pugnacity can depend on quite extraneous circumstances, such as motorization. Los Angeles, for instance, is a high-tension town, yet its singles festivities are among the most relaxed anywhere. A reason for this, I found, is that virtually everybody arrives by car. Girls don't have to face the choice between a nervous trip home by public transport and a ride with someone they may consider obnoxious. These rather bleak alternatives account for a good portion of the female resentment you meet in, say, New York, where a walk to the subway after dark now resembles an unarmed patrol through enemy lines.

One fairly effective way of getting singles soirées onto a more amiable basis is by making the participants forget what they came for, at least temporarily. This is the secret behind the popularity of the Game Room program, which started in San Francisco in 1971.

The formula, quite simply, consists of gathering random groups of unattached men and women, ostensibly for the purpose of playing games. Not traditional parlor pastimes like Monopoly, but new and exceedingly "involved" games, reflecting the temper of our times and frequently the temper of the players.

The innovators of the program were a two-girl team, Gini Scott and Helen Roberts. They had no altruistic motives—Gini designs the games concerned and Helen markets them. But what might have been a strictly commercial gambit turned into one of the happiest singles circles extant. 1722988

Miss Scott is tall and blonde, with a fringe cut, sensuous lips, and the unfrivolous earnestness of someone to whom games mean serious business. Although she refutes the label "inventor," she actually does invent her games, gleaning inspirations from newspaper headlines and creating the prototypes in her splendidly equipped upstairs workshop.

"One of my first games was *Confrontation*," she recalled. "That's on student protests. Students confront the establishment with demands for changes. One team plays the students, the other the establishment. Both sides have certain options: doing nothing, rioting, negotiating, suppressing, etc. It's a bit outdated now, really, so I'm redesigning it to make it more—well, *immediate*."

"Are all your games that topical?" I asked her.

She shook her fringe. "No, but I try and capture a current interest. I have one called *Nostalgia*—all about the twenties and thirties and early forties. Because there *is* this general nostalgia."

In the initial stages, Game Room participants were predominantly male, which didn't surprise Miss Scott. "Traditionally," she said, "women have been encouraged *not* to play games. Games are associated with competition, and women are taught not to compete. Or—if they're competing with males—to lose. But games are changing now. We're getting into discussion games, imagination games, interaction games, where winning is purely secondary. So currently our players are about half and half."

She gave one of her rare grins. "But there's one thing that hasn't changed. The women always arrive late. About thirty minutes after the men. I suppose that's because every one of them is terrified of being there first."

The Game Room has a kinship to the "oldest floating crap game in town," insofar as it constantly changes location. The night I dropped in it was proceeding in the private banqueting chamber of a famous San Francisco seafood restaurant. You could order drinks brought up in any quantity, but most of the players were far too engrossed to think of refreshment.

There were an even forty, including the two organizers, and ranged from the giggly secretarial to the pompously executive, with a couple of beard-and-beads types sprinkled in for contrast. Newcomers could choose between three group actions. I joined something called *The Lib Game*, in which players were divided into four teams: "Uppity Women," "Male Chauvinists," "Liberal Males," and "Conservative Chicks." Assignment of roles was arbitrary, reflecting neither the players' sex nor their convictions.

"But I'm *not* uppity—truly I'm not," a platinum blonde protested. "Just the opposite, really."

"It's only a game," Gini reassured her. "You're only pretending. Next time round you'll be something else."

"Oh, that's all right, then." The platinum lady relaxed. Then an even more ominous thought struck her. "But what if I have to play a man? I mean—I just *couldn't* . . ." She thrust out an impressive pair of vital statistics to demonstrate the difficulty of the task. Having accomplished this, she subsided.

The game was played by drawing "topic cards," dealing with various points of the Women's Liberation movement. Each point was presented as a demand, and the function of the teams was to argue pro, con or lukewarm, according to their assigned positions. Finally, a secret ballot vote decided which team had made the best, most logical and convincing case.

The Male Chauvinists, I regret to report, won hands down. This was entirely due to an epicene young man with fingers like prehensile frankfurters, who displayed astonishing oratorical powers. He blasted the opposition with verbatim quotations ranging from H. L. Mencken to St. Thomas Aquinas and even managed to squeeze in Kaiser Wilhelm's famous dictum about "Kinder, Kirche, Küche" being woman's God-assigned realm. Somewhat surprisingly, he turned out to be a pet-shop proprietor.

The Uppity Women ran last. Their efforts had been sabotaged throughout by the platinum lady, who felt obliged to preface every sentence she uttered with the phrase, "I don't really believe this, but . . . ," which tended to deprive them of persuasive impact. Nor was their cause aided by the presence in their ranks of a love-beaded gentleman in his forties. He interspersed each statement with five or six "like, you knows," presumably to demonstrate his youthful sincerity.

Neither of them really lost, though. The platinum doll was eventually scooped up by one of the executive types and taken to a late supper downstairs. The beaded one departed in earnest conversation with a broad-hipped brunette wearing artistic patches on her brand-new jeans, symbolizing devil-may-care poverty.

The pairing process occurred imperceptibly during the game. Somebody liked somebody's style. Or lack of style. Or dedication. Or timidity. There was one game, *Ethics*, where you even learned the participants' reactions to being given too much change at a grocery store. Afterward, you could see the sympathizers gravitating toward each other. They didn't have to flounder for openers. The game offered a fine topic on which to hang any amount of flirtation.

A mixed batch of players stuck their heads together and arranged a party for the following week. Everybody present was invited, providing they brought a bottle. About a third of those who had arrived singly left in doubles. It amounted to the highest proportion of impromptu pairing I had seen at any such event.

There were two reasons for this, the lesser being that the games took much of the naked obviousness out of the gathering. After all, you *might* have come because you enjoyed playing *Ethics*.

More significant was the opportunity for display, for the peacock ritual that has been part of the mating process since time immemorial. In a ballroom this privilege is granted only to really spectacular dancers, and even they tend to vanish in the crowd. The games, on the other hand, gave everyone a platform on which to strut, coo, bellow, preen, declaim or twitter according to inclination. The audience was nailed down and attentive, demure shyness just as easily demonstrable as flamboyance.

The formula doesn't work nearly so well when applied to out-and-out sex games. At a similar function in Chicago, I watched much the same cross-section of people play *Adultery* and *Office Party*, two of the determinedly "adult" board games currently being retailed by a company in Phoenix, Arizona. Both involve lashings of stylized hanky-panky and force players to reveal their attitudes to various forms of (cardboard) promiscuity. Far from relaxing, most people visibly tensed during the evening. They couldn't escape the thought that their game behavior would be expected to mirror their real-life morals, which put a severe clamp on their spontaneity. Few of the guests, I noticed, teamed up afterwards.

There is an object lesson in the game rooms that can be extended to the entire spectrum of singles sociability. It adds up to the fact that the mechanics of mate hunting generally work best with us when disguised as something else, no matter how transparently. Give men and women a reason—other than the real one—for gathering anywhere, and they'll make contact pretty rapidly without undue strain on their psyches. Deprive them of all pretexts and— eight times out of ten—the atmosphere becomes loaded with sup-pressed hysteria.

This is probably not the way nature intended it to be. And it still isn't among simpler, less paradox-riddled civilizations, where basic drives require no ceremonial fig leaves. I couldn't envisage a singles club flourishing in, for instance, Tahiti. But being what we've made of ourselves and unable to shed our skins, the above rule has applied to us for many centuries.

Our ancestors undoubtedly knew what they were doing when they camouflaged their proverbial "hayride" as the transportation of fodder from the fields.

two

MATCHMAKER! MATCHMAKER!

There is this story about the green-skinned, eight-armed, saber-toothed Venusian who crawled out of a spaceship onto Miami Beach one morning. The first human he allegedly saw was a stout woman who rushed up to him, shouting, "Mister, have I got a girl for you!"

The lady, of course, illustrates one of the stock characters of immigrant folklore: the marriage broker or matrimonial agent or —as she would probably call herself—"social consultant."

Under whatever label you choose, her corner of the mating trade represents the antithesis of computerized matching. With her, nothing is entrusted to science and mathematics, and everything to experience, intuition, and horse sense. Her questionnaire is usually minuscule, her knowledge of clients often encyclopedic.

Whereas the electronics department is managed almost entirely by men, her particular niche is overwhelmingly matriarchal. While the computer cupid was developed by American academicians, her brand of matchmaking came over steerage with the "huddled masses." It is the oldest, staidest, coziest, least fashionable—and frequently most efficient—branch of the business.

Matrimonial bureaus have been quite unaffected by the recent upsurge of organized matching. Twenty years ago there were about eight hundred of them in the United States. Today the total is still roughly the same, and so is the size and make-up of their clientele.

There are several reasons for this, one of them being the generally poor public image of these institutions. The public mind has them firmly linked with "lonely-hearts clubs," which—as we shall see—are entirely different enterprises.

More important, they lack any vestige of scientific glamor and aren't even tinged with eroticism. It just isn't part of their stock in trade. Nor—in the course of my round dozen interviews with matrimonial agents—did the word "love" crop up more than twice. As one of them put it: "Love doesn't really come into our business at all. It's something that grows on you *after* you're married."

Their concept of pairing is wholly out of tune with prevailing American attitudes; it appeals neither to romantics nor swingers. You might say that marriage brokers never made it really big in this country because they're too coolly realistic about their services.

They operate from the premise that the wedded state per se offers such advantages to both parties that other considerations become quite secondary. The blessings may not be so great emotionally, but socially, physically and economically they're solid enough. Never mind if your psyches don't mesh perfectly or if you don't find each other intellectually stimulating. So who wants to be stimulated for forty years? The main thing is to get married, to live together, sleep together, fight, have children, and get ahead. In the process you'll probably get to like each other. And even if you don't, it will still be better then "sitting home alone, staring at four walls."

All this may sound like the bleakest heresy to enlightened minds, but it seems to come closer to a practical formula than any of the more attractive alternatives promulgated to date. For whereas our overall divorce rate stands at one divorce for every three and a half marriages, it is one in ten among couples matched by "social consultants."

The formula itself is only a minor factor. What makes it effective is the personal touch, the way it is stretched, bent, modified, ego-tailored, and sweetened by the people who apply it. For sheer professional savvy they're in a class of their own.

While researching this volume I experienced very little difficulty passing myself off in any role the occasion required, even under the eyes of supposedly highly trained psychologists. But not once did I succeed in bamboozling a professional matchmaker for longer than thirty minutes. Then she or he would lean over with a knowledgeable smirk and inquire: "Now tell me, what are you collecting material for—an article or a book?"

Their professionalism makes everyone else in the field appear dilettantish. Most of them are elderly and equipped with only the barest rudiments of formal education. In print they frequently sound like satires of themselves, and some of their publicity brochures can be read for comic relief. But their instinct for people, their perception of the real person behind a façade, sometimes borders on the uncanny.

While the computer maters constantly assure you that they treat questionnaires as Holy Writ, the marriage brokers will blithely admit that they often disregard them altogether. "What people put down that they want is what they feel they *should* want. And if they got it they wouldn't know what to do with it," one lady explained to me. "So I use my own nose, and most of the time it's better."

Marriage brokers concentrate solely on what their title implies: marriage. No nonsense here about "swinging relationships." Even prolonged dating is anathema to them. Some of them collect only a portion of their fee in advance, the rest is payable after the wedding. It takes a really solid dose of self-confidence to make such a financial arrangement.

The single-minded pursuit of matrimony is part of their immigrant heritage. The newcomers had neither time nor inclination for much romantic dalliance. They paired off fast—especially if the girl brought a dowry. The matchmaker—whose business it was to know the essentials about both parties—saved them the effort of finding out the details about each other piecemeal.

Thus the marriage broker's forte rested on her or his familiarity with a certain group of people—a few hundred or a few thousand who came from the same village or the same province. Matchmakers thrived to the extent that these people practiced endogamy—that is, the custom of marrying within a group. As the American melting pot began to diminish this practice, the role of the matchmaker declined correspondingly. The further afield the flock strayed, the more they became removed from the matcher's sphere of action.

All matrimonial agents in this country were originally linked with clearly defined ethnic groups: Irish, Italian, Jewish, Polish, German, Ukrainian, Levantine, Slovak and Chinese—in roughly that numerical order. They retained their roles to the degree that these groups continued to observe endogamy. Which means that today they are active chiefly—but not exclusively—among Jews, Lebanese, Slavic minorities and Orientals.

But "active among" no longer means being necessarily *of* them. The biggest matrimonial agent in America happens to be a branch-water-pure WASP. A remarkably high proportion are Irish, either of the Green or Orange variety. A bewildering paradox in this business is the way in which marriage brokers contribute to the very trend that undermines them: exogamy—the opposite of endogamy—by introducing people of different ethnic backgrounds who would otherwise be unlikely to meet.

One of the great "mixers" is Clara Lane, whose establishment—from being strictly matrimonial—has veered toward the general-introduction field.

"To be sure, there's a good reason for that," she said dryly. "People don't get married the way they did. This past half year I've had—let's see—just fifty marriages. Back in the old days I was marrying them off at a rate of four or five per week. So"—she smiled a philosopher's smile—"now I've become a bit of everything."

Clara Lane is probably the oldest established matchmaker in the United States. She opened for business in 1938, and at one time had Friendship Centers dotting the entire nation. Twenty years ago she shifted from New York City to downtown Los Angeles, where she now presides over a plain, smallish office, decorated chiefly by photos depicting her aiming a Cupid's bow at the mayor of Chicago, and chatting with Tallulah Bankhead, Earl Wilson, and Joe E. Lewis.

She is a well-rounded little lady with a pair of sky-blue baby eyes beneath a dazzling white (once dazzling blonde) coiffure, and a disarmingly appreciative way of mustering male callers. Her cheerful, slightly self-mocking candor makes her come across rather like a Hibernian Sophie Tucker.

"How did I get into this business? Via restaurants. You see, I was an Irish farm girl from Iowa and I only knew two things: cooking and reading tea leaves. So I opened up a Gypsy tearoom in New York and called myself Madame Cassandra. Better than farm work, believe me." She patted my arm affirmatively.

"Now, I don't rightly know why, but I kept records of my readings. And they all had unhappy loves in them. People crying in their tea about this one and that one. And after I sold the restaurant, some Jewish friends of mine suggested I should become a marriage broker.

"So I contacted all these people with the broken hearts and announced that I was Clara Lane now. No more Madame Cassandra. And that I'd find partners for them." She gave a retrospective chuckle. "Well . . . the business got very big then. Seventy-five-hundred square feet of office space. And I retained some very high-class counselors. I had to because, you know, half the questions people asked were a bit beyond my reach. I didn't want to let on I was that dumb, you see, so I hired others to give them the right answers."

Miss Lane folded her hands over her bosom and smiled. "But after a little while—twenty years or so—you learn. Leastwise, I did. I had lots and lots of marriages. Then I had an article in the *American Magazine*. Mr. Vance Packard did most of the work on it, so don't put me down as a writer. I couldn't draw a straight line. But it brought in a lot more business, and I went into franchises. Opened up offices right across the country."

"What did you charge then?" I wanted to know.

"I charged when you got married. To me it was like playing the horses. If I got you a winner, you paid. Couple of hundred dollars."

"Quite a sum for those days."

"Oh, the men never paid that much. Good-looking guy like you wouldn't." My arm got patted again.

Miss Lane's advertising methods had all the subtlety of train wrecks. She would print lists of her available manpower, specifying quantity and vintage: 5 Attorneys (middle-aged), 1 Motion Picture Sound Engineer (young), 1 Oilman (retired colonel), 5 Ranchers (middle-aged), 20 Retired Businessmen.

Female prospects received the same treatment: 20 Wealthy Widows (all ages), 10 Registered Nurses (young and middle-aged), 1 Ballet Dancer (young), 135 Housewives.

"And who did you find hardest to match?" I asked her.

She didn't have to think about that one. "Irishmen and music lovers," she said grimly. "With the Irish we had to make a special note in our files which *county* they were from, so help me. Because you get County Mayo people who'd rather hang than marry anyone from County Cork. And music lovers—you have to find out exactly what *brand* of music they love, the exact shading. Some Bach fans, for instance, despise anyone who's fond of Chopin. Those were the toughest."

"And the easiest?"

"As a group, I'd say women from Europe. They know just how to treat a man. Particularly Germans and Hungarians. They'll take off a man's coat—just about. And before you know it, they have him at home, with his shoes off, eating apple strudel. Well, maybe American girls know it too—but they don't show it."

Miss Lane leaned forward with a confidential twinkle. "I'm not in this to educate the public. So I don't lecture clients. But I can tell within maybe a minute whether a couple will hit it off or not. Of course—nowadays I sometimes get types I never got before."

I was curious. "What types?"

"Oh—defrocked priests. Quite a lot of them. They're dolls, some of 'em, I'm telling you." She chortled quietly. "I'm crazy about one of them. We have a nun registered here, too. Former nun, really. The most beautiful creature ever to fall from grace, I'm telling you. But she doesn't want any of our defrocked priests. No, sir. She wants a businessman."

"Did you ever meet any men yourself through your business, Miss Lane? I mean—are you married?"

"Me? Oh—I was married long before I set up in business. I've been married all these years. To the same man, too. Only, he never approved of my business. He thinks it's terrible. But he's been ill for many many years. And—well, this is better than him trying to do something."

Whereas Clara Lane represents the ethnic mixer, her male counterpart in New York still caters almost exclusively to the endogamic. About 90 percent of Irving Field's clients come from Jewish immigrant families.

I had watched Mr. Field on a number of television shows and found that one of his characteristic features was missing in the flesh. He lacked his Clark Gable mustache. It was, I later discovered, painted on.

Otherwise, he lives up to his video image in every respect: the pompadoured black hair, the world-embracing gestures, the pink shirt and white silk tie, gold-rimmed spectacles, and curiously baroque speech style—like a cross between Lord Chesterton and Zero Mostel.

His office, on Manhattan's Forty-second Street, seems like an oasis of romantic tranquillity amidst the surrounding desert of hard-core porno shops and skin flicks. A floral rug, a plastic tree growing artificial oranges, the walls decked with photos of demurely smiling newlyweds.

Mr. Field claims the most perfect record of any matchmaker I have encountered. "I have arranged the meetings of more than ten thousand couples and brought about the marriages of all ten thousand. Never a case closed without results. And not one instance of divorce among them."

He has, understandably, a poor opinion of computer matchings. "What does a computer know? You feed in numbers, so you get out numbers. A cold machine—no heart and no brain. Can a computer tell if somebody has high blood pressure?"

His own pairing methods are based on personal interviews (always conducted by himself) and a formidable filing system that leans heavily on the economic status of his clients. He has them grouped into Laborers, White Collar, Better Middle Class, Wealthy, and Society. His advertised listings are equally unequivocal:

Miss, 26, $40,000, seeks gentleman 28–35
Doctor, 30, good income, seeks miss 24–27
Widow, 55, $225,000, seeks gentleman 57–65
Engineer, 32, $225 week, seeks miss 28–33

Irving Field's potential customers receive a little pink booklet that illustrates his services pictorially rather than in words. The line drawings (some depicting him in action) tell happy-end stories under vivid staccato headings that might have been borrowed from early bioscope movies: "Girl at Telephone—Man at Bar," "Worried Parents of Son and Daughter," "Couples Scene with Children in Park, One Woman Alone on Park Bench," followed by, "Same Woman Sitting on Park Bench with Husband and Child."

The section dealing with correspondence (captioned "Man, Cupid, Love Letter, Woman") features a sample communication:

Dear Jane, Your last letter telling me of your various hobbies and your philosophies of life made me realize how compatible we can be! I can't wait to meet you. I'm flying out to visit you . . .

But correspondence is not Mr. Field's big schtick. His fame rests on the personal touch, sometimes discreet enough to be conspiratorial. He is frequently approached by parents who want their daughters' (sometimes their sons') marriages arranged without their children's knowledge. He has an inspired knack for conjuring up such matches—seemingly out of the blue—without arousing the subjects' suspicion that the whole affair was ordered, organized, and paid for. I know one happy accountant's wife who delights in telling visitors how her husband had admired her from afar for months before using secret service methods to discover her name and telephone number. She will very likely go to her grave without realizing that the young man had received both from Irving Field—at her father's instigation.

Normally the procedure is rather more mundane. A gentleman (all of Field's clients are "gentlemen" or "ladies") calls at the office for an interview. He explains his wishes and gets a fairly thorough interrogation. Field's reputation as a matchmaker depends largely on his instinct for the seriousness and respectability of clients. He is rarely wrong. "A lady can accept with complete peace of mind any gentleman recommended by me," he states firmly.

The preliminaries over, Field picks out several "possibilities" from his filing cabinet. One for immediate use, the others as reserves. The couple can either meet on Mr. Field's floral rug or arrange their own tryst. Either way, Field will get a progress report on the date from both parties the next morning. If the gentleman doesn't take to the lady, Field brings out the reserves one by one. He has more than five thousand names in his register, so the supply is ample.

His usual contract period runs for six months, and he claims that all his customers are hitched by then. "Or nearly all. Some few rare cases may take a year at most." He has absolutely no Cinderella illusions and never mixes his clients' economic brackets. Judging by his results, he is probably right.

And if there is one thing Irving Field is adamant about, it's results. "I never fail," he declares, with a characteristic all-embracing stretch of his arms. "If Marilyn Monroe would have come to me maybe a day before, she would be not only alive and happy today but for the rest of her years."

One of the difficulties in comparing matrimonial bureaus is their tendency to go under variegated titles. Arlene Adams, for instance, indignantly refutes the label "matchmaker" and insists that she runs an Introduction Service. As, indeed, she does. But since her service produces an average of around three hundred marriages each year, it also makes her one of the leading matchmakers in the land. The distinction here is more than a matter of semantics. Miss Adams certainly wouldn't wish to be classed alongside the general mass of establishments currently calling themselves introduction services.

Arlene Adams' organization, based in Oakland, is the oldest of its kind in northern California, and possibly the most conservative anywhere. Her advertising breathes restrained gentility. But it pointedly features Anatole France's quotation regarding the domestic hearth: "*There* is the only real happiness."

Miss Adams is an imposingly white-haired matron, with a somewhat aloof no-nonsense manner and a way of pursing her lips at whatever subject she finds distasteful. She purses her lips a great deal. Her opening remark to me was: "I'm afraid I won't be able to help you at all." Whereupon she proceeded to help me considerably.

"As I said, we don't aim at marriages as such," she declared. "We arrange contacts between people of similar tastes and life styles. It's true, we *do* get a phenomenal number of marriages. But I regard them as . . . bonuses."

"Have you found any special attribute that your clients particularly favor?"

"Well, yes," she nodded. "Optimism. Men like women who take a positive view of life.

"Of course, few people know what they *really* want." Miss Adams permitted herself a ladylike smile. "We had a professor once, a very brilliant man—an intellectual—and he told us that, above all things, he didn't wish to meet any blondes. And for about twenty-eight evenings he dated a succession of dark beauties we introduced him to. Until I ran clear out of brunettes. So I put him in touch with a charming blonde, a nurse at the Alameda Hospital. And, you know, *she* was the one—the only one—he became interested in."

Miss Adams takes great pride in the cerebral qualities of her customers. "Intellectual" sounds like the highest mark of approval in her vocabulary, with "maturity" ranking next in line. She was the only social consultant I came across who never mentioned her clients' financial status.

She bristled mildly when I brought up the matter of fees. "I am not going to give you that kind of information." She explained, however, that she uses a sliding scale, keyed to the customer's age level. The older the client, the higher the rates. (The norm, as I discovered in a roundabout fashion, was about $240.) Her senior client had recently passed away at the age of ninety-one. But I never managed to find out what *he* had been paying.

The moral upheavals of the past decade have, apparently, not affected Miss Adams' clientele. The prevailing tone of her service is very much that of the Eisenhower era.

"We carefully eliminate people who wouldn't—er—fit in. I had one man here the other day who told me he was a swinger. Well, I didn't know exactly what that meant, but I found out." She shook her head with slow finality. "We don't take"—she cleared her throat before pronouncing the word—"swingers."

For sheer contrast, it would be hard to locate anyone more graphic than Rae Leifer. Her publicity brochures proclaim her the "Wife of a Professional Man," who "finds you a mate with amazing speed." You only have to see her office in New York's Bronx to learn the nature of her husband's métier. A dentist chair stands at one end of the room, her file-strewn reception desk at the other.

"We both use the same room, but we work different hours. So we don't get in each other's way," she said. "The house is always full of customers, his or mine. Believe me, mine look happier."

Mrs. Leifer is a short, trim, bubbly blonde who chirps away at jet speed, frequently interrupted by great gales of giggles. She reminded me of someone, and the half-forgotten image in the back of my skull kept nagging until I had it pinpointed . . . Gittel Mosca, the heroine of *Two for the Seesaw;* about twenty years older, respectably married and minus her bleeding ulcer!

Rae Leifer has at least one claim to uniqueness: Other women go to a marriage broker to get a husband; she *became* one.

"Sure, that was my only reason. When I was growing up on the Lower East Side, I wasn't meeting anybody. Well, meeting, yes, but not the right kind. All the people that went to the dance halls were from our area. And I knew that if I married one of those fellows, I'd end up living on the Lower East Side. Which I didn't want to raise children in. So I decided the only way to get out of this was if I opened up a matchmaking service. And when I'd selected someone for myself, I could give it up."

"So your husband was actually one of your clients?"

She nodded brightly. "He was the third."

"And how long ago was that?"

Mrs. Leifer giggled. "About twenty-five years ago."

She grew earnest again. "He just said he wanted a nice-looking girl, not a fat girl, and somebody that wasn't stupid. And what did

I have to offer him? And what my fee was. So I said five dollars. I didn't know what to charge. I just thought five dollars sounded all right, and then when you married you'd pay me maybe fifty. Of course, I had no girls. I had no one. I had a book, you see, with nothing written in it. I just turned the pages, like I was reading something, and kept saying, 'No, this wouldn't be any good for you.' And, 'She's not your type.' Then I told him to come back next week. I thought next week I'd have some girls.

"Besides, I needed the five dollars. For the rent of this hole in the wall I had. It was so small that if two people came in, one had to wait outside.

"When I got home that evening my mother said 'Well?' Like that. And I told her a dentist had come to see me. 'A dentist! Ohhhh—a doctor of teeth! That's the one,' my mother said. 'That's for you! Do you know where you'll live if you marry a dentist? Did you read in the newspaper about a dentist that has fifty thousand?' Well, you know, what I was looking for was a fellow who'd bail me out from where I was living. Like our bathroom was out in the hall. Two tenants shared it. So if I could meet a fellow that could give me my own private bathroom—that would be the fellow I'd marry."

Mrs. Leifer sighed. "But, I told my mother, 'What if he doesn't like me?' And my mother said, 'So try.' So, all right, I tried.

"He came in the following week, and I said I'd spoken about him to a very nice girl and she'd like to meet him. Would he come to my home and meet her there? Her name, I told him, was Ethel.

"Well, he came over and we sat and waited . . . twenty minutes . . . thirty minutes . . . Ethel didn't turn up. Then I said, well, the evening didn't have to be a complete flop; he could take *me* out for a walk. He did—he took me out for a soda. On the Lower East Side you didn't go out for drinks, you went out for sodas, see.

"Okay, two days later I rang him and said Ethel'd had a cold, that's why she hadn't come. But if he'd like to drop over to my home, she'd be there tonight. Well, we waited again . . . no Ethel. (I *did* have a girl friend named Ethel, but I wasn't going to introduce *her* to any dentist. She was very good-looking.) I suggested going for a walk again, and we did, he bought me another soda. He didn't take me into an ice cream parlor, where you got waited on at tables, we just went to a drugstore. Professional people are very stingy."

She paused, briefly, for breath. "So he came to my office again and he said, all right, could I fix him up with another girl? I went through my book again—it still had nothing in it—and finally I said, 'Look, I'm expecting a lot of girls next week. But in the meantime, why should you sit home alone? How about taking *me* out? Temporarily. I'm not too bad.'

"All right . . . we went for another walk. And he bought me another soda. My mother thought the world had ended when I got home at nine o'clock. She said: 'This is a good boy—a good boy.' And I thought, 'Well, what's so good about a good boy if I don't even get into the ice cream parlor!'

"A week later he came back, he still wanted to meet girls. And I still didn't have any. I honestly didn't have any. Things were rotten. Finally I said to him: 'What's wrong with me? I'm interested in dating someone if he's nice.'

"We had a dinner date that night," Mrs. Leifer said solemnly. "It took me four hours to get dressed for it. That day I did not bend down. I was so well-groomed, I couldn't budge. My mother washed my stockings for me; I shouldn't knock myself out." She beamed in memory of the occasion. "Anyway . . . six weeks later he asked me if I wanted to marry him. And I told him he'd have to buy me a wristwatch to show my mother that we're sort of—like—there's an understanding.

"Well"—she clapped her hands with a resounding slam—"like the next *day* everybody on the Lower East Side knew that Rae was going with a dentist! Because my mother told the butcher, and the butcher told everybody who came into his store. And suddenly a whole lot of girls came to my office wanting to meet fellows. Did I know any more dentists? Did *he*, maybe, know any dentists? The mothers came in, too. Did I have a doctor of teeth for their daughter? No? Perhaps a doctor, then? I didn't have to advertise. I had all the customers I wanted. Five dollars coming in from all sides. Business became great."

"Was that why you didn't give it up after you were married?"

She waggled the palm of her hand. "Yes, partly. But also because I found it very interesting. More interesting than cooking. I was a rotten cook. So was my mother. Anyway, I kept the business going even after I had my children. When they were babies, I always had the carriage in my room when I was matching. If the baby was yelling, I asked whoever was there to hold him. They did, too. Gave them the bottle and everything."

"Did your husband agree with what you were doing?" I inquired.

"No. He hated it. He said to me: 'You're matching everybody up, and one day you're going to match yourself up again.'"

She chuckled. "So I promised him, 'If I ever match myself up again, I'll match you up, too. And I won't charge you anything.'"

Rae Leifer's local popularity survived her move to the Bronx (where she acquired not only a private bathroom, but a maid as well). Clients still undertake the pilgrimage from the Lower East Side to consult her. I asked her whether she ever arranged first encounters in her office.

"I do—uh—sometimes. A man came in here once, and he gave me a really detailed description of the kind of girl he wanted. And I had just that type in my book. Ready and waiting. I rang her and said I had *her* fellow for her. A *dreamboat*—car and everything. Waiting in my office. To get herself all dressed up and come over.

"She got here . . . looking out of this world. What can I say? Perfection. And the man"—she put on an expression of concussed disbelief—"saw her and screamed: 'I was married to her ten years ago! And she took all the money from our joint account and sold all the furniture! You're gonna give me back that furniture—right now!' And then he went for her. I had a terrible time getting them apart, so she could run. I told him he should be calm, but he kept yelling, 'No, I want to cripple her!' It was terrible."

As a rule, however, her matchings proceed smoothly, nudged along by frequent personal touches. One of her lady clients was having a difficult time with her dates, because she had to hurry home from each rendezvous in order to walk her dog. Then Mrs. Leifer discovered that her maid happened to be looking for a pet. She promptly persuaded the client to swap her pooch for a husband.

As I rose to leave, she motioned me down again. "We've been talking so long, you must be thirsty. Wait a moment, I'll get you a drink."

When she reappeared she was balancing a tray with a glass and a bottle of ginger ale. Rae Leifer may have abandoned the Lower East Side twenty-five years ago, but a "drink" for her apparently still means a soda.

American marriage brokers, unlike their counterparts overseas, operate solely in metropolitan areas. A few of them occasionally send out representatives to work the medium-sized cities, but they merely skim off the cream in flying visits. Small towns and semirural regions remain so much wasteland as far as organized matchmaking is concerned. Frequently these are the areas most in need of it. Townlets with a couple of thousand inhabitants and virtually no eligible partners, existing in social isolation from the larger population centers.

A single matching service has so far zeroed in on this territory, and it didn't do so for profit. The Scientific Marriage Foundation (SMF) might be described as a one-man crusade against loneliness; otherwise, it is hard to pin a precise label on it. Although one of the biggest outfits of its kind in the country, it belongs to no clearly defined category and has to get a bracket for itself.

The SMF's founder and driving force is a remarkable Midwesterner named George W. Crane. A physician, psychologist, psychiatrist, syndicated newspaper columnist, textbook author, lecturer and Sunday-school teacher, Dr. Crane is an astonishing mixture of scientist and lay missionary, and his organization mirrors his own personality.

Headquartered in a converted school building in Mellott, Indiana, the SMF represents the kind of project you frequently find hailed in the pages of the Reader's Digest. Staunchly moralistic, solidly patriotic, interdenominationally religious (the Advisory Board includes a bishop, a monsignor, a senator, a rabbi, a judge, several reverends, and Dr. Norman Vincent Peale), it combines a decidedly paternalistic approach with an up-to-the-minute flair for gadgetry.

From its conception, in 1956, the SMF used advanced electronic techniques for pairing purposes. The particulars of members—age, race, religion, education, income, hobbies, etc.—were coded onto ten-holed IBM cards. Trained operators ran the cards through sorting machines, set to correspond the holed data of a card with the equivalent holes of another person of the opposite sex living within a 200-mile radius. When the machine produced two cards on which all ten holes matched, both respective clients were given each other's name and address.

The information that went on the cards was (and still is) carefully checked out by some twenty-five hundred volunteer counselors, each responsible for members within his or her geographical area. The counselors also arrange the first meeting of a pair in their own offices. The significant point here is that all of the field counselors are clergymen (sometimes women) and that their reports on specific prospects are naturally influenced by their calling. Which is precisely what Dr. Crane intended when he launched his Foundation.

Graying, mustached, business-suited, Dr. Crane, who wears rimless spectacles and usually a broad smile, could pose for a publicity portrait epitomizing the Christian American Optimist.

Some of his pronouncements have made him the *bête noire* of his professional colleagues, particularly when they dealt with courtship and marriage counseling. "A lot of our psychologists and psychiatrists are interested in the fees they get from counseling," he once stated. "They want to make a big affair out of this instead of getting down to what I call horse sense."

One of his passions is verbal simplicity, which he displays not only in his column but also in his college textbook *Psychology Applied;* perhaps the most widely adopted textbook in its field. He has been accused of "simplifying intricate problems down to comic-strip levels," but this doesn't faze him in the least. "The average word in the Bible," he retorts, "has only two syllables, so if college professors would follow the standard policy of newspapers, they would put their ideas across faster." The most celebrated address he delivered during his thirty-five years of Adult Bible Class teaching in the Chicago Temple was entitled "Jesus, the World's Greatest Psychiatrist."

To Dr. Crane there was nothing particularly complex about the inability of some people to find suitable mates. "A great number of individuals are stymied. They may have fine personalities, but their professional or social environment does not permit them to meet eligible partners."

He saw this as a major tragedy. "The founding of happy homes is the most important safeguard for both our American Republic, as well as our churches," he wrote. "Without happy homes and properly trained children, civilization will rapidly decay."

Dr. Crane was ready to put his beliefs on the line. Together with a group of like-minded conservatives, he launched the Scientific Marriage Foundation as a nonprofit "educational organization." He and his fellow directors donated their time and energy free of charge.

The nonprofit part is perfectly genuine, although it's difficult to discover the educational aspect. Prospects pay twenty-five dollars for a lifetime membership. Of this, five dollars is the fee for the field counselor, the rest goes into secretarial salaries, machinery, office costs, etc. In order not to render the members' actual quest too obvious, the SMF functions as a subdivision of its contact bureau, called the Compliment Club, a suitably innocuous title.

The SMF does not advertise, but gets all the publicity it needs from constant mention in Dr. Crane's syndicated column, "The Worry Clinic," which appears in about three hundred newspapers and topped a readers' poll of columnists in the Detroit *Free Press*. (Ann Landers ran second.) "The Worry Clinic" features the mating dilemmas of worthy men and women (usually described as "high type" or "cultured") and brings in the SMF as the obvious solution to their problems.

Although some of the membership is drawn from large cities, the majority have a small-town or rural background. And within that framework the SMF has proved outstandingly successful. Of the more than ten thousand marriages engineered by the Foundation, only 11 (one tenth of 1 percent) have so far ended in divorce, compared to the national average of 27 percent. The field counselors I spoke to also commented on the ease with which their charges "click." The first or second introduction usually results in a "promising relationship."

The Foundation's statistical accomplishment, however, may stem from its orientation rather than its methods. The SMF's appeal is quite clearly pitched at folks who share Dr. Crane's viewpoints: church-involved people with well-insulated moral codes, who take similar nonpermissive attitudes toward questions like liquor, drugs, erotica and sexual promiscuity. Which means, in any case, they belong to the segment of population that has the lowest divorce rate.

The SMF's credit lies in bringing them together, and Dr. Crane is undoubtedly right in arguing for the establishment of more non-profit mating centers in different parts of the country. Whether his brand of Sunday-school technique would work equally well with a more general and less God-loving clientele remains doubtful.

three

THE SINGLES SYNDROME

Of all the minorities currently flexing their muscles in the United States, by far the biggest is the amorphous population segment called "the singles." Generically, the term applies to some thirty-six million adults—one for every two and a half married people.

Their muscle-flexing has so far been of the mildest order. It amounted to no more than the distribution of SINGLE POWER buttons and the assembly of various conferences to air the grievances of the nonweds. But these are straws in the wind, denoting a growing consciousness of a potentially immense amount of political and economic clout.

The grievances, although not particularly harsh, are genuine. As Dr. Marie Edwards, a clinical psychologist in Los Angeles, stated: "Unfortunately, our society puts a stigma on being single." She might have added that most civilized societies have done so since antiquity.

Their attitude was only partly governed by the country's need for children to counterbalance the tremendous rate of infant mortality. It was also—perhaps chiefly—based on the fact that the family is the most efficient social unit mankind has ever evolved—combining the functions of reproduction, child care, sexual gratification and economic cooperation. From the state's point of view, it has the additional advantages of being easily controlled, of giving its head a stake in the community.

A certain proportion of eligible men have always been reluctant to shoulder the responsibilities of married fatherhood. They had to be nudged into it—sometimes quite firmly. The Athenians and Spartans branded bachelors as "those who refuse to give sureties and pledges to the state" and barred them from army commands as well as all administrative positions.

The Roman Emperor Augustus made a point of publicly berating his unmarried knights, calling them—among other things—"debased pederasts who slake their filthy lusts on their slave boys." In eighteenth-century France and Prussia, male bachelors were required to pay a special tax. Soviet Russia, in true egalitarian style, put an extra tax on the unmarried of *both* sexes—the man paying from the age of twenty to fifty, the woman only to forty-five.

The English went about it rather more subtly; instead of taxing the bachelor, they taxed his servants. The general idea was to force their master into paying such outrageous wages that he would come to consider a wife a cheaper alternative.

While bachelors suffered most of the economic harassment, the lot of spinsters was infinitely worse. In medieval times—unless they were independently wealthy—their choice lay between a brothel and a nunnery. Later centuries gave them wider scope, but simultaneously made them the objects of a virulent and savage kind of ridicule that broke the spirits of all except the toughest. That stock figure of Victorian slapstick humor—the "hysterical old maid"—had frequently become semidemented because she couldn't stand the incessant barrage of sneers and taunts inflicted upon her.

In modern America the position of singles of both genders was oddly ambiguous. They enjoyed considerable freedom and were not subjected to any official discrimination. Yet society treated them as people somehow outside the national norm, rather as if their physical measurements had been a few sizes too big or small.

They were made to feel downright alien during the years of the great Togetherness Cult, a mania birthed jointly by Madison Avenue and Hollywood, which regarded singleness as akin to halitosis, and anyone lacking offspring as either an invert or a Communist. The idea was that normal *Homo sapiens* came equipped with spouses and progeny and carried them permanently fastened to their backs, possum style. Most of the nation's facilities were geared to the family as *the* consumer unit. Family housing, family entertainment, family cars, family vacations, family games, family diets, family magazines, family everything; including prayers and hobby kits.

The winds of change began to blow during the early 1960s, about the time when an increasing slice of the family market decamped to exurbia. The prefix "single" crept into advertising jargon, timidly at first, but imbued with a chic aura of rakishness. Within five years it was adopted by every conceivable commodity, plus a few rather inconceivable ones. (One Chicago retailer announced "Waterbeds For With-it Singles," the implication being that with-it singles slept —while not alone—*very* closely together.)

Among the first grazers in the new pasture were the singles bars, also known as "Body Exchanges" or "Pettin' Places." Basically, these are saloons infused with a certain café ambiance: mostly Tiffany lamps, dark-wood paneling, and comfortable chairs or settees so arranged as to permit a maximum of impromptu mingling.

The prerequisite of a singles bar is the ability to draw large numbers of young women minus male escorts—a reversal of established saloon policy. One way of achieving this is by hiring handsome, personable waiters and bartenders—frequently junior executives moonlighting on their jobs. These usually bring in a nucleus of their own peers for a start. The rest must be left to a process the trade calls the "powder room tom-tom."

"Word spreads that a certain hangout is fine for meeting fellows," a Boston bartender described it. "So the chicks flock in. After that, it all depends how they work out together—you never know beforehand. Even after you have a good scene going, you can get it ruined inside a month by the wrong crowd suddenly turning up. What kind of crowd? Oh, guys who play rough and think they can feel the chicks after they buy 'em a drink. A dozen of those, man, and the whole business just folds."

Singles bars, in fact, have to balance on a thin behavioral tightrope. On the one hand, a certain reputation for raunchiness is highly desirable—as long as nothing actually happens on the premises. A much-repeated joke I heard from their managers was the alleged introduction formula between patrons: "Shall we have a drink *first?*" The proprietor of a certain pub in San Francisco's financial district assiduously spread the rumor that in his hostelry a number of gals turned up every Friday night bringing toothbrushes in their purses.

On the other hand, the atmosphere mustn't become too gamy. A few professional hookers can ruin the scene just as effectively as an invasion by heavy-breathing longshoremen.

"No, I wouldn't call them dating spots. They're meeting spots," explained former Chicago airline stewardess Mia Crawford. "My girl friends and I don't make dates there—not often, anyway. Mostly we just give out our telephone numbers. It's a bit like a parlor game with rules, really. Like, you can walk away from a guy after he's bought you a drink. That's okay. But after he's bought you several, you're kind of stuck. Obligated, if you know what I mean. Of course, you can always pay your share of the tab and move to another table. I've done that myself."

For those singles bars that strike just the right chord, business can be dazzling. According to an insurance-company estimate, there are 780,000 single persons living within the square formed by Manhattan's Fifth Avenue and the East River between Thirtieth and Ninetieth streets. The first actual "Body Exchange" opened in that area in 1964, when Berney Sullivan plushed up his formerly stodgy little saloon. After Sullivan's came Friday's, created by bachelor-duo Alan Stillman and Ben Benson. (It has since been followed by Tuesday's, Wednesday's and Thursday's, and the partners now have franchises right across the country.)

Then, in rapid succession, came a whole string of hostelries, including Mr. Laffs and Maxwell's Plum, where on weekend nights the action is literally wall-to-wall. Today New York's "Singles Strip" reaches almost into Yorkville, although the focal territory is still the two-square-mile enclave on the midtown East Side. (Greenwich Village is *out* since the hard-drug crowd moved in.)

From New York, the singles-bar pattern has spread to other centers, forming similar strips in Chicago's Near North Side, Boston's Back Bay, and San Francisco's Union and Montgomery streets.

These strips magnetize the most attractive crowd of young people in contemporary America. And they have developed a mode of encounter *au naturel*, delightfully free of the tortured verbal convolutions that once accompanied pickups. It works both ways; either sex is permitted to smile a nonchalant "Hi," and start from there.

Another bit of unwritten etiquette requires the girl to buy her own beer first, but expects the man to pay for subsequent rounds once a conversation gets under way. A meal—or the establishment's facsimile thereof—counts as something of a commitment.

Even the banes of the singles bars belong about evenly to both sexes. On the male side it's the nonsingle, the married philanderer sailing under false colors. He may not be able to take a girl back to his apartment, but he frequently ends up in *hers*; thanks to a superior *modus operandi* that comes from experience.

His female equivalents form what is known in bar parlance as the "Martini Mafia." These are coordinated groups of three or four girls who disperse as soon as they enter. Each lady then nails her sucker-for-the-night, who will spend the next few hours plying her with the costliest potations available, climaxed by a three-course supper. The moment the plates are emptied, however, the whole bunch reunites to march out of the place in a solid phalanx—unassailable through weight of numbers. Their regular boy friends—or husbands—are men working night shifts . . . often behind the counter of another singles hangout.

The bars have acquired a high and glittering profile that makes them appear much more significant than they actually are on the singles scene.

For a start, they remain confined to small sections within a handful of our biggest cities. More important, they cater almost entirely to young, white, middle-class post-collegians. Older men and women, and those lacking the "right" clothes and vocabulary, find themselves largely ignored. Apart from being thus geographically and socially exclusive, the bars also disqualify people who can't cope with their elbowing free-wheeling brand of *joie de vivre*; not to mention non-drinkers. All in all, they absorb a very minor portion of America's singles reservoir.

This reservoir is not only immense, but maldistributed. On a na-tionwide basis, unmarried women outnumber unmarried men; but the proportions vary tremendously according to age levels. Among young adults the female preponderance is around four to three. After the age of forty-five it rises as high as four to one, as more women be-come widows. Yet some states—especially Alaska, Hawaii, and Ne-vada—suffer a distinct shortage of women in *all* age brackets. The District of Columbia, on the other hand, has only about seventy sin-gle men for every hundred single women, while in Miami the girl-boy ratio is a fantastic seven to one (this being due to the presence of legions of airline stewardesses in training).

By and large, it can be said that the great urban centers draw many more single girls than men because female power is needed for sales, clerical, and secretarial work. It happens, therefore, that while a state's over-all sex ratio may seem reasonably balanced, it is actually heavily weighted against women in the metropolitan areas and against men in the rural regions.

But statistics are treacherous beasts that can't be trusted to paint an accurate picture of any situation, even if the figures are right.[1] Just because a city contains more lone females than males, it doesn't follow that this is necessarily reflected at all singles functions. At-tendance varies according to a bewilderingly illogical pattern. The bars, for instance, always have a clear male majority. The same ap-plies to the contact ads appearing in specialized periodicals—about which more later. At "singles weekends," however, the customary ratio is three or four women per man.

I could find no discernible reason why this should be so. The

[1] As a random example: If you read that in 1971 Switzerland's unemployment rate rose by 50 percent, you get the impression that the country has suffered a devastating economic blow. Unless you happen to know that in 1970 there were exactly thirty-four jobless men in Switzerland, which figure shot up to fifty-one the following year.

weekends are expensive, competition is frenetic, their purpose—if anything—more blatant. Yet month after month they continue to attract women who, according to their own fervent statements, "wouldn't be caught dead in one of those lousy bars."

Singles weekends have become synonymous with half a dozen resort hotels situated in New York's Sullivan County, a stretch of gently undulating countryside in the southern foothills of the Catskills, colloquially known as the "Borscht Belt" or the "Jewish Alps." They did, in fact, originate there, but have since spread throughout New England, to Florida, southern California and even Puerto Rico. Nevertheless, in the repertoire of a score of nightclub comics (most of whom rely on the Borscht Belt for sustenance) the institution remains totally identified with that particular region and its clientele.

The territory's largest resort is the high-rise Concord, a titanic edifice that could pass as the fifty-first state. The Concord has three nightclubs, a discotheque, six bands, a dining room the size of an airfield, a 1500-foot toboggan run, four indoor and thirteen outdoor tennis courts, a skating rink, three golf courses, an indoor pool ringed by sun lamps, a Night Owl Lounge for insomniacs and—periodically —orange snow.

The weekend I got there it was jammed with twenty-eight hundred singles and could dispense with the orange snow. It could have dispensed with most of the indoor entertainment as well, because the gathered stags supplied the only attraction that interested them—each other.

The management catered to their desires just short of pushing them bodily into bed. From Friday's registration to Sunday's checkout, the motto was "*Mix!*" You mixed on the dance floor, in the pool, along the bars, around the lobbies, at the wine-tasting, the graphology lecture, the bridge tournament, and during what appeared to be a permanent game of "Simon Says" proceeding in one of the lounges. We were goaded into greater mixing efforts by a social hostess with a smile tattooed on her face, reciting at intervals: "If you mingle, your spine will tingle, your pockets will jingle, and you won't stay single."

The age of the guests ranged from the early twenties to the late fifties. The men dressed with extreme casualness, but the women seemed to have brought one wardrobe trunk each. Some of them changed attire four times a day, never repeating an ensemble in forty-eight hours. Without exception, they were as jittery as neon lights, punctuating the weekend with sudden explosions of door-slamming, tear-brimming rage.

My roommate, a veteran of five weekends, explained their behavior to me. "It's all this competition. Makes them flip their wigs. You better watch out—give one of them the slightest encouragement and you'll be stuck with her for the weekend."

His name was Max, he was thirty-three, a salesman, and lived in Brooklyn with his mother. He had a nervous tic on the left side of his face and the remarkable ability to blush with his ears. During most of his stay he wore a green sweater with bright-pink pants. He displayed great masculine camaraderie from the moment we met. "Anytime you want the room for a bit of screwing, just push this in the door and I'll keep out." He showed me a red thumbtack and added: "But don't take all night about it."

I went to one of the lobbies the patrons called "the meat market." A girl sat down beside me. She wore a phosphorescently turquoise miniskirt, a platinum hairpiece, and the eye make-up of a Balkan spy in an early Erich von Stroheim production. We spent the next fifteen minutes strenuously lying to each other. I told her I was divorced, and she told me she was a fashion model. I told her I was a corporation lawyer, and she told me she came up here to relax. It went on that way until the social hostess appeared, blowing a bosun's whistle and advertising us to *mingle!* We mingled.

Later, Max buttonholed me. "You're from Manhattan, aren't you? Well, lay off that broad. She's G.U."

"What's that?"

"Geographically undesirable. Lives in Long Island."

If the girls were tense, the men were breathtakingly rude. I heard one cavalier introduce himself to an overweight brunette with the words: "Listen, why don't you go on a Stillman diet?"

A young man of elephantine proportions, chewing a soggy cigar, broke into an all-girl conversation about Chinese acupuncture by hollering: "Aw, cut out dat smart talk and maybe you'll get husbands."

The ladies gave almost as good as they got. At dinner a matron with inch-long eyelashes and a plastic butterfly on her silver lamé gown surveyed the vicinity and said loudly, but to no one in particular: "I'll have to see about another table. Just once I wanna sit with some class people."

If whatever raged outside was the war between the sexes, this was nuclear combat. And all present had paid between seventy and eighty dollars to participate, not including transportation costs.

The tone persisted through a dinner dance, a calypso party, a cocktail mixer, and a disc session with free wine, possibly because nobody drank enough to get mellow. Enough, though, for me to hear some fairly unvarnished female views of the setup.

"My mother makes me come up here one goddamn month after another. *She* pays for it, so I don't have an excuse. Why? Because I'm going on for twenty-six, an old maid already. Well, just look at these jerks—*look* at them!"

Her neighbor looked, as ordered, and nodded, her jaws chewing rhythmically. "Yeah, they're terribly few this week. So perhaps it'll be better next month."

A girl with a voice like a caress, who did freelance PR work, gave me another angle. "The older women are the worst here. They just about trample you underfoot hurling themselves at guys. And most of them don't even want sex, just compliments. What I mean is they'll pay with sex for a few flattering words. Anything to keep their egos intact for a little while longer."

"And the men?"

She made a curious grimace, something halfway between sympathy and disgust. "A lot of *schlemiels.* They all want to go to bed with you immediately. If not here, then back in the city. But they're piss-scared of *any* kind of commitment. Emotional or anything. They don't even want a real hot affair, for God's sake, just a quick lay."

Yet despite her observations—and mine—the singles weekends produce a steady crop of marriages. Mostly by a delayed-action mechanism. A girl will give her telephone number to eight or ten men over the weekend. Perhaps half will actually ring her for a date, half again may take her out repeatedly, *one* may stick around for keeps. It's a way to make the law of averages work on her side.

The Concord's neighbor is the smaller, more *gemütlich*, but equally hectic Grossinger's, which, according to its billboards, HAS EVERYTHING. A singles weekend at Grossinger's costs sixty-five dollars, including meals that are not only Gargantuan but excellent. When the guests aren't actually eating they're kept entertained "from dawn to yawn," and frequently a good while longer.

Grossinger's specializes in participation programs on all levels. One gathering invites patrons to thrash out requests and complaints with the management in open assembly. Another features amateur contests of singers or instrumentalists. When I looked into the resort's nightclub, I noticed that paying guests were taking turns to replace the professional go-go girls in their glittering display cages for long and arduous stretches.

I asked one of the volunteers, still dripping sweat from her exertions, if she'd enjoyed her stint in the cage. "Hell, no," she panted, "but with a thousand women here, how else are you gonna make guys *notice you!*"

The logical extension of the singles weekend is the singles tour. These excursions have been around for years, but only recently have they reached proportions that make certain travel agents depend on them for survival.

Essentially these are packaged, conducted, prepaid and pretipped group jaunts, lasting from seven days to three weeks, confined—ostensibly at least—to the unmarried. They range from $154 hops to Hawaii to bus-and-boat zigzags through seven European countries, costing around $700 plus air fare. They serve the same purpose as the weekends, sometimes even the selfsame clients—the so-called "runners" who race the singles circuit from the Catskills to Capri.

But there *are* differences and they loom very large on that ultimate of singles enterprises: the cruise. Around half a dozen shipping companies are currently conducting singles cruises. One has actually teamed up with a computer outfit to produce the quintessence of mating games, played with more or less captive participants.

In 1969, the Greek Line began to sail singles cruises to the Caribbean in conjunction with Operation Match (see Chapter 4). The idea proved so successful that the company now runs three such tours a year, booking about 700 passengers per trip, filling every inch of cabin space of its white 26,300-ton luxury flagship *Queen Anna Maria*. And this despite the fact that Operation Match president Steve Milgrim frankly admits that, with this small sample, the computer can't do a proper job and the whole matching procedure "is conducted in a fun spirit for the basic purpose of acting as a social icebreaker . . ."

Passengers answer the usual questionnaires beforehand. Once embarked, they receive lists of those people the machine has paired them with. Long lists, containing up to forty names. During the first day out the constant refrain on board goes, "Are you on my list?"

But they quickly learn that life afloat has its own rules, quite unconnected with computer listings. The first is that, although one class, the vessel boasts an elite fringe—the occupants of single cabins. Single cabins cost $600 for nine days (compared to $300 for the cheapest double) and entail considerable erotic privileges. Whereas the twin-berthed proletarians must hunt for sex crannies among the life rafts, the stateroom aristocrats can conduct their amours in bed. At leisure.

The composition of the passengers is apt to come as another surprise. Women usually outnumber men—but not among the largest age group on board, those between twenty-five and thirty-five. There the ratio is more likely to be two males per female. The higher up in the age span, the lower the male ratio descends.

Here, however, a totally unforeseen factor intrudes: the crew. The presence of several hundred sturdy seafarers can play havoc with the dreams of men banking on the numerical law of supply and demand. Officially, the ship's personnel is forbidden to fraternize, but the ban holds good only as long as they are on duty. After that, it becomes about as effective as Prohibition.

This works particularly in favor of those Junoesque ladies who are most frequently advised to go on Stillman diets. Greeks generally adore heavy women, and buxom blondes—the buxomer the better—

may wind up with relays of passionate Cretans, who don't need dictionaries to get their point across.

The initiative doesn't necessarily rest with them. On a proportion of women travelers the crew acts like catnip—to the virtual exclusion of fellow singles. Stewards, bartenders and the muscular shipboard masseurs are particularly in demand. Ladies have been observed slipping them fifty-dollar bills as inducements to break the nonfrat regulation.

Other deductions from the ranks of available partners are the "sickies" and the drunks. The former term applies to the permanent *mal de mer* invalids, who get seasick the moment they climb up the gangway and remain in that condition more or less uninterruptedly until they crawl back on land. The second embraces two distinct categories of liquor fiends. One is totally harmless, if useless. They are the men (always men) who simply went on the cruise in order to imbibe peacefully. They retire to a bar and emerge only for meals and slumber, now and again inquiring vaguely: "What's the weather like out there?" The latter, however, can become a nerve-grinding nuisance after a few days. They are the men and women who can't cope with the constant liquor supply flowing at dinner, in the staterooms, at dance and cocktail parties, but can't stay away from them either. They become hostile, hysterical, incapacitated or destructive at every given function, ruin tableware and evening gowns and the fun of everybody within reach, and always require several bodyguards to get them out of trouble and into bed. No one and nothing can persuade them that they can't hold their liquor, and their rampages usually last as long as the cruise.

Which brings us to another fact of shipboard life: the inability to get away. Once a particular menace has you targeted, there is practically no escape from his or her attentions.

"We had this character on board we called The Prince," related Lorna Taunis, a pretty manicurist from Lansing, Michigan. "The Prince was a walking arsenal of joke gadgets. You know, plastic ink blobs and imitation turds and squirting flowers and bleeding fingers. And when you weren't looking he'd switch your glass for a dribble glass. Or he'd stick a cold slimy kind of plastic lizard on your neck.

He must have brought a trunkload of those things. Laugh? He'd practically kill himself. Only not really, worse luck. Well, you just couldn't duck that creep, no way. We had a kind of alarm system set up, four of us, we'd sound the 'early Prince warning.' Mostly he got through, though. I swear he could multiply himself like an amoeba."

Getting away, however, is not a major concern for people on singles cruises. The important thing is to get closer. And the entire ship's program is aimed to accomplish just that.

From the "round robin" meals (anyone can sit at any table) to the nightly balloon dances, the *leitmotif* is proximity. The balloon dances, in fact, resemble ritualized coitus performed amidst a circle of spectators, like Watusi mating ceremonies. Except that the female does the grinding. Several men have inflated toy balloons hung over their nether portions. An equal number of women are unleashed to catch them, clasp them in their arms and—by rubbing hard against the appropriate parts—pop the balloon. As an inhibition shedder it beats deck tennis.

In case some inhibitions still linger, there's Charlotte Antin, the cool and exquisitely poised blonde social directress, giving lectures on dating behavior for women over forty. "You can't just sit around waiting for the man to make the advances," she tells her audience. "*He* is the commodity in demand, not you . . ."

Certain inhibitions, of course, remain unassailable, just as there are men and women on whom not even tropical-ocean moonlight can graft sex appeal. Singles cruises have wallflowers, but they have decidedly fewer of them than most mating functions. About halfway through the voyage a special chemistry takes over, melting reserve, transmuting active dislike into resigned toleration and fanning minuscule sparks into fair-sized glows.

The glows may not last past landfall (although Mr. Milgrim assures the passengers that within twelve months 7 or 8 percent of them will be married to someone they met on the cruise), but their warmth will linger at least part of the way through the bleak winter season at home.

Cruises are both the most expensive and most elaborately organized facet of the singles spectrum. At the opposite end of the scale range the singles parties, which get by on the barest minimum of structuring. As a matter of fact, their main attraction is the apparently casual nonchalance with which they are thrown together, although the nonchalance is more apparent than real.

Singles parties are such purely metropolitan phenomena that most people living outside the New York, Chicago and Los Angeles areas don't know the meaning of the term. It signifies a party—afternoon or night—at which only unmarried adults gather. Sometimes by personal invitation, more often by following advertisements appearing in specific publications.

The vogue began in the late 1950s and reached its present peak ten years later. At the moment, you can scan the columns of New York's *Village Voice* or the Los Angeles *Free Press* and line up a couple of dozen of these gatherings for any given weekend.

They are the epitome of free enterprise, requiring merely a biggish apartment, a record player, large quantities of paper cups, and a resilient nervous system. Anyone can throw them and charge whatever entrance fee the market allows. Which, at the moment, is between two and three dollars, depending on the neighborhood, the reputation of the hosts, and the presence or absence of such supplements as coffee cake or hors d'oeuvres. Since liquor regulations forbid the sale of alcohol on unlicensed premises (and the admission charges *could* be construed as constituting sales), the entrepreneurs usually compromise by dispensing anonymous concoctions called "punch," which may or may not contain an eyedropper's measure of spirits.

In the pioneering days of these ventures the hosts were invariably young bachelors, and very much in evidence. In the words of Jerry Farbin, who helped usher in the vogue around 1958: "I made about twenty bucks clear profit on each party, and I always got the best looker to stay the night. She not only took care of my Saturday sex, but she'd also help clean up the mess next morning. Sometimes she made my breakfast too."

Since then, however, the atmosphere has become more detached. The hosts are now frequently married middle-aged couples, whose only purpose is to rake in the gate money and keep anxious eyes on their breakables. Since competition is fierce, they may insert inducements into their ads, promising "College Graduates Only" or "Professional People" or "Writers, Musicians and Artists." In practice these baits are blithely disregarded. Not once, at any singles party, was I asked at the door to reveal my academic status or means of livelihood.

The parties get a wide cross-section of ages—probably wider than ordinary shindigs, which usually attract a limited chronological span, about the same age as the hosts. Unfortunately, they also get the kind of individuals who would never be *invited* to a normal gathering. And some of them have to be experienced to be believed.

At one function, held in a home in Westwood, Los Angeles, I had trouble finding the house number, which was hidden behind palm branches. A little man loomed up beside me, looking rather like Charlie Brown grown wrinkled. "What the hell are you looking for, the number? It's right in front of you, for Chrissake! You blind or something?" He had the tone of voice you'd expect a Pekingese to develop, given human vocal cords.

We entered the house together. At the door the little man kept a firm hold on his two one-dollar bills while he peered into the living room. There were about twenty people inside. "Well, when is everybody coming?" he yapped. The hostess assured him that more guests were expected. He let go of his money, shaking his globular head dubiously. "That's what they always say. Afterwards nobody turns up."

He sat down comfortably and proceeded to comment on the furniture and his fellows: "If there's one thing I can't stand it's them Mexican blankets," he announced, pointing to one. "Ah, well, they're cheap, that's something." His pudgy index finger wandered to a rather scruffy young girl standing nearby. "Hey, miss, listen, I'm in dry cleaning, and I reckon *you* need a bit of dry cleaning." He let out a Pekingese laugh. "I'll give you special rates. On account it's a *big* job."

His unmarried state, at least, was never in doubt.

The astonishing thing is the number of really attractive guests of both sexes who turn up; admittedly for different reasons. I asked a svelte, raven-haired Chicago secretary why she chose parties she had to pay for.

"Because it would take me about a month to meet as many bachelors as I meet here in one night," she said gravely and frankly. "I think it's worth the door money."

"How do you know they're bachelors?"

She laughed. "Oh, I've learned the signals. Like—you ask a man where he lives, right? If he's single, he'll tell you in detail. A married man gets evasive. He'll say, 'Oh, not too far from here.' Something like that."

"Any other signals?" This was becoming instructive.

"Plenty." She thought for a moment. "When a guy asks your phone number, you ask his in return. Bachelors give their home numbers. Married men give you their office numbers. Another thing—vacations. A single man will go to Europe for two weeks. Or to Mexico. A married man, with a family—he goes to the beach."

The authentic bachelors produced other motivations, but with equal directness. "The girls you meet here are the easiest to make. If you can't score at these parties, you can't score, period."

My informant was a tall, cerebral-looking veterinarian named Ivan, who claimed that he had never yet departed alone from a singles party. Judging purely by his performance that night, he was probably telling the truth.

"There's something about paying their way in that seems to make women—well, vulnerable. Weakens their defense mechanism. Or maybe they just don't want to have wasted three bucks," he added.

"It's a contradictory setup." Ivan launched into what was obviously a well-trodden topic. "You have a basis of perfect equality: men and women paying the same admission and gathering for the same purpose. This seems to produce a certain—uh—recklessness in girls, a what-the-hell posture. Okay. But at the same time they feel —how can you describe it?—kind of *exposed*. As if they'd been stripped naked in front of an audience. Just by being there. Now, when I approach them—casually, like—and say, 'Drop over to my pad for a drink,' I play on both these feelings at once. Appeal to the recklessness and simultaneously offer rescue from exposure, you get me? It's hitting a psychological solar plexus. Seven times out of ten they'll come. And I mean gals who normally wouldn't dream of climbing into the sack at a first meeting."

What struck me about Ivan's attitude was the underlying assumption that he automatically came out the winner in these encounters. As if he were relating a series of car swaps in which he traded jalopies for quality vehicles. It apparently hadn't occurred to him that in each deal *he* was the jalopy.

Strangely enough, the women I asked about it tended to agree with his concept. Most of them were likewise convinced that these arrangements somehow worked for Ivan's benefit. It was a textbook illustration of the state of affairs historian Max Lerner called our "moral interregnum." The old standards have all but evaporated (singles parties would have been unthinkable thirty years ago), but the dual morality that governed them still lingers. We have simply adopted different operational methods to improvise along until the new standards arrive. Meanwhile we remain stuck in the predicament immortalized by Dorothy Parker:

> *Higgamous Hoggamous, women monogamous*
> *Hoggamous Higgamous, men are polygamous.*

If women really *are* monogamously inclined by nature (rather than conditioned to it), sexually untrammeled situations will always place them at a disadvantage. But we can't be certain by any means that monogamy constitutes an inherent feminine trait. It doesn't appear to be among those Pacific tribal societies that attach no importance to it. The next decades will show just how deeply rooted a characteristic it is with us. We may be in for a few surprises.

At the moment, America is experiencing a unique attempt to transfer the singles-party notion to everyday life. This is embodied in an entirely new form of community known as singles complexes. Currently these are still confined to California and Florida, but it seems purely a matter of time until the idea spreads northward and eastward.

They have been dubbed "a cross between country club and fishbowl"—meaning they are big on facilities and weak on privacy. But privacy ranks very low on the list of their tenants' priorities. The tenants are middling-affluent singles, theoretically of all ages, in practice mostly between twenty and forty. The dwellings are called complexes because they consist of a multiplicity of buildings, spread over ten or twelve acres of landscaped grounds, housing up to five hundred people. The facilities—which come with the apartment key—may include swimming pools, whirlpools, basketball, tennis and volleyball courts, huge clubhouses, billiard rooms, gymnasiums and saunas, indoor golf ranges and, above all, parties. Organized and catered parties that spread and spill over lounges and patios, in and out of apartments and into swimming pools and may continue from Friday night to Sunday dawn.

Advertising for these complexes, while never mentioning sex, has a faintly orgiastic undertone: "FUN PADS for Young Adults" —"No Way To Miss!"—"Live There and *live!*" Most of them employ full-time activities directors to run the ceaseless round of cook-ins, barbecues, amateur theatricals, lectures, card tournaments, ping-pong matches, water ballets, discussions, disc sessions, luaus, art classes and parties, parties, parties . . .

A lot of action for the money, considering that the furnished apartments rent at around $135 for a studio and $220 for two-bedroom units. But the action has a distinct fraternity-sorority flavor, reinforced by the housemotherlike presence of the social directress. "More like Stanford than Sodom," as a former tenant put it.

"You get people wandering in and out of your pad all the time," he remembered. "Of course, you can just lock your door, but then they have you marked as antisocial. There's another thing too—you can't switch partners easily. Once you've had a relationship with a girl living there—well, you keep running into her, at the pool, in the lounges, everywhere. That's not so pleasant when you're with another chick. So I went back to an ordinary apartment after a year. Less swinging, but a lot more private. If you stick around those complexes too long, they become a kind of crutch. Substitutes for the real life in the world outside."

Ponytailed Evelyn Norris, who still lives there, disagreed. "I think this is an ideal place—until you get married, anyway. I used to hate going home to my lonely apartment and shut the door and feel all isolated, nobody caring what happened to me. Here—even if you just have a cold, people come and inquire how you're doing."

There is also an additional factor, which Evelyn failed to mention. In every singles complex opened to date, the male population predominates by two to one!

All of the preceding developments point to a growing awareness in this country of singles as a distinctive social group. They are being looked upon less as folks suffering from a passing aberration of life style, a kind of lingering pubescence. One of the reasons for this is undoubtedly the much-proclaimed specter of population explosion, which has blown some of the virtue out of family founding per se. Another is probably numerical. The U. S. Census Bureau figures show that in 1970 some 45 percent of women under the age of thirty-five were unmarried for one reason or another, compared to less than 38 percent in 1960. An increase of 7 percent over one decade is an economic verity not to be ignored in a consumer-oriented civilization.

But while singles are gaining increasing social recognition, they still suffer discrimination where it stings worse—financially. Since 1948, when Congress instituted the joint tax return for married couples, the disadvantages for single people in the same income bracket as marrieds have grown apace. Today a childless couple earning $10,000 pays $1620 in income tax. An unmarried person earning the same salary must pay $2090—roughly 4½ percent more.

This is not only unfair but is *intended* to be so. As Californian C.P.A. Denny Flynn explained to an interviewer: "The tax structure is geared toward family development. This has been a basic American fact for so long it has become a sort of tradition."

Bearing him out are numerous recorded statements by Congressmen proclaiming that if single people's tax rates were reduced it would encourage them to live together without marrying. The Government would, in effect, be abetting promiscuity.

The argument has a quaintly archaic ring, reminiscent of the time when Queen Victoria's administration opposed the introduction of a Saturday half-holiday in England on the ground that it would "foster idleness and dissipation among the labouring classes."

Bankers may not take a moral stand on the issue, but they frankly admit that they consider singles poor risks and make it more difficult for them to obtain loans. Which in turn makes it harder for singles to acquire property, thereby helping to keep them "poor risks."

As a minority group the singles therefore have some legitimate complaints. The astonishing thing is that so far they have only found one solitary champion in the press. Who, as it happens, is married.

The sole exception is Merla Zellerbach, a columnist for the San Francisco *Chronicle*, who has also authored books on subjects like mental institutions and prisons. Her concern with singles may have something to do with the startling fact that in the 1970 U. S. Census, San Francisco was found to contain one of the nation's highest proportion of single people over the age of fourteen —41 percent.

Her one-woman crusade is not so much concerned with singles as such, as with the loneliness and exploitation that frequently go with their single state. Her column, *My Fair City*, has become a regular platform for the needs and grievances of the unmarried.

"What first drew my attention to this problem? Well, about five years ago I received a letter from a colonel. He wrote that he was attractive and well-to-do and divorced. 'How do I go about meeting women?' With his permission I printed the letter and his address in my column. I think he got something like three hundred calls the first day."

She smiled, but added quickly: "It wasn't funny, really. After the colonel's letter I received hundreds more—from men and women —all wrapped in that terrible cocoon of isolation. I just hadn't any idea that so much loneliness existed in this area."

Merla Zellerbach's crusading instinct awoke. But unlike her dog-matic fellow columnist Dr. Crane, she didn't mount the morality charger. Instead, she joined with some of the more articulate letter writers and formed what they called—for want of a better name—

The Organization. This is an expanding group of unattached individuals who get together regularly to talk, dance, hike, visit shows—but mainly to get together. The kind of loose-slung, inexpensive, pleasantly nondirected solitude breaker that *could* exist everywhere, but doesn't.

In June 1970, Merla and her husband, author Fred Goerner, followed this up with a pioneering venture that may represent the shape of things to come. The Singles Information Service (SIS), among other functions, acts as a consumer guide for singles. It uses volunteers to compile and publish information of special interest to singles: computer dating, taxation, crime (much higher against single people than marrieds), lonely-hearts clubs and encounter groups. The SIS compiles bulletins comparing and evaluating services, issuing blunt warnings against those it considers rackets.

At the moment, the SIS is still in a decidedly embryonic stage. But it can serve as a model for a nationwide network of such units operating at the consumer level, which would diminish the easy pickings currently enjoyed by the loneliness hucksters.

Loneliness, like illness and idealism, is a highly exploitable state. In our uprooted society it has reached the proportions of a national malaise, with a locust swarm of shysters, quacks, religious cultists, pseudo psychologists, faddists and cranks battening on the afflicted.

It is also an exceedingly dangerous condition. Adolf Hitler, it may be wise to remember, rode into power largely on the votes of lonely women, each and every one of whom he promised a man.

four

THE ELECTRONIC CUPID

In February 1965, the town of Cambridge, Massachusetts, became the scene of an enterprise that may one day rank as a milestone in this country's social history. That month, two Harvard University undergraduates launched a scheme they had christened "Operation Match." It entailed nothing less than the automation of the hallowed American ritual of Boy meets Girl.

The two young men distributed questionnaires (printed on credit) among the students of neighborhood colleges. Recipients were asked a set of rather basic questions about their personalities and their preferences concerning members of the opposite sex they would like to date.

The answers were fed into an IBM 1401 computer (rented from a local service bureau). The machine collated, tabulated and grouped the information and regurgitated the presumably likeliest dating candidates for each individual. Then the selections were sent to the participants, together with their telephone numbers. The rest was up to them.

The organizers of the project charged a modest three dollars per matching, hoping to defray costs and possibly break even. Neither of them was prepared for the furor that followed.

Within six weeks, some eight thousand local collegians had dated their computer choices. Over the next eight months, as word spread through the nation's campuses, more than ninety thousand students signed up. Romantic results varied considerably, but the process was echoed by a fanfare of publicity that—properly harnessed— might have generated a medium-sized war.

Press reporters, TV and radio pundits, magazine writers, gossip columnists, marriage counselors, sociologists, clergymen and sexologists swooped down on this latest college craze (it beat panty raiding by miles) and deluged the public with details. The subject was ideally suited to word play, and the air grew thick with tags like "condenser couples," "digit dolls," and "transistor trysts." The peak was probably scaled by a southern radio evangelist who referred to the participating coeds as "those Brides of Frankenstein."

While the avalanche did little to clarify the mechanics involved, it established the term "computer dating" as an American household phrase. And it wasn't long before the nonacademic world picked up the idea.

First came several East Coast resort hotels specializing in "weekends for singles." The resorts hired the services of Operation Match for a bargain ten dollars and offered them—as a gratis inducement —to weekend patrons. Then, almost overnight, there appeared a mushroom crop of organizations selling computer dating as their sole commodity. The fees charged for the service doubled—quadrupled —then shot up in geometrical progression to the four-figure level. Apart from more elaborate questionnaires and testing methods, the process remained virtually unchanged. The entrepreneurs in charge had simply discovered what the market would bear.

At that stage the youthful founding fathers of the scheme retired from the scene, slightly dazed by what they had wrought. Operation Match is still flourishing, but today it has added an "Inc." to its title and become a strictly commercial enterprise, unconnected with Harvard except by lineage.

It would be risky to call any one person the *inventor* of computer matching. As is the case with most technical innovations, there are several candidates for that honor. At least one outfit in New York and another in Toronto were already using IBM cards to classify and match clients searching for romance. CONTACT, also a college foundation, was organizing high-school "Computer Dances" at which prospective partners checked their degree of compatibility by means of mutually punched tabs.

But there is no doubt that Jeff Tarr, the undergraduate who concocted the original questionnaire for Operation Match, rates as one—perhaps *the*—pioneer in the field. When I looked up Mr. Tarr in 1971, he had turned twenty-six and was newly married.

"No, I didn't meet her through a computer," he hastened to assure me. "Matter of fact, I've been completely out of the game since 1967. I don't even know what they charge these days."

Tarr is a slightly built and supple man with a shock of wavy dark hair, impeccable diction, and a penchant for statistics. "You know," he said, "when a classmate and myself started this project of matching up college kids, we thought of the whole thing as a kind of social experiment. We never considered it as an ongoing, money-grubbing business."

He flicked an invisible speck from his shirt cuff and added reminiscently: "It was fun, though. I was dating a lot of the participants myself. For a while there I thought I was quite a lover."

"How did you compile your questionnaire?" I asked.

"Well, I had taken several psychology courses and was also quite proficient in mathematics. So I put the two together. The basic idea was to divide our clients into general groups according to certain chief characteristics. Height and age were the most obvious, religion also to a large extent. Geography—where the kids lived—was another big factor. Then interests, tastes, opinions, habits, etc. Given a pool of around ten thousand boys and girls, we could break it down into ten separate groups of a thousand each and match them one against one."

"Did you need a computer for that?"

He shook his head. "Actually, we didn't. The project would have worked just as well without one. The mechanics of it didn't require any computer." He gave a faint grin. "The computer was —well, let's say a business gimmick. And that's really all it was."

Tarr may have been right from the strictly technical point of view. But sociologically the machine proved a decisive factor. Far from being a mere prop, it was responsible for changing public attitudes toward a new development that seems destined to play a major role in our altering life style. The development is organized, indexed, cash-in-advance matchmaking—the "Mating Trade"—and it took the computer to get Americans to feel comfortable with it.

Although the demand for such a service was colossal, so—at first—was popular distaste for it. One reason for this was the American romantic tradition, which recoiled from such a cold-blooded procedure as contrary to the ideals of a Hollywood-nurtured generation. Another was the deeply rooted suspicion that anyone participating had to be a misfit, an oddball or a loser. Those who did preferred to keep very quiet about it. Eight years ago, when I first wrote on the subject, I had a hard time getting people to talk about their experiences. This time round, the difficulty was making them stop. The transformation occurred with the advent of computer dating.

Almost overnight, organized assignations became chic, *in*, the latest conversation points. The college kids, who started the trend, did so mainly as a lark and rarely came back for a second helping. Instead, their elders took over with a vengeance. Within three years the average age of computer daters rose to thirty-five for women and thirty-eight for men, and for them it was no lark.

It was the "scientific" aspect that had done the trick, appealing as it did, to the American public's unbounded faith in gadgetry and electronics. In the minds of a multitude the computer was an omnipotent divinity, capable of producing long-dreamed idols from its memory bank. If not at the first try, then surely at the third or tenth or thirtieth.

Sometimes that faith seems jusified. "Yeah, I suppose you could say that I met my ideal woman through a computer," nodded Harold, a rotund, thirty-seven-year-old cost accountant from suburban Towson, Maryland.

"Her name's Doris and we've been married—oh, going on for three years now. I lived way out of Baltimore here and I just wasn't meeting any girls, period. So I invested—let me see—three hundred and sixty dollars in a matching service. Expensive? Sure, but worth every cent; in my case, anyway. Well, sir, I got me three or four real duds at first. I don't even wanna talk about 'em. Doris was the fifth, and she turned out just what I'd always hoped for in a woman. In *every* way, if you get my meaning. The point is—without that computer I wouldn't have had a change in hell of ever meeting her."

Harold, though well-satisfied, obviously regarded his $360 as a heavy investment. But by current standards it is not even middle-weight. Of the 200-old computer matching outfits now in operation, there are still some—a very few—that charge $10 or $15 per selection. The average, however, lies around the $500 mark, and the figure goes up—depending on the company—to $1000 and more! I know of one case in which a Bostonian matron shelled out $3477 in order to meet "specially selected college professors and business executives." She didn't meet any, and her file is at the moment in the hands of the police Fraud Detail.

The very high fees are usually not standard figures printed plainly on a contract form. They come about through a subtle adding-up process: so much more if the client is over fifty, an extra $100 "investigation charge," interest rates if the client pays in installments . . . and presto! we have a four-figure bill.

Some of the costlier outfits concentrate on selling elaborate "social referral" schemes, extending over five years or longer. Their salesmen, a highly specialized breed, use a technique of emotional pressurizing similar to that employed by certain dance studios and funeral parlors.

"I'd followed up an ad run by Compatibility in *Life* magazine," a girl named Liza told me. Liza is twenty-eight and resides in Buffalo, New York, where she works as a dental nurse. A thin brunette with wispy hair, regular features and no bosom to speak of, she is not so much plain as forgettable. She doesn't register.

Everything about her—looks, personality, opinions—seems to have been stamped out by some slightly blurred die.

"A man from Compatibility came to see me a few evenings later," she went on. "Not young, but very nice-looking. Like a doctor, you know, with gray temples. Well, he told me, he said what was wrong was that I'd been meeting the wrong *class* of fellows. You know, not my *caliber*."

She crumpled a piece of Kleenex in her moist palms. "He said they had hundreds of thousands of members and they'd put my personality profile in their computer and come up with a whole row of guys who'd match me in—I think he said thirty areas. Not just one or two men, but a whole string of them. All checked out and tested and screened. All compatible with me. My caliber.

"Then he gave me a test right away," said Liza. "About fifty questions it was. You know, about my character, and about sex, and my religion—I'm a Catholic—and like that. He said I was very *positive*.

"They had this social referral program that would guarantee me between five and ten introductions a month for five years. It sounded pretty good. He filled out a contract, but I got a shock when I saw the price. It was four hundred and ninety-five dollars. I just didn't have that kind of money."

The Kleenex in her hands was a soggy mess by now. "Well, he talked some more—must have been a couple of hours. He explained how I was just tapping in the dark, meeting fellows by chance, the wrong kind of fellows, not my *caliber*. And here they could line up maybe two men a week for me—you know, the *right* kind, scientifically tested. With that many possibilities I couldn't miss." She thought for a moment and added: "I remember something he said. He said, 'You can't cuddle money.' That's right, you know.

"Oh, and it didn't matter about me not having the cash. I could start meeting fellows right away and take two years to pay. Or was it three years? Anyway, I signed up."

"Did you get your introductions?" I asked. "How were they?"

"Oh, yes, I got plenty of dates." She hesitated, a look of bewilderment in her vague blue eyes. "Only . . . well, it's hard to explain really. Those men—the fellows that turned up . . . I don't know how they matched them with me. It seemed like—like, well, pretty much the same kind I'd been dating before. Only more of them."

Compatibility, one of the largest and hardest-selling computer companies, was also among the first to run into legal trouble. Under a pair of exceptionally dynamic heads, Donald Cornish and Mel Zahn, the organization had spread out into thirty offices from coast to coast and prospered sufficiently to treat its area managers to a sales conference in the Bahamas.

But in 1970, New York Attorney General Lefkowitz launched an investigation of the company. This move followed sworn complaints by seventy-five persons who alleged that they had become the victims of deceptive advertising and fraudulent sales practices.

The tenor of the complaints was consistent. All of the men and women involved stated that they were continually supplied with partners who didn't meet their stipulated requirements concerning age, religion, education, appearance and tastes. In other words, they weren't *matched.* One female rock and pop addict, in fact, kept getting her very antithesis—men entirely devoted to classical music.

Don Cornish was inclined to put the blame on overeager salesmen, ready to promise anything in order to collect the $100 commission Compatibility paid per deal. "You must realize," he told an interviewer, "that a lonely single person is fodder for the good, tough, direct salesman who is determined to pin her in a corner."

But Compatibility wasn't the only electronic cupid in trouble. In California the attorney general's office moved against another high-priced outfit, Matchmakers, on similar grounds. And at the time of writing, proceedings are under way against five smaller companies in three different states. One of the incidental risks in mentioning these legal maneuverings is the amazing similarity of company names throughout the entire field, which could lead to dangerous confusion. There is, for instance, a Compramatics, Inc. operating in Crystal City, Virginia, and a Compramatics in nearby Washington, D.C. Both firms sell computer dating, and both charge around $500 for their services. Otherwise, they have no connection with each other.

One inescapable conclusion I reached after surveying the field was that a great many companies don't use a computer at all. The computer crops up only in their advertising. Even Compatibility's actual contract forms never mentioned the word computer.

I approached one large outfit in northern California with questions about the make of their particular machine. "Make?" said the manager. "Yeah, well, it's down in Los Angeles."

"Yes, but what make is it?"

"Oh, different kinds. We use different kinds." And, after a moment's pondering: "They're all very modern. We use only the latest models."

Oddly enough, the vintage of the apparatus could not conceivably make any difference to the result obtained. When I asked computer executive Howard Rigi about this he merely laughed. "Given the usual number of participants," he explained, "the whole process is just a delusion. You cannot get specific matchings from programings based upon multiple determinants and on a people-pool of, say, six or seven thousand. At minimum—I say minimum—several hundred thousand subjects would be required. And there can't be more than a couple of companies in the entire country who have that many."

Yet the magic exuded by the word "computer" is stronger than all the technical reservations of the experts. Especially since few, if any, of the computer clients have even the haziest notion of what precisely the machine does.

What it does is simply sort piles of punch cards, coded with information, and pair certain male with certain female cards according to programed instructions. These instructions are based on areas corresponding to the clients' attributes and desires. If a given number of these areas—or points—match, the people they represent are considered "compatible." The number of points required for a match is called a parameter and may be large or small, according to the will of the programer. There are no government standards laid down for matchmaking.

Compatibility, for instance, gave its clients sixty-four possible areas and applied a parameter of thirty-three points. That's a pretty generous ratio, but it still left thirty-one areas unmatched. And if the traits most important to the client happened to fall among those unmatched areas—well, that was his or her bad luck.

This setup contains so many variables that I could spend the rest of this chapter describing nothing else. The entire procedure rests on the quality and depth of the questionnaire, since the information to which the computer responds is derived from it. The questionnaire in turn depends on the skill of the persons compiling it. Even if they are highly qualified, there is no guarantee that more than a fraction of the results will actually be fed into the computer. Because the more explicit the matching instructions, the fewer matches the machine turns up. Which is not exactly to the company's advantage.

Sometimes the variables are entirely beyond the computer's control. There was the case of the young man in Boston who enrolled with Data-Mate and received one date. Whereupon he wrote the following letter:

"Congratulations. For ten dollars I now have the name and address of my cousin who I've gone through school with for the last four years. Keep up the great work. Too bad I don't have a sister."

The most obvious weakness of the system, however, is its inability to gauge attraction. At its scientific best it can only weigh a certain limited range of psychological and physical factors and conclude that two people are *compatible*. Frequently this means nothing whatsoever in terms of human relationships. How little compatibility may count was shown by this letter addressed to another dating outfit:

"Your computer was right. Mitzi W. and I like all the same things. We like the same food, we both like the opera. Mitzi likes bike riding and so do I. I like dogs, and so does Mitzi. Actually, there was only one thing we didn't like—each other."

As a general rule, the higher the fees charged by a company, the more elaborate are its questionnaires and testing rituals. While these offer no guarantee as to the results, they provide wonderful window displays. This does not imply that the preliminaries are mere eye-wash. Only that clients have no way of discovering how much of the information gleaned is ever utilized.

I have seen checklists containing up to five hundred questions, some of which could be answered in four different ways. They may span the entire gamut from favorite colors to masturbatory habits, from ideas on underwear to credit rating, from classification of family background (five choices) to If-you-could-make-yourself-invisible fantasies.

I was asked whether I found "unshaven feminine armpits" offensive more or less in the same breath as the number of symphonies composed by Beethoven. One southern California organization went into the minutiae of racial descent with mathematical fervor. Was I Caucasian (85.7 percent or more), Chinese (25 percent or more) or Negro (3⅛ percent or more)?

The written quizzes are frequently followed by two, three or more personal interviews with staff members, plus one or several sessions with a psychologist. To top it off, there may be an investigation of the candidate by private inquiry agents, often involving the questioning of neighbors, friends and employers.

Most of this is done chiefly to demonstrate to clients that they're getting their money's worth. But what finally happens to all this personal data is a moot point, in more ways than one. Since matchmakers spring up, close down, amalgamate, relocate, or sell out to each other with dazzling rapidity, their confidential files are liable to end up in entirely different hands than they were intended for. There are no laws—not even a code of ethics—to provide safeguards.

Despite this plethora of questions, only one company (one of the cheapest) currently allows subscribers the luxury of indicating the *degree* of importance they attach to each matching item. Meaning they can state that they particularly wish to be matched on the basis of religion or education or height, etc., thus making reasonably sure that these points, at least, go into the computer.

The firm is Icebreaker Inc., which charges a standard $15 to all participants and operates from a small, stuffy, badly cluttered office on New York's Broadway.

Icebreaker was founded in 1968 by Arthur Winston, a young ex-marketing specialist, whose matter-of-factness represents quite a change from the usual entrepreneur type in his genre. I had no trouble elucidating from him that his company rented a Control Data 31–50 computer once a week and that in the past year they had processed twenty-five hundred clients.

"Of course, the whole matching process is still in its infancy," he said, adjusting his glasses. "We have to use a lot of plain common sense and my partner's training—he's a psychotherapist—to get results."

"What kind of results did you get so far?"

"About ten matchings per subscriber since we started four years ago. But what interests me most are the statistical results." He tapped a stack of charts on his desk. "For instance, our natural intake is 55 percent men as against 45 percent women. Now, that's the reverse ratio of the usual proportion in this business. Why? I wish I knew."

Winston drew out a chart, warming up to his subject. "And here. The average age of our clients is thirty-two—four years under the general average. Again, I don't know the reason. Now this"—another tap on the chart—"is more normal: 96 percent are white. Computer dating hasn't caught on very much with blacks yet. And more than half are Jewish. That's normal for the Greater New York area. This will probably change when we expand into Philadelphia next year.

"But you know, what I'd really like is to run a nationwide survey trying to establish complementing male/female profiles. Only I'd need a government grant for that. I've offered my data to several agencies already. But so far"—he shook his head—"no luck."

When Winston mentioned what he called "natural intake"— meaning his clientele—he had put his finger on the sorest point of the entire industry. A matching computer can only match the material it gets, and the quality of the customers—in terms of matability—is often way below par.

This appears to vary from company to company, from region to region, according to no discernible pattern. The nearest thing to a guideline might be the fact that the caliber of the male clients tends to be somewhat higher in states with a shortage of eligible women: Alaska, Idaho, New Mexico, Wyoming, and the Dakotas. The female norm, however, shows no geographical distinctions at all, but mutates from one outfit to another with total inconsistency. Perhaps the particular pitch of a company's advertising has something to do with it.

When a matching service's clientele is bad it can be truly dismal. One unusually honest matchmaker (whose name I promised not to mention) informed me that the average age of his female subscribers is thirty-nine and that about 78 percent of them have been previously married. His men, on the other hand, are mostly over forty, and 64 percent of them were never wedded. To summarize: He was trying to mate a majority of widows and divorcees with a majority of confirmed bachelors.

While the above picture may be regarded as the gloomiest going, it is by no means unique. And throughout the computer-dating world women in the higher age brackets outnumber men by an uncomfortable margin. (Later we'll come to other branches of the mating trade where the position is reversed.)

Most of the screening devices are contrived for the sole benefit of lady clients. Salesmen continually harp on the ingeniousness with which their services sift out drunkards, drug addicts, psychotics, ex-convicts, and the already-married. In many instances, women told me that their main reason for paying the extravagant fees demanded was the belief that they were buying protection from such "undesirables."

Unfortunately, they weren't. Whether the screens are not applied rigorously enough or are simply ineffective, the fact is that the "undesirables" have no difficulty getting through. Their ease in doing so seems to bear no relation to the amount of precautions a company claims to take.

The absolute maximum in sifting measures was claimed by a San Francisco outfit called Unité Unlimited. They first drew my attention through their ads, which were little gems. Under the heading *Date with Dignity*, they presented a cool low-key approach to people who already had their share of casual dates, but wanted something more: ". . . meaningful relationships, whether or not marriage is your goal." Just in case the reader's linguistics weren't up to it, the ad also explained that "Unité" was pronounced "U-Ne-Tay" and meant "to bring together" in French.

Unité's offices were a plush, pastel-colored suite in San Francisco's most luxurious business block, the Fox Plaza. Deep carpets, a tastefully chic blonde receptionist in the waiting room, and a breathtaking harbor view through the window. William J. Winslow, the president, received me from behind a statuette of Rodin's "Thinker" on his desk.

"This," said Mr. Winslow, sweeping the room with a gesture, "is *not* a dating service. Nor a matrimonial bureau, although marriage, of course, frequently results from our arrangements. We are a *matching* service in the truest sense of the word."

He dressed appropriately for the head of a matching service. Everything on him matched—shirt, tie, handkerchief, cuff links. Even his business suit blended with his desk. In an indefinable way, Mr. Winslow matched his entire office décor. He is a fair, chunky man, with a brush cut and a rapid, slightly twangy voice that sounds as if he were reading a permanent list of instructions. It didn't surprise me to learn that his field used to be personnel placement.

"We are definitely not the place to come to for casual daters. No, sir." He shook his head vigorously. "Here is one of our contract forms. Note the number of personality tests and checks we apply."

The list was impressive, almost intimidatingly so. First came a personal interview (several, if required). Then a written psychology test. Then a medical examination. Then a "confidential character and background investigation." Finally a private consultation with a licensed psychologist.

"Do you have a psychologist on your staff?" I inquired.

Mr. Winslow smiled thinly. "We couldn't afford to pay the salaries these highly qualified people would rate. But we enlist their services on a regular basis. Here—if you like—is the name of one."

"And who does your confidential investigations?"

"A private firm of inquiry agents. Very efficient. Let me read you one of their reports on a prospective client." He cleared his throat:

"Neighbors comment on his politeness, friends state that he drinks in moderation, is affable and even-tempered. Leads a steady, routine life. Punctual in paying bills, highly esteemed by his employers." Winslow closed the folder. "An excellent prospect. Quite excellent."

I opened my mouth for a question, but he held up his hand. "One more thing. After all the tests are in, we hold a special staff conference on the acceptance of each client. All the interviewers and checkers participate, each one writes a recommendation, We even consult our receptionist—she's watched the client in the waiting room. She has no special qualifications, but she contributes a—er—woman's intuition. That counts a lot sometimes."

I asked whether he rejected many applicants.

"Yes, I'm afraid so," Winslow nodded gravely. "We are highly selective. We don't, I'm sad to say, accept cripples or alcoholics. No men under five feet four inches, nor women over six feet tall. Nor anyone more than 20 percent overweight. And, of course, nobody who's mentally unstable."

"Then, how many subscribers do you have?"

"I'm sorry, we do not reveal such figures."

I tried another tack. "What's the sex ratio of your clients?"

"I'm sorry, we can't reveal that either."

He was more forthcoming about his fees. They ranged, he explained, from $285 to $475, depending on the "marketability" of clients, a general attribute involving their age, appearance, income, and several other factors. The easier a person was to match, the lower the fee.

Mr. Winslow, I learned, lectured extensively before civic groups and schools, and distributed a colorfully illustrated booklet entitled *Modern Dating*. Its author was one Garner Ted Armstrong, who heads an evangelizing sect somewhat to the Fundamentalist right of Oral Roberts. Couched in what you might call Dick-and-Jane prose, the volume contained an even-handed mélange of fact and fable, a million or so exclamation marks and a few perfect jewels of statistical misinformation.

Winslow seemed slightly uncomfortable when I queried him on the booklet. "Well, no, it doesn't actually reflect my own views. But there are very few books on dating available. *Suitable* books, I mean. Also, we got these free . . ."

Several months later I heard that Unité Unlimited was embroiled in a legal hassle with one of its clients. I went to see her.

Sandra, as we'll name her, a social worker and anthropology student, lived in a charmingly rustic, book-lined apartment in Berkeley. She turned out to be rather different than I had expected: petite and curvaceous, looking younger than her age, her polite reserve laced with a dash of dry humor.

"Unité told me that I had to join their five-year program because I was over forty," she began. "When they mentioned that it cost four hundred and seventy-five dollars, I said 'Oh, no.' Then the man there came up with the idea that I could pay two hundred seventy-five now and two hundred in six months, without any interest. That was okay with me."

She gave a wry smile. "Well, my first match introduced himself as a fireman. He sounded a bit funny over the phone, but at that point I didn't know the reason. When he appeared, there was something about his clothes. They weren't just casual. They were, well—odd.

"I didn't catch on to what was wrong with him until our second date. When he arrived he could only just stand on his feet. He'd been drinking all day—wine, he said. During the evening it dawned on me that this was a fairly permanent condition with him. He was an alcoholic. He told me he'd had a whole series of motor accidents through drinking. And that they'd threatened to fire him at work if he had another accident. I didn't want to see him again."

She raised a forefinger. "That was Match Number One. Let me tell you about the second. He was neatly dressed and well-behaved. Nothing wrong with him. Except that he was shorter than me—and I'm five foot two!"

"Did you get a third match?" I asked.

"I sure did," she said. "And, boy, he was really something." Sandra's third match opened proceedings by talking uninterruptedly for forty-five minutes. It seemed that he had been a child prodigy—a mathematical genius—and had gone to Stanford University at age twelve. By the time he was twenty-five, he revealed, he was a millionaire. Regrettably, he had to spend all his millions on his wife's treatment for cancer. Which explained why he was currently both widowed and impecunious.

Later he became a director in a vast electronics conglomerate. He was forced to leave, however, because the company kept stealing the patents for his numerous inventions. He also used to gamble at the Lake Tahoe Casino, he confided. But there again he was foiled. For he had worked out a system whereby he won such astronomical sums that "they"—the casino bosses—forced him to stop.

"What do you say to somebody like that?" she shrugged. "He came on so—so completely paranoid—that I got scared. Among other things, he kept saying 'don't' for 'doesn't,' and that made all these— these fantasies—sound even weirder. I sure was glad when he left."

At that stage Sandra balked at paying the remainder of her fee. In fact, after being scientifically paired with a full alcoholic, a near-dwarf and a semipsychotic, she wanted her money back.

Unité insisted that she pay the residue: first in a series of increasingly sharp letters, finally by way of a summons handed to her personally at seven o'clock in the morning. It demanded $200 "plus legal expenses." Sandra thereupon contacted a firm of attorneys, who filed a cross-complaint on her behalf. She was ready to fight the case in court.

It never reached that point. In October 1971, Mr. Winslow sold Unité Unlimited to a southern California computer service called Amalga-Mating. The pastel-hued suite in the Fox Plaza closed down, though Winslow continued to direct various other enterprises in different locations.

Amalga-Mating welcomed its newly acquired members with a circular informing them of the takeover. Enclosed was yet another Compatibility Questionnaire, the biggest of them all. It contained 109 questions (each with 5 alternative answers) and embraced bathing habits (daily, weekly, biweekly?) as well as the frequency with which the member changed underwear.

Ludicrous mismatches have convinced many people that, as a technological blessing, computer dating ranks somewhere alongside the *Titanic,* the *Hindenburg* and the Edsel. Yet its concept is sound enough. The flaws lie in the application.

The most basic is the numerical aggregate. The system just won't work effectively if the pool of participants is too small or too lopsided in its sex balance. This could be easily rectified by a law compelling companies to publish the *current* size of their membership.

Catch two is a tougher proposition. It stems from the clients' inability to discover what they actually get for their fees—as distinct from what they are promised. Their position is not exactly unique. Anyone taking his or her car for a "thorough mechanical overhaul" faces the same problem.

Some kind of governmental control seems the only possible remedy. The Better Business Bureau (BBB) has shown itself quite unable to cope with the torrent of complaints. Two of the most blatant scalping outfits I encountered in my research blithely referred me to their sterling record with the BBB.

In January 1971, the New York State Attorney General conducted a hearing on the subject, listening to more than forty witnesses. The best-qualified among them was Stephen Milgrim, a principal of Operation Match, which now has 114,000 subscribers. Mr. Milgrim told the meeting that legislation was absolutely necessary "to correct the many abuses in the industry." It could start by licensing the services. At the moment we can't even ascertain how many of the twenty-eight dating organizations in metropolitan New York actually have access to a computer.

Yet despite all this, computerized mating remains a promising method of tackling the results of social displacement. And not only in America.

Soviet Russia currently suffers from a similar population shift. There the role of our suburbs is played by gigantic new industrial complexes frequently built in remote regions and woefully devoid of mingling facilities. *Literaturnaya Gazeta*—the closest thing to an avant-garde publication the country boasts—suggested a remedy: state-run matchmaking institutions, using computers to bring together optimal partners. A landslide majority of readers' letters favored the idea. The establishment, however, was not amused.

Pravda, official voice of the Communist party, reacted with a blast of brimstone. "Electronic and mechancial pairing," it thundered, "is contrary to Soviet social morality and proletarian dignity. One does not see why a periodical should propagandize on its pages a proposal so alien to our mentality."

Literaturnaya Gazeta, duly chastised, shelved the discussion. But it may have found consolation from being in distinguished company. Not so long ago *Pravda* had delivered much the same verdict on the introduction of psychoanalysis.

five

DATING CLUBS
AND LONELY HEARTS

Spread before me were the snapshots of nine women, all looking ominously like those pictures displayed in post offices under the heading WANTED BY THE FBI. The reason for this did not lie in the ladies' features but in a photographic copying technique that somehow imbued every face with an expression of frozen criminality.

The snaps came two weeks after I had completed a questionnaire and paid $15 to the Yale Photo-Dating Service of New York. According to the company's brochure, their system was developed "to fill the need of people who feel they are too individualistic and complex for the impersonal computer dating services to match." Instead of a machine, I learned, the matching was done by "trained professional consultants."

The women in front of me supposedly possessed the physical and mental characteristics I had claimed to desire on my form. Each of them had also received my picture, address and phone number. The brochure made it clear, however, that "Men should phone or write to contact the women first as a prerequisite to formal dating."

I selected three whose looks seemed interesting, and decided to leave the rest in abeyance. This turned out to be a purely theoretical scheme, because in due time all of the remainder contacted *me*. One with a five-page letter explaining that she was not currently available, but had been available last month and *might* be available again a month hence.

I certainly couldn't complain about the quantity of prospects supplied by the service. The quality was another matter. For whatever the attributes of the ladies concerned, none of them bore even a passing likeness to the profile outlined in my questionnaire.

My first choice appeared to be in mortal terror of me over the telephone. Most of our initial conversation was devoted to finding a rendezvous place that would offer me no opportunity to attack her. She eventually settled for a lunchtime meeting in a midtown café, where at that hour you needed a shoehorn and a hand grenade to gain entry.

We sat eying each other across the plastic tabletop, while loaded trays kept circulating above our heads. The girl's name was Edith, she was in her late twenties and wore a look of permanent incredulity, like someone who has just found a three-holed contact lens container. She worked for IBM, which, she confessed, was "a big firm." That was nearly the sum total of information to be wrung from her. She countered every subsequent question by whispering, "Why do you ask that?"

I invited her to ask *me* something in turn. Edith ruminated at length, then inquired: "Do you take sugar in your coffee?"

We parted shortly afterwards.

My second telephone assignation proved quite a contrast. The lady at the other end said she'd be delighted to meet me. Anytime— providing it was for dinner. She knew just the place, too. A middling expensive Italian dine-and-dance hostelry supplying what the Mafiosi call "cops' food" to the piped accompaniment of Mantovani's diabetic strings.

She arrived wearing a dress of luminiferous lilac stretched over layers of foundation garments, plus exactly as many rings as she possessed fingers. Her voluptuous figure was starting to run riot in several directions, and a helmet of reddish-golden curls nodded roguishly whenever she moved her head. Her name was Mildred.

"You sure talk funny," she said by way of openers. "What's that accent?"

"Australian, mostly."

"Well, you learned English pretty good," she conceded. "I met an Austrian once, and you could hardly understand a word of him."

Mildred was the widow of a textile wholesaler, who had left her childless and well provided for. He had been, it appeared, a man of considerable cultural accomplishments. "He'd play you anything you wanted on the piano. Gershwin, Liberace—anything. And we had books all over the house. Books *that* thick"—She indicated a ten-inch tome with her hands.

Since his demise, Mildred's life had become a more or less continuous hunt for a replacement of similar caliber. Mainly through dating clubs, occasionally on singles weekends. "You can't imagine the types of people I've put up with. Culture? They don't know the meaning of the word even." She shook her head vigorously, the curls trembling in unison. "Honestly, all men think about these days is clothes and money. Books—hah! Pianos? They wouldn't know which end to play on."

We got up to dance. She ran a bleak eye over my Harris Tweed jacket. "Eddie," she said—"that was my husband. Eddie always wore silk suits. Made him look like—uh—*somebody*. People respected him."

On the dance floor she severed all connections with me, so to speak, going into a series of independent sweeps, twirls and bobbing dips, concluding each of her private frenzies by shouting "whee" and flinging her arms wide. After she had knocked two breadsticks and a salt shaker off an adjoining table, I managed to recapture her and place her under light restraint. Some of the ringside diners applauded.

"You have dynamic energy," I told her.

"Me? Aw—this is nothing," she said, panting slightly. "You oughta see me when I really cut out. I could keep this up all night." She began to sing, "I could have danced all night—I could have danced all night—la da de deedledum da," in a fair contralto, while the music played the theme from *A Clockwork Orange*.

I pleaded tiredness and herded her back to our table. "You don't have much stamina, do you?" Mildred said. "Eddie—that was my husband—he must have been about ten years older than you. And he'd outlast *me*. Whatta man! That was before his first coronary, of course."

"Of course," I agreed.

Mildred suddenly beamed across my shoulder and arose with a rush that sent our serviettes flying. She strode over to the next table and seized a gentleman by the arm. "Aren't you Mr. Frinelli?" she demanded. The man tried to get his arm free. His name, he protested, was Berkowitz. Mildred released him reluctantly and returned to me, shaking her head in an unconvinced manner. "He sure *looks* like Mr. Frinelli," she murmured. "That woman with him isn't his wife, though." She brightened. "Maybe that's why he wants to call himself Berkowitz."

While pondering the menu it became clear that Mildred held strong views on the subject of cholesterol. She firmly vetoed two dishes I wished to order for myself, on the grounds that they would kill me. I was finally allowed sole in lemon butter, but only if I omitted the mashed potatoes. She also harbored unaccountable grudges against most wines, insisting on a certain brand of upstate New York champagne that tasted the way feet feel when they've gone to sleep.

After our dinner had crawled to a close, Mildred indicated that the night was but a pup and that she and I were going to paint the town. She actually used that expression. I excused myself, saying that I had to fly to—er—Pittsburgh early next morning. Overcoming the temptation to tell her that I was about to join the Foreign Legion.

"Aw, that's too bad," she pouted. "Well, gimme a buzz when you get back, okay? We'll really howl."

I went off in search of a hamburger. Sole sans anything is not my idea of a meal.

The third of my photo-dating selections had a languidly amorous voice and invited me to her apartment immediately. "We can go out for a drink afterwards," she yawned. She wasn't quite sure of her house number, but the place had a yellow doorway. Or was it green? "Anyway, you can't miss it."

She lived in the sleaziest part of the West twenties in Manhattan, the street lined with unbroken barricades of cast-off furniture, scorched mattresses and garbage cans in varying stages of putrefaction. All the bells at her house had been ripped out, except for one, which gave you an electric shock when pressed.

She opened the door, wearing paint-spattered jeans, a gray sweater which had "Sing Sing" printed across the bosom, and no bra. She was tall, broad-shouldered and graceful, with blonde hair falling to armpit level and sleepily smiling green eyes. Her skin had the texture of dirt-streaked ivory.

"I wasn't expecting you," she said enigmatically. "Welcome."

The apartment looked as if the Viet Cong had recently used it for an ambush. It wasn't so much littered with debris as buried in it. The fittings were unrecognizable beneath a lava crust of towels, coats, underwear, magazines, newspapers, sheet music, pillow cases and torn envelopes. There was a smell—not altogether unpleasant —of mingled bacon grease and marijuana.

The girl made a charming gesture of invitation that embraced her entire abode. I entrenched myself, digging through several layers of matter before striking something solid to squat on. Smiling silently, she began to excavate jazz records from various places, which she put on a player entombed somewhere else. We listened for a long time while she continued to bestow beatifically remote smiles on me.

Eventually she murmured, "You smoke, don't you," groped among the ruins and produced a stash of weed. She rolled two neat joints and handed me one without further questions. A look of worry crossed her beautiful and grubby brow. Her smile faded.

"Yeah, well, listen," she said, "when I smoke I can't screw. Like it turns me off. Some people's mouths get dry, with me it's my pussy. You sure you don't mind?"

I assured her that I didn't.

She gave me a grateful smile and closed her eyes—a picture of total repose.

We may have imbibed grass and jazz for one hour or several—I don't know. Time had departed on a different track. At length I decided that I'd better depart myself. I touched her shoulder.

She opened her eyes and gazed down at herself in astonishment. "Hey, look," she said, "I'm wearing all my clothes." The discovery seemed to please her. "You going now?"

"Yes. And we didn't even have our drink."

The worry crease reappeared on her forehead. You could see her trying to focus on something concrete and immediate. When it snapped into place with an almost audible click, her serenity returned. "Oh, listen. Before I forget. Will you lend me fifty dollars? It's for rent and stuff."

"Sorry, no," I said.

She smiled. "Okay. Well, drop around again. Soon maybe. I think you're nice."

She went back into somnolence. A blonde goddess, slightly shopworn, reclining upon clouds of junk . . .

After absorbing this trio, I began to doubt whether anyone at Yale had even read my questionnaire, far less did any matching on the basis of it. But that, I later discovered, was not the problem.

Dating clubs, even the most conscientious of them, face a predicament similar to that of the French small-town mayor who explained to Napoleon why there had been no cannon salute from the ramparts on the occasion of the Emperor's visit. He said that the ramparts were old and might crack from the concussion; the powder was wet; the houses were wooden and might have caught on fire; he hadn't heard of the visit in time; the horses might also have been frightened. And, at the end: *"Enfin, Majesté, il n'y a pas de canon."* ("Finally, Your Majesty, we have no cannon.")

Like monsieur, the mayor, dating services can only offer what they have. And what they have includes a lamentably large proportion of undatables. This is a general condition, shared by clubs throughout the nation, regardless whether they charge clients ten or two hundred dollars.

By their very nature, dating services attract casuals, transplants, the chronically rootless, the socially maladroit, and the plain curious. Since their official *raison d'être* is dating—not matrimony—very few of their members join in expectation of anything durable. Although I was repeatedly told about them, I have not been able to track down a single case of anyone getting married through a dating club.

They lack the aura of scientific glamor surrounding the computer outfits. Being, by and large, cheaper, they also tend to draw clients who are either financially strapped or just not willing to spend much. In no other branch of the mating trade did I hear so many complaints from women whose escorts for the evening had blithely suggested that they go Dutch. The crowning piece in that direction was probably achieved by a cavalier in Madison, Wisconsin, who contacted a lady by telephone one Sunday afternoon. "He asked me to go for a stroll in the park with him," she related, "and said he'd meet me by the entrance. When I thought about it for a moment, he snapped: 'Come on, make up your mind. I'm ringing from a pay booth and I don't want to waste another dime.'"

Despite earnest efforts, I couldn't even work out an estimate of the number of dating bureaus functioning in the United States. As a breed they represent a statistician's nightmare.

The Manhattan telephone directory, for instance, lists twenty-three such enterprises. But closer investigation revealed that no less than ten of them share the same address: a small, musty office on either Broadway or Forty-second Street, depending on which entrance you choose. This is also the headquarters of Scientific Dating Service, Inc., and I couldn't help wondering whether that "Inc." embraced all the others as well.

The Scientific Dating Service, which calls itself cryptically "The Original and Largest Personalized Dating Service Since 1961," is run by Ronald Melstein. I knew Mr. Melstein by sight if not in person, having occasionally seen him stroll around the Times Square area wearing a placard proclaiming "Guaranteed Dates."

I telephoned Mr. Melstein, explained what I was doing and asked for an appointment. His response was anything but enthusiastic:

"So you want to interview me? Sure, I can tell you everything about dating services—everything. I started the first one over eleven years ago. And I've got files on *all* the services. The point is—what do *I* get?"

"Well—you get a mention in my book," I ventured.

"And what's that worth, I ask you? How do I know how many copies you'll sell, huh?" Mr. Melstein pondered for a moment. "Tell you what," he said. "Why don't you go on television? The David Frost Show! I'll go on with you, and I'll tell you *everything*. That way we'll *both* get something out of it. Okay?"

Since I have not yet made the David Frost Show, I am still unable to say whether that Broadway address harbors ten dating firms or merely the one advertised on Mr. Melstein's sandwich board.

An equally bewildering situation exists in Washington, D.C. There a total of twenty-one dating, introduction, computer, social and matrimonial agencies are housed at the same office on K Street, Northwest. They all belong to one Harold J. O'Brien, who—for good measure—also operates a chauffeur service. Similar setups thrive in Detroit, Chicago, Houston and Minneapolis, rendering any kind of body count impossible.

With dating clubs so inextricably entangled, it is not surprising that members frequently find themselves carried on the rolls of organizations they never joined. A Chicago electrician named Lezinsky enrolled with an outfit called Rapid-Date for one month in 1969. The company dissolved a year later, leaving nothing behind except a recorded telephone message: "This number is no longer in service." Since then, however, Mr. Lezinsky has been receiving calls and letters from ladies who were given his particulars by four other dating services, all of whom claimed him as a "carefully screened client."

I know from my own experiences that handing a completed form to one dating bureau often results in the same information becoming available to half a dozen more. This is due to the swapping or selling of membership lists, a practice rampant not only among dating agencies but among computer services and lonely-hearts clubs as well. Occasionally it reaches such proportions that you get the macabre feeling of dealing with *one* gigantic, nationwide, all-embracing cartel, which—like those legendary gray banking "gnomes of Zurich"—runs everything.

This is not meant to cast aspersions on the fair number of outfits that take considerable trouble over their matchings. The Zipo Clubs, with neat, ultramodern branch offices all over the West Coast, work out the problem in geometrical terms. Their patrons' tastes, characteristics and attitudes are printed on graph charts, which can be studied and compared by the participants themselves. The charts illustrate five patterns—Social, Cultural, Conformity, Religious, and Sexual—and in combination *should* reveal a reasonably accurate personality profile.

They are compiled on the strength of lengthy questionnaires on which applicants can mark four alternative answers to queries like, "Do you believe that sinners must suffer eternal hell?" or "Should secretaries have lunch with male colleagues?" The graphs emerge looking like industrial-production tables in four colors, the scoring lines zigzagging from a bottom 10 to a top 90, showing at a glance whether you're a lowbrow or an esthete, libertine or puritan, traditionalist or Brave New Worlder. They are sent out to other Zipo Club members in the age bracket selected by the applicant for perusal and possible follow-ups. Supplemented by photographs, they constitute a serious effort to take the blindness out of blind dating.

In practice, however, it doesn't work quite so well. Applicants *will* lie, sometimes outrageously, conveying portraits of rectitude and artistic sensibility whose resemblance to their real selves is not even coincidental.

And no amount of graphic geometry can help dating services over the fact that they simply can't get enough members of the specifications most in demand.

These are passably attractive girls under twenty-six and men in their forties who are, a) genuinely unmarried, as distinct from merely separated, b) not paying out most of their income in child support and alimony, and c) not beset by crippling personality problems.

"It's fairly easy to cope with the sex bugs," a youngish widow in Philadelphia told me. "It's the other hangups that floor you. One man I met through a dating service was a compulsive counter. He had to count everything, all the time. His small change, the number of cars parked in a street, how many people there were in a room—just everything. Most of the time he couldn't talk, he was that busy counting.

"Oh, and I had another guy, he seemed very nice at first. Well-dressed and polite and highly educated. He was a watchmaker. We went to a drive-in movie and he held my hand all during the show, like a college kid. Afterwards he kissed me. Well, I opened my mouth just a little—you know, making it a bit passionate—and he hit the roof! Called me a filthy animal and God knows what else and screamed that I had filled him with germs. All the way home he kept wiping his mouth with his handkerchief. He never called me again."

Others find the "sex bugs" not so easily manageable. A New Jersey matron in her late fifties, staunchly Baptist and rather nervous, invited her blind date over for afternoon tea, following a telephone conversation during which he had charmed her with Bible quotations. On arrival, he was wearing a raincoat. When he removed it she saw that the entire front portion of his trousers had been artistically cut away, revealing him in all his glory. The lady had a screaming fit.

Most dating clubs still charge economy fees—somewhere between $12 and $50 for enrollments up to a year, regardless of the number of contacts established. But a few have pushed boldly into the luxury bracket, basing their rates on a more elaborate show of interviewing and very little else.

One of them was Matchmakers, a Los Angeles agency that folded tents in 1970, after several of its clients took their complaints to the attorney general.

Mrs. Lisa Goodwin filed a deposition in which she declared that on top of paying $295 to Matchmakers, she had to add another hundred dollars "investigation fee." The person investigated was herself —more exactly her income and credit rating.

In return she received a total of eight referrals. Of the men listed on the referral slips: Two were found to have nonexistent addresses, five had never heard of Matchmakers (one said he had registered with *another* bureau for $10 and never been interviewed at all), and one told her that he was only interested in dating younger women and—what's more—had stated so in his questionnaire.

This record is as unusual as the fees that went with it. What was customary were the ads that first attracted Mrs. Goodwin's attention. They promised "a dramatic and exciting change" in her life, which runs true to the phraseology employed by nearly all dating and introduction bureaus.

Similarity of advertising is largely to blame for the inability of most people to distinguish between matrimonial agencies, dating bureaus and lonely-hearts clubs. Yet all three operate differently, and anyone considering participation would do well to keep that in mind.

Dating bureaus, regardless of size, will maintain premises of some kind and at least see and interview their patrons, no matter how superficially. Lonely-hearts clubs work almost exclusively through post office boxes, which makes their designation as "clubs" rather mystifying. Whenever I followed up a street address given in their ads, it always turned out to be just another mail drop.

Their titles are usually mere trademarks (such as "Mother Eve"), and with some you can exchange letters for months without learning the actual name (or sex) of your correspondent. Fortunately, there are ways of tracking them down. The easiest, I found, was to slip ten bucks to one of the girls employed at the mail drop. Invariably, she would remember the name—sometimes even the address—of whoever collected the letters. It's an old, old reporter's ploy.

As a rule, though, the operators manage to preserve the anonymity. I met one entrepreneur in Boston who informed me with quiet pride that he had been handling about eight hundred clients a year for the past decade without catching a glimpse of any of them. "Who," he added pithily, "would want to?"

Lonely-hearts clubs, then, are simply mail-order houses whose merchandise happens to be human. Their stock consists of address lists and photographs—often years old—which they supply to all applicants in exchange for a two- to twenty-dollar fee. Most of them don't even pretend to assess their customers' mating potentials. Those that do often leave you wondering at what particular grade they dropped out of high school.

One outfit called "Lucky'n Love," located in Flushing, New York, proclaimed that it "has done many years of research in Psychology, Marriage Councelling [sic], and the compatability [sic] factors that go into successful person to person relationships." Its questionnaire inquired whether I had attended "grammer school," expressed myself "reguardless" of others feelings, suffered from a "disabilaty," had a "mathamatical bend," enjoyed "rhodeos"—and finally promised me "satisfacxion."

I only hope they are luckier in love than in their spelling.

The fee structure in this field fluctuates according to some quite unfathomable design, which seems to have no relation to the law of supply and demand. I have paid as little as $5 for a large selection of glossy photographs, and as much as $18 for a single short slip of badly printed addresses.

Overall, the rates are the lowest on the entire mating mart. Two dollars sent to Booster in Homestead, Florida, will get you either a list of 100 eligibles eighteen to twenty-nine years old or 150 over-fifties. Joyce Dee, of Jackson Heights, New York, offers 100 New York City gals (all ages) for three dollars. The same amount buys you 500 romance seekers of either sex from Social in Chicago. The bargain bonanza, as far as I could establish, comes from the Ohio Club, which advertises "1000 Lovely, Lonely Ladies" for seven dollars.

This price economy is made possible by the fact that lonely-hearters operate with minimal overheads. Although a few—such as the National Mailway Clubs—involve biggish organizations, the great majority consist of just one person working from his or her private apartment, requiring no other equipment than a filing cabinet and a tongue tough enough to endure considerable stamp licking.

In Miami I encountered a husband-and-wife team, the Klingers, who ran a lonely-hearts club on top of flourishing mail-order lines in luminous crucifixes, hair restorers, hard-core pornography and orthopedic shoes. They have since switched to real estate.

Apart from low running costs, another price-reducing factor is undoubtedly the stupendous competition involved. Currently some fifty periodicals—not to mention daily newspapers—carry columns and entire pages of lonely-hearts ads. I counted ninety-three different ads in one issue of a single publication. Scanning them is like dipping into an ocean of liquid saccharin. The key words are "Lonesome" and "Love," and what follows below reads like the product of a typewriter ribbon bathed in treacle. Sex hardly ever intrudes; it's always romance, enduring passion, Cupid's arrow, entwined hands, hearts beating as one, whispered endearments and something called "twosomeness." Money—or rather "means"—strangely enough, is permissible. Several ads announce "Wealthy Women!!!" in assorted batches of fifty to one hundred. Occasionally also "Gentlemen of Means!"—but with fewer exclamation marks and minus any mention of the quantity available.

My personal favorite, imbued with a delightfully sinister tang, was perpetrated by the United Circle Clubs of North Carolina:

> If you want to make the right move toward ending your lonely days write us & we will go to work for you at once . . .

There is a tradition among sociologists that lonely-hearts clubs must only be described at the receiving end of an indignantly trembling index finger. They are invariably pictured as unmitigated evils that owe their survival entirely to public lethargy.

The truth is that lonely-hearts clubs are no more inherently wicked than, say, patent-medicine sellers. The proportion of sharks among them is certainly no higher than in the used-car trade, although they do seem to harbor more incompetents. Their hyperbolic advertising claims are no more strident than those unleashed by the detergent industry—not to speak of cosmetics. And if their continued existence really depended on public lethargy, it must be slothlike, for the lonely-hearters have been active in America since the 1870s.

The reason for their dismal repute stems from their involvement in an area of special sensitivity—equaled only by the medical profession, the police, and perhaps the undertaking business. Social scientists *expect* them to take other than a purely commercial attitude toward their work, and are constantly shocked on discovering that they don't.

The club operators I talked to seemed genuinely puzzled by this. Why, they argued, should they be held responsible for the prevalence of heartbreak among their clients any more than an automobile salesman should be blamed for traffic accidents? As Mrs. Klinger pointed out to me: "Our forms state clearly—in pretty big print— that we don't check out clients' credentials. We just pass on whatever they put on their entry slips. If they can't use a bit of elementary caution in dealing with the people they meet—well, that's not our fault. It means they're just plain dumb."

In her own fashion she had put her finger squarely on the root of the trouble.

I don't know whether lonely-hearts subscribers are actually more obtuse than the general population, but they certainly behave as if they are. Men and women quite accustomed to prudence in business affairs will toss circumspection overboard when dealing with perfect strangers whose object is—purportedly—romance. No matter how often they hear that clubs do not investigate their clients' characters, they still cling to the nebulous belief that these have— somehow—been vetted.

Their simplicity is staggering. It can be, as we shall see in a later chapter on crime, hair-raising. The easiest marks seem to be folks with pronounced religious convictions. Anyone spouting a few random clichés concerning their particular dogma achieves an almost hypnotic effect over their brain cells. It is no coincidence that every one of the famous lonely-hearts murderers—from Henri Landru to Raymond Fernandez—chose to wrap himself in a religious cloak.

This attitude, however, is less connected with low IQs than

with high levels of desperation. For whatever the club operators may say, the great majority of their clients—perhaps 70 percent —are women over forty, usually with very limited attractions. Those advertisements announcing a half-and-half male/female membership are concocted in the spirit of the old Hungarian cavalry recipe for chicken and horse goulash: Take half a chicken and half a horse . . .

The age and educational brackets stated in the listings are merely those claimed by the members. The operators accept no more responsibility for their accuracy than they guarantee the vintage of their photographs. For them it is simply a case of *caveat emptor*: Let the buyer beware.

Just how little the *emptors* will *caveat* was demonstrated to me by the ten ladies I met and the dozen more I corresponded with through club channels.

Initial contacts are made by a standard method that hardly varies from club to club. You receive large sheets of numbered snapshots accompanied by lists of skeleton data about each picture. A sample listing might read:

> Mary B., Sewing teacher, 42, 5'4", 127 lbs., Widow, Brown hair, Blue eyes, Lutheran, Own home, Good savings. Likes music, conversation, cooking. Hartford, Conn.

Now, chances are that Mary will be forty-eight in reality, that she'll weigh around the 140-pound mark, and that her photo was taken at her son's wedding six years ago. The bit about her savings will most likely be correct. Lonely-hearts ladies rarely seem to fib about money—the men nearly always do.

In writing to twenty-two such Marys, I discovered that the more insincere my approach, the more positive their response. Ornately curlicued compliments and unctuous sentimentality worked best, especially when it involved flowers on a mother's grave and the little ole church of one's childhood. Humor was out, unless clearly marked by quotes. Poetry went over big—the ghastlier the better. The worst thing to do, I found, was to type a straightforward letter in clear, grammatical English. Typewriters, in their minds, were irrevocably linked with business. Anyone using them for intimate epistles obviously lacked emotional refinement. Precise phrasing was apt to strike them as "cold."

But by avoiding such pitfalls it was possible to establish amazing accords by mail. By the time we got around to an actual meeting, the ladies invariably assured me that they felt they'd known me for years. What they actually knew about me was nothing—not even my real name.

At that stage their behavior frequently became so trusting as to be scary. A librarian in Utica left me alone in her apartment half an hour after my arrival in order to buy some ice cream. The place contained two valuable cameras and a gold bracelet. Another —on equally brief acquaintance—asked me to pick up her purse, which she had left in her car. The purse held her credit cards, a silver cigarette case, platinum lighter, and about sixty dollars in cash. I began to feel envious of the wonderfully easy lives thieves must lead.

Occasionally I experimented to find out just how far my pen pals would allow themselves to be drawn into potentially dangerous situations. The answer was simple—all the way. After writing two grotesquely false letters to a theater cashier in Philadelphia, I asked her to accompany me on a camping trip in the Adirondacks. She agreed by return mail, adding that she harbored no qualms, since "we both feel about life the same way." She had never so much as laid eyes on me. I disappointed her sorely by canceling the trip.

Once or twice I made mild attempts to point out the carelessness of their behavior to my partners. One replied that she was sure our club wouldn't enroll "anyone nasty." What made her so sure? Well, there were all those testimonial letters in her brochure. I drew her attention to the fact that all those glowing testimonials bore signatures such as "Mrs. C.W.A., Macon, Georgia," and could just as easily have been composed by the operators themselves.

From that moment on, her attitude toward me chilled noticeably. I had revealed myself as a "cynic."

But such risks are mild compared to those taken by other members, who appear obsessed by an almost lemminglike urge for self-destruction. They turn up in "Special Offer" listings, retailing at around thirteen dollars, cozily described by one Pittsburgh club as intended for "Genteel people who wish to meet persons of means and the culture that goes with it." Their data always reads very much to the point:

Divorcee, 5'6", 145 lbs.; just received gigantic settlement; wishes help to forget.

Widow, 44, 5'4", 130 lbs.; husband left her plenty; a big business needs good manager.

Lady Doctor, 40, 5'4", 140 lbs.; has $80,000 home, fine income, car; will share all.

Widow, 5'7", 150 lbs., just received $25,000 insurance; lonely, very generous.

It doesn't take much imagination to see green eyes lighting up in urban jungles and the carnivores licking their chops. None of whom, to be sure, will jeopardize their meal by making "cynical" observations.

Earlier on, I mentioned a high level of desperation as the chief motivating force behind these listings. By this I didn't mean to create the impression that the women concerned are either spectacularly plain or incapable of functioning socially. This applies only to a fraction of the younger ones. The very ugly, the grossly overweight or the psychically unbalanced are as much a minority among lonely-hearters as everywhere else.

The desperation of the average club member stems largely from a *lack* of distinctive features, from utter *ordinariness*, physically and mentally. The majority, as we have seen, are middle-aged and either widowed or divorced. Thus they belong to the population group for which the fewest eligible males are available, where the competition for partners is toughest. Possessing neither outstanding looks, personality nor intelligence, their chances of a successful rematch are minuscule, especially in the smaller communities. Their limitations also bar them from certain sublimatory outlets such as art, study courses or politics. You cannot really blame them for waving the one asset they may have: money.

Added to all this is a peculiar form of moral disorientation that often plays havoc with their emotional balance. Their original courtship and flirtation days—the years in which they learned to relate to men—were governed by sexual codes which, they hear, no longer apply. Finding themselves thrust back into the fray after an interval of two decades or more, they mostly lack the flexibility to adapt the new concepts to their own natures. The result is that they either remain frozen in the moral posture of the early 1950s or hurl headlong into frenzied promiscuity—pathetically embarrassing because of the absence of real erotic temperament. Potential Messalinas don't, as a rule, join lonely-hearts clubs.

Their craving is not so much for sex as for personal attention, for the flattery that goes with seduction and for the intimacy that should follow it. It is precisely this need—and their inability to fill it—that renders them dangerously vulnerable, sitting ducks for any male with an oleaginous pen and ulterior motives.

In this particular niche men have all the advantages that come with being a scarce commodity. The ratio between the sexes here must be at least five to one in their favor, probably much higher. But even for them, it's by no means safe sailing.

Milwaukee boasts a club called Action, which specializes in an intriguing turnabout arrangement—women and girls are expected to contact men first. For an entry fee of twenty dollars, a man's particulars are circulated among female members, and he can sit back and wait for approaches. Some of the proposals I received in that fashion had the innocuousness of baited fishhooks.

A farmerette, who had inherited a fair-sized spread in North Dakota, offered me the management plus half the profits of her property, providing I invested one thousand dollars "goodwill money" in the deal. Since I had claimed no farming skills of any kind, the lady must have placed an uncommonly high value on my benevolence.

A Los Angeles woman sent me artistically undraped pictures of her pretty daughter, aged fourteen. In her letter she assured me that she was "very modern and broad minded" and believed "that three people can have more fun than two." A stakeout for a spot of blackmail if ever I saw one.

One of the neatest tricks I heard about was pulled on a fifty-three-year-old carpenter in Chicago, whose name is Stanley but who likes to be called Stash. He received a charming, if ungrammatical, letter from a lass in Cicero, photo enclosed. Although, only twenty-two, the girl wrote that she preferred "fatherly types" as boy friends, particularly if they could "do things with their hands"—craftsmen.

Stash looks younger than his age and is rather vain about his full head of hair and tall, outdoorish build. He has a dry, cracker-barrel brand of humor and chuckled as he remembered for my benefit:

"She was a kind of a hippie, I suppose, but a real nice looker. Only wore pants, though. I never saw her in a dress. She was living in this godawful dump of a joint—three rooms, and all the furniture must have come from the Salvation Army. The moment you sat down on anything, it broke.

"Well, I fixed that place for her like you wouldn't believe it. Worked on it every weekend for months. Couple of months, anyway. I fixed her chairs and tables and her bed, and I built her a whole dresser. Brand-new mirror and everything. Oh—and I repaired her rocking chair, too. You could really rock in it after I got through."

He grinned wryly. "Yeah, sure, she was mighty nice to me while I worked. Fed me meals—she was a godawful cook, but I didn't mind. I guess I was kinda stuck on her there for a while. Stuck enough to swallow that pizza she made. Tasted like dog shit with garlic. Yeah, she did sleep with me. Once. That was all —just that once. The rest of the time, I dunno, she had her periods or a headache or a cold coming on or something. To tell you the truth, I was working so hard most of the time I was too tired to care much. But we were really gonna rock once I had her place in shape. That was the idea, anyway. *My* idea. She had different ones.

"Because the moment I'd finished—before the varnish was dry even—that little bitch dropped me. But cold. Wouldn't talk to me on the telephone or nothing. I think maybe she wanted a qualified plumber next. Or a dentist. On account her teeth weren't so hot."

At this point one may justifiably ask what has kept the lonely-hearts syndrome ticking all these years. If the clubs offer only delusions, why are hundreds of them still in action after a century of being denounced, exposed and condemned? The answer is that they survive for much the same reasons the numbers games do. Everybody knows that most players lose, but also that *some* of them win. And for the unlucky majority there is always the thrill of the game.

The aggregate of matches achieved by lonely-hearts clubs may be small, but it exists. And for hundreds of thousands of people those letters represent the only spark of excitement in lives that would otherwise be nothing but a succession of pages torn from a calendar.

In tracking down some of the marriages accomplished via the club route, I found that they always involved certain personality types. People of modest expectations, who didn't hope for much and were willing to settle for less. People like the small, mousey post office clerk, who dug out her original listing for me, an entry remarkable only for its patent lack of tinsel:

> Michigan widow, 39, two children, not pretty but affectionate and loyal. Will make good wife for sincere, loving man. Money, looks, or religion immaterial.

Although the listing ran for years, she told me, it only drew two responses. "One was from a fellow in Indianapolis. I don't know what happened to him. He faded out after one letter. He probably got onto something better.

"But the other kept on writing. He lived in Flint, not far away from me, and he worked as an engraver. No, he wasn't a great letter writer, but kind of steady. I got used to hearing from him. All about his job and his dog and the movies he'd seen.

"The funny thing was that he never suggested the two of us meeting," she said. "I wanted to, all right, but I felt a bit shy about, you know, pushing it. So we just wrote back and forth for —oh, must have been eight or nine months. And all I'd seen of him was his picture. Then I got kind of fed up."

She shook her head, still mildly astonished at her own boldness.
"I went over to Flint and visited him. Just like that. Uninvited.
Well, and then I saw why he hadn't wanted to meet. He had a
bad limp—he'd never told me about it. He'd had it since birth. It
bothered him a lot.

"Well, you know, it took me months before I could convince him
that it didn't bother *me* a bit. And that was the honest truth. I
couldn't have cared less. Once I got it across to him, though, he
kind of blossomed out. Became a different man, almost. We found
we had lots in common. Like being lonely. We were married, let me
see, just three years and five months ago. Yes, it's worked out
pretty well, I'd say. About as well as well as anyone has a right to
expect. And maybe just a little bit better."

six

THE AD MARKET

San Quentin convict. I am 26 yrs old, Hawaian, doing time for robbery. I'd dig hearing from chicks that aren't hung up on middle class Amer. type life! If you're into the communal organic bag, that's outasite. Saying what you think and feel is beautiful! Don't know anyone from Ca. as I got busted right after coming from Hawaii, so it'll be an experience for me too. Will answer all. Peace! Stephen K. Ani, Box . . .

The above advertisement, which appeared in a 1971 issue of the Los Angeles *Free Press*, is not typical of its genre. Very few of the estimated 120,000 contact ads printed annually in U.S. publications originate behind bars. But it is indicative, in a mild way, of the immense latitude currently enjoyed by this particular branch of the mating trade.

The accent here is on *currently*, because such a degree of permissiveness did not exist eight years ago and may no longer prevail by the time you read this. It rests, as we shall see, on rather precarious foundations. But at the moment it is safe to state that the American ad market offers greater freedom of expression than any of its modern equivalents—with the possible exception of the so-called Weimar Republic in Germany.[1]

This does not imply that the field has been given over to prurience. The great majority of advertisers—including the convicts—still couch their quests in phrases that wouldn't offend a church journal. The point is that certain desires, formerly coded in abbreviations and euphemisms, can now be expressed in plain English.

Not *all* desires, by a long shot. I have yet to see an ad inviting participation in bouts of, say, necrophilia or coprophagia or vampirism or any of a dozen other fancies not mentioned by Dr. Reuben. But if a sadomasochistic gentleman with transvestite tendencies wishes to be scourged while wearing pink lace panties, he is at present permitted to announce the fact, if only in specific segments of the press.

The classified *Confidential* and *Personal* columns today provide scope that not long ago was confined to medical textbooks—but in a strictly departmentalized fashion. From that viewpoint, the entire media falls roughly into four sections:

1) Daily newspapers and conventional magazines. Will run friendship and matrimonial ads of the most innocuous kind only, usually tucked away somewhere between Real Estate and Missing Pets.

2) Weekly tabloids of the *National Graphic, Keyhole, National Informer* and *Midnight* variety. These feature up to six full pages of mating ads. While unmistakably clear in meaning, they are not very frankly worded and hint at rather than state their cases. The exception here is the biggest of them all, the *National Enquirer,* which prefers faith healers, outer-space creatures and White House hassles, and leaves sex ads to its smaller competitors.

3) Mating magazines, which are a world unto themselves. They span the entire spectrum from the cutesy-flirtatious *Peeplpickers* to the dryly informative *Singles Register* and the jovially pornographic *Response.* Although all of them contain *some* editorial matter, this consists merely of random crumbs sprinkled between the classified portions that form their bulk.

[1] The Weimar Republic was the short-lived democracy established between the departure of the Kaiser in 1918 and the arrival of the Führer in 1933.

4) The Underground press, subterranean in name only, since you can buy it at most metropolitan street stands. Divided between the ostentatiously carnal, like *Sex* and *Screw*, and the revolutionary-psychodelic, like the *East Village Other* and *Berkeley Barb*. The ads of the former delight in four-letter words, the latter in self-consciously bad grammar. Both are often undistinguishable from washroom graffiti.

Each of these sections would provide material for a fat and learned doctoral thesis, and probably will one day. In combination, they represent the most free-wheeling—and risky—form of mating enterprise going. Whether you place or follow up these ads, you're strictly on your own, with not even a semblance of an organization to provide guidelines.

This is undoubtedly the reason why the ad pages are for women what lonely-hearts clubs are for men: a seller's market. The Personal columns frequently find themselves so short of feminine appeal that some offer to take ladies' ads free. Men pay a minimum of five dollars for twenty-five words. Even quite pedestrian female inserts will draw a dozen or more replies. Intriguing ones may get over a hundred, plus a permanently busy line if advertiser were naïve enough to give a telephone number.

Very few do so. Routinely, the responding letters will go to a code number. If the advertiser replies in turn, it is frequently under an assumed name and from a post office box. And since the re-spondee's missive may have used a similar cover, the ensuing exchange sometimes proceeds like a game of blindman's buff until one of the players decides to drop the camouflage.

The motive behind all this anonymity is fear. Partly of kooks and criminals, but chiefly of the law. Because there is always the chance that your romantic correspondent may be wearing a badge.

The law makes it a criminal offense to send "obscene material" through the mails. Since obscenity, like beauty, lies in the eye of the beholder, it has been found almost impossible to prejudge what, precisely, constitutes obscene mail. The result is a form of justice that strikes as haphazardly as a hailstorm. Some writers remain unscathed while busily dispensing vanloads of lavatorial bawdry, others get nabbed and hauled into court for a single blue-tinged line.

The Chief Inspector of the U. S. Post Office Department once declared that "The seal on a first-class piece of mail is sacred." This is not only somewhat less than true, but also irrelevant if the recipient of the letter happens to be a postal or FBI agent. Both authorities will plant provocative "blind" ads in periodicals, goad correspondents into revealing their purplest thoughts, and then arrest them. It's simply a variation of the standard practice used by plainclothesmen on prostitutes, but it has cost many otherwise respectable citizens their jobs as well as their reputations.

These official "blinds" are only one among several kinds that plague the market. The most numerous phonies are actually hatched by the magazine managers themselves to alleviate their chronic scarcity of tempting female ads. In some of the more *risqué* columns these may account for a fair share of the contents. With practice you can learn to pick them out. They always proclaim extravagantly lustful beauties agog to tackle all comers. Gratis.

The C.O.D. offers—which proliferate in the glossy papers—are even more easily identifiable. Usually they contain certain key words, such as "generous" or "model," to indicate the professionalism of the deal. Some may not actually mention any *quid pro quo*, but are phrased so as to leave no doubt. You also find the same ones cropping up all over the territory, like landmarks. One of them is the "Amazon" (pictured wearing high boots, riding crop, and a ferocious smile) who "seeks dwarfs or other physically handicapped males to act as my chattels." Her photo, enlarged and framed, graces the wall of the New York publishing firm that runs it most frequently.

Equally obvious is the perennial Florida lass, "Young, beautiful, very passionate, travels to California often on business. I would like to mix my business with pleasure . . ." According to my last count, her ad had appeared twenty-nine times, which gives some indication of the scope of her business as well as her pleasure.

Others, unfortunately, are quite impossible to spot. They come from a species of literary voyeurs, belonging to either sex, who get their jollies through the perusal of red-hot correspondence. They demand that all replies be "frank, stark, unblushingly revealing" and often answer in kind, but they have no intention of ever meeting pen pals face to face. When pressed for a rendezvous, they simply fade out.

Finally there are the party orators who want letters merely to read aloud to their buddies. They can be indefatigable, because these recitals are usually their only contribution to an evening's fun. Having gathered one batch of mail, they will switch to another publication and collect a fresh lot. Unless you run into their ilk accidentally (as I did), you never encounter them in the flesh—which may be an advantage.

Fake ads have become so ubiquitous that a special guide bulletin now operates from San Jose, California, for the purpose of exposing at least a percentage of them. For a two-dollar fee, *The Exposé* sends out constantly revised lists of photostats showing phone numbers, date offers and party invitations that have proved duds or traps. The catch is that this estimable service runs an ad column of its own and *may* just be acting in a spirit of competition.

The overtly salacious offers, however, make up only a minor portion of the ad field. The major part consists of straightforward appeals for partners, sedately worded and passably honest. Considering the general state of our mating situation, they should be highly successful. Strangely enough, a great many of them aren't, particularly those inserted by men. It's not easy for a male to appear both attractive and on the level in ten lines of telegram prose.

Girls, as mentioned earlier, are showered with replies. But unless they know exactly how to phrase their ad and where to place it, the response may not be at all what they wanted.

Among those who obviously didn't know either, was a girl now famous in subculture circles as "The Fat Redhead." She had placed an ad, bearing that signature, in New York's *East Village Other*. Identifying herself as a college student on vacation, she announced that she wanted a summer love affair—no strings attached—with a nice, virile partner. As ultimate proof of her innocence, she also supplied her phone number.

Some weeks later she called the whole thing off in another ad that has since become a minor classic of its type. A kind of pulp version of Molly Bloom's much-banned soliloquy from *Ulysses*, scaled down to classified-column levels.

She began by apologizing to a couple of likely prospects who called her once, but—apparently—never called back. Then:

> But to the others—which includes the two lesbians, the under-25s and the over-40s, the numerous ones who dialed my number and hung up as soon as I said hello; the 35 or 40 of you who made dates with me and never arrived (and that includes the gentleman who bragged about the size of his penis); the wife-seekers, the much-married, and the man who was so nuts that all he thought about was his sexual organs; and the men who couldn't get it up when I was panting for them. To those who looked so ugly I couldn't get past their faces, let alone their tight pants; to the masturbators, who wanted what I did not want as a fairly normal lass. The ones who wanted to be beaten, whipped, hurt, kicked—to hell with you! To the men who bragged about how much money they had—with their small penises—please stop phoning me!
>
> To the doctor who wanted to rape me—as he opened my door. To the salesman who had nothing to sell in his pants. To those who could only talk garbage language, thinking that would excite me over the phone, to hell with all of you! To the faggots who wanted me for financial, not sexual, support, go to the same place. To the junkies, acid heads, hippies, creepies—go!

The lady's lament proved nothing so much as her ignorance of the ad world. For she had chosen a medium with a *deliberately* wide-open pitch, addressed to an audience that finds most of the above-mentioned specimens significant, at least not irritating. Had she taken the trouble to study the field a little, she might have scored bull's-eyes in one of several other publications.

She would probably have done very nicely via the *Black Book*, which rates as the New York *Times* of dating mags, and with some justification. The *B.B.* is simultaneously restrictive and expansive, meaning that it confines itself to advertisers whose wants are reasonably ordinary while allowing them the space necessary to describe them. Its ads can often be read for sheer entertainment value:

> Copywriter, slightly out of his mind, 24, 5'11", 190 lbs., clean-cut Caucasian, college grad, desires with breathless impatience a cute, blue-eyed, Scandinavian-type blond, 19–24, approximately 36–21–35, who's uninhibited, unaffected, warm, considerate and beautiful in mind—for perpetual, possibly permanent, fun-loving times. I faint when surprised. Please send photo.

This is a brief effort; the lengthy ones can run to 300-word essays costing $24. But it illustrates the general tone of the booklet: chatty, breezy, eccentric, yet essentially square. The *B.B.* boasts a great many individualists and some oddballs, but no self-proclaimed deviates. By encouraging openings like, "I'm a brown-skinned Afro-American, 25, and considered incomparably beautiful . . ." and, "Disgustingly sober Ivy League Ph.D. . . ." it accomplishes what none of its rivals do—gets readers to grin and relax.

The publication is owned by the possibly unlikeliest duo ever to have spawned a successful enterprise. Otto Heinrich von Wernherr is a miniature tycoon at thirty-one, with Peter Lorre's accent and Henry Kissinger's energy, who—besides *Black Book*—operates a telephone-attachment company, a firm manufacturing "SMILE" buttons and bumper stickers, and a dress factory in Delhi, India.

He supplied the drive and the capital; his partner, Bruce Price (who calls himself "Jason Pike" on the masthead), the editorial skill and imagination. Von Wernherr launches business ventures. Price writes novels, ponders about Life, and crusades against the current journalistic habit of using nouns as adjectives. At present he is working on a futuristic volume about a man searching for his father in the year 1979.

A tall, gruff, bearded young Virginian, who wears open shirts and a hat, Price has so many interests that he finds it difficult to stick to one point for longer than about a minute.

I asked him when *Black Book* was founded.

He stroked his hair with a characteristic gesture, as if he were massaging his thoughts. "Well, there was this friend of mine, Von Wernherr," he said with a trace of a southern accent. "Now, he's

very, very industrious. Likes to work, make money. I met him—
in a bar, at a party, I've forgotten where—and he kept discussing
what sort of businesses we could start. So, in the fall of 1967, we
started the book. It was my idea. I got it when I was in the Army.
Just because I didn't have anything to do then, I joined everything—Mensa, dating clubs—everything. So I knew the mechanics.
But it was his push. You'd better mention that."

"Where did the name come from?"

"That's a cliché—you know, someone's 'little black book.'"

"Do you get many complaints from people about their letters
not being answered?" I asked.

"Not many, no. But some. The trouble is that some people think
we *own* our advertisers and that we can *make* them answer. I'll
give you a classic situation. You'd better get this right. Is that thing
on?" He pointed to my tape recorder. "Right? Okay. Listen. If
somebody is a cab driver in New Jersey, and he's short, and he
writes to ten girls who live on the East Side and want to meet
tall professors and lawyers, he's just not going to get any answers.
And people keep doing it. They'll write, 'I'm not quite what
you want, but maybe you'd like to meet me anyway.' That's un-
fortunate. It's also a complete waste of time."

"But when—"

Price held up his hand. "It's really bizarre. There are people
who expect us to tell advertisers, 'Write to him—he's a nice guy!'
But it doesn't work that way."

"How does it work, then?" I wanted to know. "I mean what kind
of ads—and replies—have you found most effective?"

He stroked his hair tenderly. "Precise ones," he said. "A lot of
people feel they must write as if they were advertising toothpaste—
attractive all the way. That's wrong." Price shook his head. "A
listing should act like a magnet and a filter at the same time. The
best ads are simultaneously offensive and defensive. They say: here
is what would be great, and there's what I *don't* want. Take my own
ads, for instance . . ."

"Excuse me—you run ads for yourself too?"

"Sure." Price didn't smile. "Same ones for two years. But what

I was saying—mine are *extremely* selective. That's because I don't want a whole lot of letters. Just a couple or so per issue."

"Did the girls who answered meet your qualifications?"

"Weeell—not exactly." He grinned thoughtfully. "I asked for superwoman and they weren't quite—superwomen. But I met some pretty nice girls that way, just the same. But, as I said, my listings weren't designed to get a big response. Others get a dozen or more replies. We have one advertiser—a doctor, he's still one of our clients—he hauls in twenty letters per issue. He's our record, I think."

He tapped the open booklet on his knees. "The point is, though, that you should make your answers just as precise as the listings. You've got to really *read* those ads. Study them. See if they apply to *you*. That's the whole idea of those long pieces we run. People have the space to either sell themselves or hang themselves. But if you're haphazard about your replies, then there's no sense in all those details."

At times, however, even exhaustive study won't reveal the person behind an ad. I learned that from a lady who claimed she desired contact with "someone to share my enthusiasm for theater, foreign films, opera and art," with the forceful proviso, "Momma's boys stay away from my door."

Considering myself qualified for the former bracket and untinged by the latter, I wrote to her. She turned out to be pleasingly proportioned and polite. As to her enthusiasms, she kept them locked deep within her ample bosom. She refused to talk about them. Nor, for that matter, about anything except her cathedral-sized father fixation.

After an entire evening on the topic, I had the distinct feeling that it was pouring out of my ears. Every attempt to switch subjects foundered on her well-bred but iron determination to do no such thing. By eleven o'clock I was acutely aware of every nuance of her relationship with her papa—and absolutely nothing else. The world seemed strangely shrunken—just her, me, and Daddy.

"Tell me," I ventured while en route to the door, "why did you put that bit in your ad about Momma's boys?"

She looked at me wide-eyed. "Because I can't stand grown men who are tied to their mothers' apron strings. And you meet so many of them these days."

I left with the hope that I'd never encounter her father. I knew everything about him, including the fact that he goosed his secretaries and peered into his handkerchief after blowing his nose. It could prove embarrassing.

Black Book listings, while occasionally misleading, are always clear, even to novices. In other periodicals advertisers employ a kind of erotic Esperanto that reads as if it had been lifted from textbooks on anthropology and electronics, garment catalogs and pet manuals. It takes practice to decipher this jargon, and sometimes you wish you hadn't. But it is highly advisable to know what the ads are about before following them up.

Thus a "Student of French, Greek and Roman cultures" indicates a person who enjoys cunnilingus, anal intercourse and whipping. A "TV gal with ultra-strong high voltage AC/DC generator" means a female transvestite able to turn on to both sexes. "Rubber, leather and silk aficionados" are various brands of clothing fetishists. "Polaroid fan" stands for an expert in dirty camera snaps. "Satin lovers" and "Mauve models" are homosexuals; "Strict restraint disciplinarians," sadomasochistic bondage enthusiasts. It's also useful to realize that "animal lovers" and "dog fanciers"—some of whose ads promise "trained German shepherds"—are practitioners of the ancient bucolic custom of bestiality.

At first I believed that this code lingo was due to editorial censorship. In that I was quite mistaken. The advertisers simply prefer their terminology. Partly because it lends itself to abbreviations, but also because it screens out the rank innocents. If a lady knows the meaning of the term "vibro addict," she is likely to be one.

This slightly coy argot is the *lingua franca* of about a dozen glossy magazines, where it comes accompanied by the most uncoy photographs imaginable. Until recently, art editors made a point of disguising the advertisers' pubic hair. Now they're shown warts and all.

Seniority in this realm belongs to the *Continental Spectator*, which made a somewhat more genteel debut in 1963. Over the years it shed most of the G-strings, and today it has become difficult to tell the nude models from the equally nude advertisers. Although most (not all) of the bare skin is feminine, the majority of ads actually emanate from couples seeking either groups or threesomes. If you also deduct the girls desiring girls and the boys wanting boys, it leaves the straight solo heterosexuals with not much ad space to romp in.

The *Spectator*'s general manager, who bears the flamboyant name of Fortunato Fuda, is the first to admit this imbalance.

"You see, we started as a bulletin for swinging couples," he confided. "I had a girl friend then (I'm married now) and we knew so many swingers that I brought out this single sheet of information for them. Well, it kinda grew and developed into the *American Club* bulletin. Only, you see, there already was a club with that label, so I had to change the name. But most of my clients are still couples. And most of the single gals you find in there get their ads in for free. That's because I can never get enough of 'em. Don't ask me why—that's how it is with all the books."

Mr. Fuda is short, swarthy, and a former restaurant maître d'. "I made more money in my old job, but I have more fun now," he said, waving an expressive palm at the solid rows of pinups——barefooted up to their chins—decorating the walls of his Manhattan office.

"Does my wife object to me running this mag? Hell, no!" Mr. Fuda chuckled. "Matter of fact, she helps run it. Look—that's her." He pointed to what passes as the *Spectator*'s editorial—a chattily libidinous column signed "Linda Lee."

The *Spectator* retails at three dollars a copy and has a circulation of about eighteen thousand—huge for its field. If any of its ads can be termed *typical*, the two following are:

Attractive married woman, 27, has husband's permission to enjoy French and Greek cultures with sincere, discreet men only. Your home or mine. I never wear any panties under my miniskirts. If you don't think I mean it, try me.

On the accompanying photo the lady does, in fact, wear panties. But no miniskirt—or anything else.

For a second sample *sans* picture:

Obedient, submissive, good-looking, generous male available to white or black dominating, forceful, demanding female tyrant for part-time or permanent training, subjugation, etc.

On closer investigation, it appeared that several of the advertising lovelies were selling their charms, and not at bargain rates, either. When I told Mr. Fuda about this, he gave his best maître d' no-tables-free shrug.

"What can I do about it?" he posed philosophically. "Sometimes we get complaints about girls charging money for dates. Then I send her a letter and stop running her ad. But we don't get many complaints. I guess most guys are happy with what they get."

The *Spectator*'s diametrical opposite in terms of pictures and ad contents is a sixteen-page quarterly called *Cupid's Destiny*. It gives the impresion that even a bared shoulder might cause the paper to curl in protest. Tennis shorts rate as extreme exposure. Sex or related matters seem of no concern to its advertisers, who continually insist on their preoccupation with "good clean fun."

The bulk of them fall into two categories: "homemakers" ("housewife" is a dirty word) in their forties, with anything up to eight children; and men in all age groups and of such overpowering wholesomeness that they make Pat Boone seem vaguely dissipated.

But *Cupid's Destiny* has a few peculiarities of its own. It is produced in Brooklyn, New York, by a Reverend Dr. Harry Marmel, who, apart from romantic bliss, offers his readers a remarkable business proposition. For a fee of ten dollars, he will make anyone an ordained minister, giving them the credentials to a) perform marriages, b) visit prisons, and c) establish their own church and form their own congregations.

They can also become missionaries of the "New Truth," with the task of enrolling fresh members. In return they not only receive twenty dollars for every five applicants, but also promotion in rank—i.e., to Vicar for ten new members, to Monsignor for twenty-five, and to Bishop for fifty.

In his brochures, Dr. Marmel draws attention to the advantages obtainable for just that ten-spot:

> We can advise you how to register your own church. Once your church is properly established, you may transfer all your property to that church and not be required to pay property taxes.

Nor must it be assumed that the Doctor of Divinity offer entails any arduous preparation. In fact, it entails no preparation at all:

> Immediately, upon receipt of your application you will be ordained and sent your credentials and Doctor of Divinity.

And in case of any lingering apprehension on the part of the prospective D.D.s, the good Reverend also assures them that:

> No Schooling is Necessary.

Somewhere between the two extreme strata just described lies the great mass of mating mags. They cater to neither satyrs nor saints but to the unspectacular house-and-garden variety of sinners to which most of us belong. Their numbers are impressive, their contents bland to the point of insipidity. Every city above half a million inhabitants has three or four of them, and they all read oddly alike, as if produced by a journalistic computer. Even their titles give the impression of having been birthed by the same features editor on an off night: *Singles Critique, Singles Register, Single Scene, Single Life, Adam & Eve, He & She, Single Search,* etc. ad infinitum.

All of them adopt a mildly hysterical whoops-a-joy-we're-having-fun attitude toward the mating game, which is not reflected in their ad columns, where cold reality reigns. Their articles—always on the subject of mate hunting—are of awe-inspiring banality, conveying incontrovertible verities such as that you meet more people by going out than staying at home; that looks aren't everything; that marriage doesn't necessarily bring happiness; that you learn more by listening than talking; that men and women have different attitudes toward sex; and that reading helps your conversation. One, I recall, used eight hundred or so words to explain that close-proximity dancing is apt to arouse physical desires.

I don't know whether anybody actually reads these profundities. In any case, they serve only to fill out the staple diet—the mainstay —of these journals: the ad pages.

They have a sober, level-headed approach that strikes you immediately. The listings are neither titillating nor depressing, they don't dangle baits or expound philosophies or adopt poses. They might even be called dull. But their lack of histrionics gives them an air of sincerity that comes as a blessed relief after breathing the bagnio perfumes of the "adults only" glossies.

You can nearly always depend on their genuineness. If a man announces that he is looking for a wife, then a wife is what he wants; otherwise, he would have stipulated "girl friend" or "playmate." And aside from moderate understatements about their age and weight, the women appear pretty much how they describe themselves. This is no stalking ground for Casanovas or hookers or sexual acrobats, and the proportion of kooks is much the same as in any cross-section of the populace.

Euphemisms are used sparingly, unerotically and—as I discovered —often unintentionally. Liking the "finer things" means enjoying an occasional live play or concert. A girl who's "adventurous" is conveying the fact that she goes camping and fishing. A "gourmet cook" is someone who can make cheese fondue, and a "traveled sophisticate" anyone who has ever sat in the *Café de la Paix.*

For those who find this style too prosaic, there are a few genteel yet determinedly droll publications, like the California *Peeplpickers.* In this handsomely produced booklet, male and female ads come illustrated with little boys and girls licking lollypops, and most of the listings resemble drippings from a sugar press. A favored opening is, "Hi, there, little girl . . ." and one matron of fifty-five introduced herself as an "Ageless Madcap Divorcee . . ."

At intervals advertisers resort to poetry, and some of their verses (like those of the nineteenth-century temperance bard "The Great McGonagall") seem destined to become collectors' classics:

All week this hombre labors with steel
   Come weekend I seek an unusual gal for real.
Have peppy bus, powered by Porche [sic]
   Am 57, 5–11, with old divorce . . .
Any of these descriptions-interests fit?
   Then let's communicate.
Send photo and I'll reciprocate.

Most of the mating magazines are Lilliputian enterprises, catering to narrow geographical areas and beset by distribution and finance problems. The contacts they offer are confined to their ad sections. But in 1972 there was a development that may be the forerunner of a vastly more effective approach.

That year saw the creation of a conglomerate in San Francisco, fusing a computer-dating outfit, a social club and a travel agency with a mating journal. The first three units—Computer Match, Inner Circle and Travelsphere—were the contributions of London-born Michael Gordon, who is now president of the entire setup. The magazine, *Singles Press*, came from a young Texan named Tom Evons, who had managed to maintain exceptionally high standards while running it on a shoestring.

The all-round advantages of such a combine are obvious. It can advertise its clients, computer-match them, provide a setting of social functions, send them on economy-rate trips, and publicize all these activities in its own periodical. It has, furthermore, one of the proportionally biggest markets in the nation—San Francisco's 250,000 unattached citizens.

Similar mergers will probably appear throughout the country within the next few years. As competition for the singles market grows fiercer, the smaller computer companies, as well as publications, may find independence an unprofitable luxury. Their rate of attrition is already grim—and the recent business recession has accelerated it ominously.

But there are some journals that fit into no conceivable combination, no matter how *laissez-faire*. They would lose their uniqueness, and with it their special appeal for advertisers who consider themselves unique, at least as far as the mating trade is concerned. One of them is the Los Angeles *Free Press*, whose ad from prison I quoted at the start of this chapter.

The *Freep* (as readers like to call it) is one of the original "Underground" sheets of America and has remained true to its heritage in spite of becoming a plump fairly prosperous weekly, sold at newsstands and by legions of more or less freaked-out vendors of all sexes. The *Freep* can't be termed a mating mag by any means; it contains excellently written articles, plus some of the most acid-loaded art criticism going. Yet its backbone—and the sole reason why thousands of bourgeois suburbanites buy it—are the eight pages of classified ads in each issue.

Their piquancy is not confined to the "personals." The mail-order columns feature items like penis exercisers, "French ticklers," Japanese vaginal vibration balls, recipes for making LSD and DMT, adjustable chastity belts, rubber dildos, whips, straps, "fanny paddles" and harnesses, and bumper stickers proclaiming "First Wipe Off Your Dick—Then Zipper Your Reagan."

Under "Personal" you'll find what amounts to a survey of human sexual proclivities—from the tenderly romantic to the near-gruesome, with certain comic elements mixed in;

> Keith the rapist can make you fall in love by gently removing your panties. Anywhere . . .
>
> DIRTY OLD LADIES. Quiet wht. male, 20, loves sex with single mature buxom woman 45–65.

Sometimes the pitch is so divergent as to be mildly confusing:

> CHOCOLATE & VANILLA. To bi females who liked mixed treat, he 19 energetic b/m, she 24 buxom very bi. Mixed couples, bi fem. Try us, you'll like us!

But the gross here—as in the entire ad field—consists of men seeking female sex partners—holding out inducements ranging from rent-free apartments, cabin cruisers, movie roles, private airplanes, overseas travel and dress allowances to skiing lessons, "cosmic enlightenment" or Herculean reproductive organs. One of the intriguing peculiarities of the antiestablishment *Freep* is the number of executive types who choose to advertise in it.

I had a collaborator respond to some of the listings—an attractive and enterprising lass named Midge, whose past career included selling the *Herald Tribune* in the streets of Paris and *Encyclopedia Britannicas* in Morocco. On my behalf, Midge followed the mating call of a Malibu Beach architect who had described himself as "five feet eleven inches of suntanned manhood, hung like Priapus, with mind to match body and many interests."

Her report sounded a little *triste*:

"He was a nice fellow. Handsome, if you like them a bit on the stout side. And his beach house was dreamy. Cool and white, with a Mexican touch. Painted tiles all over the place, and those—what d'you call them?—those leather wine flasks.

"Well, yeah, he *was* hung, all right. Only, he couldn't *do* anything with it. God knows, he tried. What I mean is—you know—the tent pole kept collapsing. Poor bastard, he got so mad he almost cried. I thought he'd bang it against a wall, he was that furious. He told me he'd been divorced last year. I think he's still in love with his wife. Or maybe *that* was the reason she walked out on him. How do I know!

"Anyway, we finished up talking about Ingmar Bergman movies. He'd seen every single one, some of them three times. Well, what I mean is—what else *could* we do . . . ?"

I followed up a couple of the scarce female ads, with equally instructive results. One was from a San Gabriel housewife, "Pretty and slender, happy outlook. I wish someone would spend occasional evenings with me."

The ad left just enough unsaid to be challenging. I met the lady on neutral ground, in one of those plastic coffee shops along Sunset Boulevard, where the coffee tastes as if it had a grudge against you. She was pink and blonde and dimpled, with a slight lisp that gave her speech a babyish quality, although she must have been in her early thirties.

Yeth, she confirmed, she would love to entertain me, say, next Thursday, but I'd have to leave before midnight, for sure.

It took a lengthy interrogation before I learned the reason for the midnight curfew. She was married. Her husband, a lathe operator on shift work, arrived home at 12:30 sharp. "And then he's too tired for anything. Weekends he works in the garden, and *that* makes him tired. I just gotta have thomebody who isn't tired all the time, like my husband."

Needless to say, he didn't know about wifey's advertisement.

My second response was to the possibly most original announcement of its kind ever to appear in the *Freep*:

> Striking redheaded virgin, 26, wishes
> to change her status. Helen

Establishing mutual contact with Helen proved a time-consuming job. I got the feeling of a long, long line stretching ahead of me. The hunch became a certainty when she finally granted me a one-hour chat in her tiny Burbank apartment. Her phone was off the hook and she frequently glanced at her watch. While not exactly striking, she looked pert in an undernourished way, with rather becoming freckles and nervous little creases around her mouth.

I made about ten minutes of small talk before she cut me off.

"Look," she said in a flat Boston-Irish voice, "let's not beat about the bush. What you want to know is am I or aren't I, and why did I run that ad. Right?"

"Right."

"Okay, I'll tell you. You can believe me or not, that's up to you. I *am* a virgin and I need some money for a certain purpose. None of your business what it is. You can find out yourself if I'm telling the truth. It'll cost you two hundred dollars."

I looked at her sharply and she deadpanned back, so perfectly that I'm sure she must have practiced it in front of a mirror. "Well, are you curious or do you just want to waste time?"

"Thank you," I said, sounding as regretful as I could, "not quite *that* curious."

She nodded once. "That's what I thought."

I never did solve the riddle of the redheaded sphinx. But I would like to know just how many did.

In order to gauge the response, Midge and I manufactured an ad which—at a dollar per line, standard type—combined broad appeal with maximum truthfulness:

Good-looking, sensuous girl, 29, fed up with pseudos, neurotics, and phonies, wants straight, bright, uninhibited man to share mutually enjoyable experience. Contact P.O. Box . . .

Neither of us were prepared for the deluge we unleashed. During the next two weeks, Midge received a total of 509 letters! Just reading and sorting them was a full-time job. We filed them away in a descending order of categories, starting with "Possibles" and ending with "Psychos."

Strangely enough, the last file wasn't anywhere as bulky as we had expected. The proportion of fully fledged sexual psychotics is much larger among readers of the glossies. Those that came, however, were often of phantasmagoric obscenity; they seemed to be drooled rather than written on the paper. Even in our nonchalant age, they are only partially quotable:

One of the letters began:

"I'm a real red-blooded tall Joe that's not often found these days. I have a cock so big I can hit you over the head with. What I like is great big tits and a tight hot cunt, lots of hair, the hotter the better. I can do lots of things with my cock you'll enjoy, as I'm very healthy. All women enjoy . . ." (Here followed four closely scrawled pages of sex activities, including analingus, oral-genital contacts, and a mysterious variation he called "Black Mammy hump.") The missive concluded with unexpected formality: "I hope you will give me an opportunity of meeting up real soon. Yours sincerely . . ."

Other letters went in a similar vein, some describing mutual masturbation, others bondage, beating, biting and tickling techniques, while one gentleman demanded to be "trodden on all over, with you wearing spikey heels." Several asked for Midge's used panties and soiled Tampax. One boasted that he regularly had wet dreams.

About a third in this category contained nude photos of the senders, the pictured physiques ranging from impressive to pathetic. Two Polaroid candids showed the correspondents having intercourse with their wives (in color). The most unusual of all came from a young machinist in San Diego. He asked to be hired as a weekend maid. "My only reward shall be the pleasure of serving you and catering to your every cruel whim." The enclosed photo showed him in a very brief parlormaid's costume, wearing black mesh stockings and wielding a feather duster. He had a noticeable five o'clock shadow. In a postscript he added: "While I'm on duty I will want you to call me Josette."

Surprisingly, though, most of the answers in general were neither indecent nor overtly immoral. A good many were sweetly sentimental like the one penned by a former Catholic priest, now working as a landscape gardener: "I am thirty-two years old and I want you for my *first* lady friend." Or: "My gal married someone else while I was in Vietnam and I need someone to say all the tender things to I'd been saving for her."

At least a hundred came on expensive business stationery with corporation letterheads. About the same number were inked or penciled—often illegibly—on lined exercise-book leaves. One was illustrated with an excellent self-portrait of the writer. Midge went out with him in due course. ("No, he wasn't an artist, but an engineer. Very entertaining guy. Only he wanted me to migrate to Israel with him—and I'm not even Jewish.")

Midge used her own system of responding to the responses. She marked the letters according to a three-, two-, and one-star priority order, rang the given phone numbers in that sequence, and fixed appointments if the men sounded reasonably pleasant. Her reports to me could have filled the rest of this book:

"Yes, he really does have a sailing yacht and a British sports car. Also three ex-wives and a pile of bread. Runs a furniture store. A real tiger, that one. Bit old for a lover, maybe, but—we'll see . . .

"Boy, was *that* one a drag! He's an advertising executive and spends every minute selling himself as Madison Avenue's gift to girlhood. Talk about diarrhea of the vocal chords. And all he wants, actually, is a one-night stand . . .

"Sad case. Directs TV commercials and thinks the pressure is giving him an ulcer. *I* think his problem is that he's basically homo-sexual and won't admit it to himself . . .

"His name's Dean. He's a composer and has a beautiful beard. Terribly broke, so I paid for my own drinks. Very idealistic, puts women on pedestals—the goddess syndrome. Wants me to come and listen to his music. Maybe I can get him to dedicate a piece to me."

When I left Los Angeles, Midge was still busily dating her correspondents. No longer with research in mind, but strictly on her own volition.

The full risks of our procedure didn't dawn on me till later. That was when I learned that some years ago a certain "Eric S. Galt" had put an ad in the *Freep*, calling for "a passionate married female for mutual enjoyment."

The FBI discovered that his real name was James Earl Ray. He is currently serving a life sentence for the murder of Dr. Martin Luther King, Jr.

seven

UNWED MOTHER—
SINGLE FATHER

In a recent newspaper column San Francisco journalist Merla Zeller-bach mentioned her friend Myra, who was dating an older man. "He's only got one fault," Myra was quoted as saying. "He's never been married. There must be something wrong with him."

Several days later, however, and with great relief, she learned that the man had actually been twice wed, twice divorced. Now, she explained, she could "fall in love with confidence."

This anecdote serves as a perfect illustration of the extent to which the stigma of divorce has been eliminated in our society. Its disappearance proceeded at roughly the same pace as the national divorce rate climbed. In 1900 there was 1 divorce for every 12.7 weddings, and the act was looked upon with grim disapproval in the average community. Fifty years later the rate had gone up to 1 divorce per 4.1 marriages. In 1970 it stood at 1 for every 3.4 weddings, and San Mateo County, California, registered the world's divorce record, with 70 out of each 100 marriages dissolved in court.

If public disfavor had remained at anything like its old pitch, almost 5 percent of America's entire population would be social outcasts. Since the number of divorced and separated persons is now around 10,000,000, the annual number of divorce cases is nearly 700,000.

But although ordinary citizens no longer view divorce as an outrage, they tend to draw several false conclusions from divorce statistics. One of those conclusions is that marriage per se is going out of style.

If anything, the opposite is true. According to U. S. Census Bureau figures, people marry more frequently than ever before. Six out of seven divorced persons marry again—and often again and again, sometimes their previous partners. As an institution, marriage is more popular than at any time in our history, except for the "'till death us do part" portion.

The second widespread error consists in equating a high divorce rate with a weakening moral fiber. The two manifestations *may*, of course, occur simultaneously, but there is absolutely no connection between them. Thus one of the most dissolute and licentious realms on record—the French Empire of Napoleon III—had an insignificant number of divorces, simply because the law only permitted them in exceptional circumstances. On the other hand, the stringently puritanical Wahabi Muslims—who don't smoke, drink neither coffee nor alcohol, punish theft by mutilation and adultery by death—treat the matter so lightly that any husband can shed his wife by clapping his hands and proclaiming, "You are thrice divorced."

The reasons behind America's climbing divorce rate have little to do with moral issues. This is shown by the fact that only about 5 percent of American couples live together out of wedlock. In England, Germany, Italy, Scandinavia and Australia—where the divorce ratio is much lower—the number of unmarried householders is three or four points higher.

One of the most important—and least recognized—divorce factors was pointed out by Dr. Marcia Laswell, Professor of Psychology at California State Polytechnic College and a practicing marriage counselor:

"Our ancestors had an average married life of twenty years. They didn't have time to be bored or unhappy. Many didn't live long enough to see their own children grow up and marry. Today, the average American marries for the first time around twenty to twenty-two—and with a life expectancy now well over seventy, you are talking about fifty years of married life, which is a very long time to commit yourself to live and remain intimately in love with another."

A rapidly increasing proportion of divorces takes place after eighteen to twenty years of marriage—that is, *after* the normal span of our grandparents' wedded lives. And it is precisely this group that now faces the toughest corner of the mating mart.

They were married in the early 1950s, during a period when fecundity was fashionable and the average couple had three or four children. The younger of these children are now in their mid-teens —the most difficult age—with only one parent to try to cope with them while simultaneously casting around for a replacement mate.

To make matters worse, the lone parent is apt to be in very tight economic circumstances. For, contrary to popular belief, divorce in America is much more common among people in low-income brackets than those in the medium and upper strata. The divorce rate of farm laborers, for instance, is nearly twice as high as that of professional people, and unskilled industrial workers have the highest overall proportion of broken marriages in the land.

But poverty is merely one problem, and not necessarily the biggest. Social isolation can be even more demoralizing. This was how Barbara Olney summed up her position: "Sometimes, for weeks and weeks, I feel like I have no face. Like I'm walking around with a bag over my head."

Mrs. Olney is small and sharp-featured, her skin stretched taut over prominent Slavonic cheekbones. Her eyes, her voice, her gestures all have a curious tiredness that isn't physical. She lives in Highland Park, Illinois, has three daughters, and works in a Chicago tie factory.

"You want to know about my life? Well, I can tell you," she said. "It's just me and my kids, that's all. I've got no friends. I've got nobody. At the factory, it's all women. The friends we had—like before my divorce—they were all my husband's friends. Guys he went bowling with and their families. Yeah, sure, I got neighbors. But their wives are scared of me—I might get at their husbands." She gave a quick, very wry grin. "So they don't invite me in much. And around where I live there's nowhere to go to meet people."

She shrugged. "I can't go into town at night by myself. Where's there to go, anyway? Besides, I don't want to leave the girls at home alone. The youngest, Jeanie, she's only eleven. So I stay home, just about every night, and watch television. Weekends I clean up the place, do a bit of washing, or I take Jeanie to the zoo. She likes the bears best. Christ, I never knew you could feel so goddamn old at thirty-six."

Mrs. Olney didn't consider moving. She couldn't afford it. But for tens of thousands of newly single mothers this is the primary decision to confront. Most of them originally migrated to the suburbs with their husbands, mainly for the sake of their children. Now those children are rooted there. Shifting them to different schools and surroundings would constitute a major upset in their lives. Yet such a break is just what their mother needs in order to rebuild *her* life. Should she, therefore, put her own requirements first?

In less child-oriented civilizations adults may take their priority for granted. In America such a move often results in devastating guilt complexes—traumas that continue to bedevil parents long after their children have adjusted to their new environments.

The chief sufferers are women, because divorce courts—in nine cases out of ten—award custody of children to the wives, and because widows outnumber widowers by four to one. But there are many more solo fathers struggling to bring up families than is generally known. And their plight can be worse.

I know of a healthy thirty-one-year-old college graduate in New York who was forced to become a welfare father. His divorce left him in charge of four children, aged four to nine. For two years he had been unable to hold a steady job because he couldn't find anyone to take care of his kids.

He applied for, and received, a housekeeper from the Department of Child Welfare. The woman was competent enough when she

showed up. Frequently she didn't, never bothering to warn him beforehand. He lost two jobs through having to stay home on those
days.

The Department then sent him relays of babysitters to enable him
to go out and look for work. They numbered thirteen in all—of
whom ten spoke not a word of English. Two of the remaining three
were available only at night, not a suitable time for job hunting. The
third quit on the spot when told she would have to be paid by the
city. Her reason was that she would be "dead and buried" before
she saw her money.

The man's caseworker told him on several occasions that he
shouldn't work, but stay home with his children. "If I were to do
that," he said, "I would be forty-five before I'd be able to work again.
Who the hell is going to hire a forty-five-year-old man who hasn't
worked in sixteen years?"

This is admittedly a drastic example—for a man. For single
mothers in the lower economic regions it is almost the normal situation. And for everybody it is the price we pay for what psychologist
Dr. Joyce Brothers termed "the streamlined mobility of the nuclear
family." A family stripped down to its basic components, shorn of its
erstwhile three-generation encumbrances in the form of resident
grandmothers and maiden aunts. These peripheral adjuncts may
have been infernal nuisances at times, but they became godsends
whenever one of the marriage partners dropped out. They kept the
unit functioning by providing extra hands (and adult companionship) for whichever remained.

Their absence is never more sorely felt than at the start of the
big-city summer, which can be the roughest period in the single
parent's year.

This is when the barred, peepholed, triple-locked apartment becomes a claustrophobic trap, the desire for escape overwhelming.
One of the traditional American middle-class escape channels is the
rented summer house on a beach or in the mountains. But this is a
family tradition. For most singles it means sharing a place with up
to half a dozen others, splitting the rent and enjoying alternating

weekends of breathable air. And the one rule that nearly all of these seasonal co-ops enforce is *No Children.*

If single parents wanted to get in on such an arrangement, they had to make it with each other—which they did, very haphazardly, for years. But in 1967, a New York free-lance photographer named Joel Kovitz put it on an organized basis. He gathered a group of seventeen parents, with twenty-four children between them, and rented a large house in East Hampton for the summer. The idea caught on immediately. The following year Kovitz organized eighteen housing combines. By 1970 the number of single-parents' houses had grown to thirty-one, and the scheme was spreading throughout New England and the Midwest.

Participants can usually choose between taking full shares or half shares, the latter meaning they can come out on alternate weekends only. The price of full shares currently wavers between five hundred and a thousand dollars, Memorial Day through Labor Day, depending on the quality and location of the house. It entitles the parent to a private room, to be shared with one or two children (most combines balk at larger families), plus kitchen privileges.

"It can be a wonderful setup if you're lucky," a three-summer veteran named Vera told me, "and pretty hellish if you're not. It depends partly on the weather, partly on the organization, but mostly on who you're in with."

Vera, a plump and jolly brownette from Flatbush, was once married to a genuine and fairly successful gangster. Theirs was a happy marriage until the husband reformed and became a fanatical Seventh Day Adventist and teetotaler. When Vera went on imbibing highballs, he started beating her up for the good of her soul. After a year of that, she left him, taking their fifteen-year-old and nearly uncontrollable daughter with her.

"What are the main friction points?" I asked her.

"You mean in the house?" she said, returning to the topic from which she had strayed. "Oh, much the same as everywhere—food and sex." She smiled like the full moon. "Say you go in for communal cooking—everyone contributes equal sums of money for grub. Some of the smaller eaters may complain that they shouldn't have to contribute as much as the gluttons.

"So maybe then everybody brings their own supplies. And they put labels on everything with their names on them. Well, the younger kids can't read what's on the labels, and they'll drink someone else's milk or eat their cookies and things. And then there's a row."

"Where does the sex come in?"

Vera giggled. "Where doesn't it? One of the single daddies makes a pass at a single mummy. They're sharing a house, so why not share a bed? Somebody else gets moral about it. Or jealous. So you have another row. Or tension—silent tension. That's worse.

"Or somebody doesn't come home all night, then sleeps most of the next day. Well, who makes breakfast for her or his kids—maybe lunch too? That's how you get friction. Specially from those who aren't making out so good themselves."

She added earnestly: "But I'm just giving you the minus points. That's not fair, really. I've had two wonderful summers, and only one was kinda mixed. That's a good average. So I say, three cheers for Mr. Kovitz. If he hadn't thought up the whole scheme, I'd have been stuck in Flatbush."

Joel Kovitz's house-sharing scheme operates as an offshoot of the largest single-parents organization in the country. Parents Without Partners (PWP) is a typical American self-help movement, with all the virtues and weaknesses inherent in such bodies. Founded in New York in 1957, it now embraces some 60,000 members in several hundred independent chapters throughout the nation. These chapters, in fact, are so ruggedly independent that they frequently seem to advance in different directions.

PWP is based on a humane, nonsectarian and very liberal platform that aims to include *all* single parents—widowed, divorced, separated or never married. Incorporated as an educational, nonprofit body, its manifest function is "to learn better ways of helping themselves and their children cope with life in the one-parent of divided family." Members leave the organization when they marry, but are welcome to rejoin if they get widowed or divorced. Several have done this two or three times.

Originally, PWP concentrated on the problems of the children, and still gears most of its educational programs to their needs. But over the years the parents' problems began to loom uppermost (after all, they run the show). Since these problems stem largely from a dearth of social life, PWP has taken on a predominantly social character.

In a normal month the Manhattan Chapter, for instance, arranges about a dozen functions for children and fifteen socially flavored events for their elders. In a PWP Newsletter article, member Inge Schick gave her definition of *limbo* as, "When you have to play bridge with three other unattached creatures of your own sex." Today the organization's efforts are chiefly devoted to rescuing its flock from such a plight.

Since the membership is heavily weighted on the female end, the social highlights are those that attract outsiders: "Coffee & Conversation" evenings held in hotel lounges, dances, and cocktail parties thrown—sometimes lavishly—in private homes. Although the shopping around is just as hectic as at singles gatherings, the atmosphere is decidedly not. You get a warmly *personal* welcome instead of an admission pass, and those "meat market stares" are kept discreetly veiled. In place of tap-water "punch" and packaged pretzels, there's good scotch and man-sized martinis and often the kind of buffet spread designed to give you nostalgia for home cooking. Members call each other "Shnooks," and "Chicky" and "Bubelee," trade kisses and positively radiate bonhomie around the compass.

Below the festive glaze, however, caldrons bubble and stilettos flash. Mingle with the men and you'll be lucky to hear one kind comment passed about any of the women. Join the ladies and you'll hear most of the males present flayed alive.

"These men all tell you they're attorneys or account executives," one henna-haired matron informed me confidentially. "Then it turns out they work in the post office or in button factories. For their uncles yet."

I inquired what was basically wrong with working in an uncle's button factory. Or the post office, for that matter. The lady standing next to us gave me a vibrato blast only slightly mellowed by a Viennese accent:

"Vat's *wrong* with it? How can you ask even? Look around you, pliss. Look at this apartment!"

I looked around. It was a beautiful apartment, providing you ignored the china cherubs on the mantelpiece.

"You see?" snapped the vibrato lady, gesturing with her empty glass. "It is a milieu—a style of living—you understand. Or perhaps you don't understand. My husband—God rest his soul—vas a stockbroker. *He* had that style. I am accustomed to it. It iss a need for me, you understand. How can you expect that kind of style from a . . . a . . ." She groped in her vocabulary, but the best she could find was ". . . a button maker?"

The hennaed matron nodded Amen. "I should lower my standards," she cried, "for that lot?"

I took a close look at them. They were both edging fifty. They were plain, demonstrably uncharming, strident, and not terribly pleasant. Neither of them was likely to attract any more attorneys, account executives or stockbrokers. If they lowered their standards and remarried several rungs down the economic ladder, they would probably not be happy. The question was, Would they be unhappier than they were now?

It reminded me of a story about the two versions of hell. Seems that St. Peter offered a minor sinner the choice between going to a German or an Italian Hades.

In the Teutonic Inferno, in daytime, buxom blondes served out piles of knockwurst and sauerkraut and huge steins of beer to the accompaniment of sweet zither music. At night, though, you were nailed to a wall by your ears and had your fingers crushed with pliers while being drenched with oil and set ablaze.

The Italian variation in daytime meant luscious brunettes handing out heaped plates of pasta and flagons of red wine, while Neapolitan baritones sang their most enchanting folk songs. But at night the treatment was the same as above.

The sinner quailed. "I can't see any choice," he groaned.

St. Peter looked around quickly to make sure no one was listening and whispered: "Take my advice, brother, pick the Italian Hell. They are always running out of nails. They keep losing their pliers, and the oil they use is so watered down that it won't light. Even if they manage to find the matches."

The point about the two ladies was, Which was *their* Italian hell?

This dilemma is quite typical of a great number of upper middle-class women in the ranks of PWP. They had married well in their youth. Their children are grown up and mostly elsewhere. They are financially secure, socially active, but bored, frustrated and often bitter. Their male equivalents in age and income level want younger women, and usually get them. The men who might be interested in them are either considerably older or considerably poorer. They are intelligent enough to realize that, but not so intelligent as to reconcile themselves to it. Somewhere, they feel, there *must* be a man like the one who married them when they were twenty-five. They probably meet him every week. Only now, he's sixty.

Most PWP chapters suffer from pronounced rifts between younger and older members. The issues involved go beyond sexual rivalry. The crux of the conflict is that the senior members' children are grown and independent, whereas those of the juniors are still very much on their hands. Consequently, the older set favors adult functions; the younger parents want more activities in which their kids can participate.

In at least one branch this had led to an open breakaway movement. In November 1970, the then president of the West Los Angeles Chapter, Barry Spanjaard, took a group of dissidents out of the organization and started his own Young Single Parents Club (YSPC). Today he has over a hundred members and is expanding.

Barry Spanjaard is a squat, ebullient New Yorker of Dutch descent, with a seventeen-year-old son and enough energy to drive a power plant. He lives in a compact Hollywood bachelor pad, lavishly decorated with Army shooting medals, miniature liquor bottles and awards naming him "Salesman of the Year." Nobody in his house seems to lock his door. Spanjaard led me in and out of apartments belonging to assorted hippies, an author, and a trio of dance-hall hostesses. He knew everybody. But he grinned when he warned me against describing his current residence: "By the time your book comes out, I might be married again and living somewhere else." His reasons for walking out on PWP? "I think they're a great organization. They do some wonderful work. But, you see, at forty I was the youngest male member in our group. All the others were in their fifties and sixties. So they thought of it largely as a body where adults can get together and meet—each other. My idea was to involve the children."

Although the YSPC is very child-conscious, it certainly doesn't neglect the adult angles. Its selection of speakers at the monthly lecture meetings frequently cause raised eyebrows. They have included a medical expert on venereal diseases, the head of the Hollywood police vice squad, the president of the American Sexual Freedom Movement, and the Mother Superior of the Immaculate Heart College.

Among single parents, these organized bodies come in for at least as much antagonism as enthusiasm. A number of potential participants, I found, were put off by the pervasive Boosters' Club atmosphere, the nickname tags, the bridge-and-bagels syndrome that characterizes some branches.

"I belonged to PWP for about half a year before going AWOL. I'm still surprised I stuck it that long." My informant was a young forceful commercial artist named Audrey, who lives in Detroit with her two small children and has strong ideas on her status.

"Listen," she said, "I joined with the notion that we were there to get a few things done that badly need doing. Boy, what a laugh! You should have seen our monthly meetings. Most of the time the chairwoman couldn't even get members to sit down and listen to the business at hand. No, sir! Even while she was reading committee reports, they were jockeying around for positions, trying to sit next to someone who looked kind of promising. Yes, and the men were worse than the women—all five of 'em."

She lit a cigarette and blinked her deceptively gentle eyes against the smoke. "The trouble is that those people just aren't concerned with the real nitty-gritty issues. Like—putting pressure on local authorities for some decent, cheap community day-care centers. That's what we need—not those lousy cocktail parties."

The "nitty-gritty issues," however, are far too intricate to be solved by any number of child-care centers, though these would undoubtedly help. Most of them are rooted in the unequal positions of unwed mothers and solo fathers.

Where parents are actually living with their children, the handicaps seem about even, perhaps a bit harder on the men. But most single fathers only see their children on visiting days, while most mothers have them around permanently. And for them, child support and alimony notwithstanding, life can be a bout of not-so-silent desperation.

Socially, an unattached father, no matter how moth-eaten, is usually considered an asset. He experiences little difficulty getting invitations and introductions, even if he's known as a shattering bore. But a single mother to be in social demand must be outstandingly attractive or rich or notorious in some fashion, which leaves the great majority out in the cold. Somehow her married acquaintances fail to ask her to dinner by herself. And again and again party invitations require her to bring a date if she wishes to be welcome. (If she *had* a date she probably wouldn't want to go in the first place. And it takes truly colossal nerve to show up alone despite the proviso.)

Her love affairs, too, are fraught with difficulties the childless never even think about. Do they make love at his place or at hers? If they pick his pad, she has the unenviable choice between obtaining a sleep-over sitter (hard to get, expensive and unreliable) or tottering home around dawn, more or less unfit for the day's work. Or do they make it a fast eye-on-the-clock job, which may satisfy her neither physically nor emotionally?

Her own abode entails a variety of risks likely to dampen anyone's passion. Few mothers possess that most essential of technical requisites: a good bedroom door lock. And there is no experience more unnerving to the average male than being caught *in flagrante delicto* by an inquisitive youngster. Even the possibility of this happening, plus the need to avoid unusual noises, can render men impotent and women frigid.

Then there is the question of what to do in the morning. Spirit him out of the place before the children wake up? Or introduce him as a house guest or "uncle"? As a rule, men don't have the slightest desire to face coolly quizzical offspring stares after having spent the night with mummy. Most of them know enough about Oedipus complexes and father fixations to cringe at the thought. On the other hand, they don't relish the idea of getting out of a warm bed at six o'clock on a Sunday morning. Either way it's a bleak finale.

The entire concept of handling their lives as mothers *and* sexually active women is perplexing and often contradictory. Many single mothers waver between the extremes of totally isolating their boy friends from their children or expecting him to play weekend father for them. Some become resentful if he *tries* to meet her family; others are deeply hurt if he shows no interest in them. And the emotional havoc that may result from introducing whole series of "uncles" to young children needs no elucidation.

If the children are older, other dangers arise. Sons can be homicidally jealous of their mothers. And police blotters the world over are full of cases where Momma's beau ended up by bedding her newly nubile—and exceedingly curious—daughter.

But before single parents can get around to handling affairs, they have to make contacts. In this area the advantages of the man— although real enough—are more psychological than social. Husbands don't sever their links with the single world as completely as many wives do. Through their jobs, for one thing, they remain in midstream while their spouses frequently get left behind in the shallows. They rarely acquire the strange antagonism some wives seem to develop toward their unwedded acquaintances—a mixture of contempt and distrust—which helps to isolate them within an exclusively married circle. I've never heard of a man harboring such an attitude toward bachelors.

Men, in short, usually stay one degree *less married* than women. Regardless how long their wedlock has lasted, they don't find the process of meeting, dating and mating as alien and awkward as divorcées or widows. A great many, in fact, find it wildly exhilarating. It's freedom, rejuvenation—a second lease on life!

For most women the first plunge back is, to put it mildly, a very nervous occasion. A poised and erudite Chicago divorcée gave me her account of the experience:

"After leading a domestic life with a man for fourteen years, as I did, it seemed—well, sort of silly to go out on a *date*. Like play acting. I was used to eating with a man, sitting around in dressing gowns, sleeping in the same bed, seeing him at breakfast. It was such a *familiar* routine. You get so used to *not* putting on a front. And there I was, going somewhere with this *stranger*. What could we talk about? Was I supposed to be reserved or open? Should I ask him all kinds of intimate questions or wait until he told me something about himself?

"This probably sounds infantile—but I really didn't know what was expected of me. Or rather, I'd forgotten. My own dating period—God, that was centuries ago! This man was as close to a blind date as you could get—I'd met him for about a minute at a friend's place—so I felt like I was tapping my way in the dark.

"Another thing"—she gave a slightly embarrassed laugh—"I didn't know how I was supposed to handle the sex angle, and all that. Did you kiss on first dates or what? That was the trouble, you see: I'd forgotten the *rules* of the game. Anyway, they'd changed while I was out of circulation.

"Well, what happened was we went to a drive-in movie. And during the show he put his hand between my legs. I didn't want him to do that but—honestly—I thought maybe that was the routine thing these days. That he'd think I was medieval or something if I pushed him away. So I just sat there like a clod and let him go ahead. Pretended I wasn't noticing."

She shook her head. "Well, after a while I noticed all right. As a matter of fact, I became *very* aroused. I guess I should have worn a panty girdle or something, but I didn't. So, by the time the show finished, I was—well, very hot. He must have known it because he drove straight to his place, didn't ask questions or anything. We made love there. It was quite good, too. I mean he was a good lover. But all the time, while we were lying there, I kept on thinking: *How did I get into this, for God's sake?* Was that what *usually* happened? Or would he think I was a nymphomaniac or a slut?

"It ruined the whole affair for me. He rang me a few times afterwards, but I felt I couldn't see him with this question in the back of my mind."

There are numbers of organizations concerned with getting the divorced and widowed back into circulation. But so far only one has tackled the task of helping them become *fit* to circulate. The Transition Institute in Berkeley, California, was founded by a Canadian, Jack Crickmore, himself a divorced father of two. Crickmore, a lean and intensely cerebral man, wears his long hair in a pigtail and sports an elegant little goatee. His background is as unusual as his speech pattern—he mixes academic eloquence with casual four-letter words. In his time, Crickmore has been a cadet at the Royal Military College of Canada, an engineer, businessman and student of theology.

The Institute deals with various kinds of transition, such as aging and retirement, but its specialty is the change from twosomeness to single life.

"The main problem of divorcees," said Crickmore, "is becoming what we call *meetable*. And that problem can be divided into three areas: past, present and future. The past—that is the crap they carry around on their shoulders. The feeling of failure, resentment against their spouses, et cetera. How do they integrate all that shit into their lives?"

He adjusted his spectacles. "The present is how they feel about themselves *now*. Any kind of divorce or separation will emphasize negative attitudes toward ourselves. It doesn't necessarily create them, but it will reinforce them. Feelings of being inadequate or unlovable or unworthy. And how the hell can we get to know anyone if we feel that we ourselves aren't worth knowing?

"Now, the future can be equally in the way. If I go around with my mind focused solely on finding another mate, kind of programing myself for that objective, then I won't really meet *people*—just items that may or may not fit into my agenda. And that, again, is an alienating operation, preventing me from being reachable or ever reaching anyone else."

Crickmore sees the start of the solution in dispelling the aura of loneliness that envelopes so many divorced people. As he puts it: "You carry your loneliness before you wherever you go. And it's contagious."

His Institute functions in workshops averaging fifteen people, usually two thirds women. Participants pay an initial ten dollars, then thirty-five dollars for a workshop weekend lasting two full days.

It always starts with coffee around 9 A.M.—lots of coffee. An hour later, members cluster in small groups. Their object is to share—verbally—in each other's concerns. Sometimes there is a long silence before someone begins, haltingly: "I'm having this really hard time coming out of my shell . . ." Or: "All I seem to be thinking about is my money problems. Money, money, money, all the time . . ."

Others nod, smile creased little smiles of recognition, interject—"Yeah, that's exactly how it was with me . . . for years." You can feel some of the barriers melting in a warm flood of mutuality. People look at each other. A man shakes his head in disbelief. "You know," he mutters haltingly, more to himself than to the group, "I never guessed there were so many others—in the same boat . . ." He lapses back into silence. But a piece—a tiny piece—of his wall has crumbled.

There is no pressure on participants to "open up" unless and until they feel like it. The Institute doesn't go in for shock situations or group compulsion or psychodramas. It doesn't hand out approbation or disapproval. It merely establishes a sense of shared experience, the idea that "You aren't the only one."

Ruth MacIver, a slender blonde woman who acts as Crickmore's assistant, gave me an idea of the importance of that feeling. "I first came here as a member, after I'd gone through my divorce," she said quietly. "And I felt like—I wasn't a complete human being any more. Like I was only half a person, almost a freak. Then I saw there were other people—mature, intelligent people—who felt about themselves exactly as I did. I can't tell you what a comfort, what a source of strength that was."

The workshops use very little gimmickry, but they occasionally include a device known as The Script. Two people pair off, and one tells the other the story of her or his separation—as detailed as they want to. Then the partner tells the story back, in the first person and as verbatim as possible, with no interpretations allowed.

"And what does that accomplish?" I asked.

Crickmore grinned. "A lot of things. First of all, it allows people to *tell* their story. And to someone who's actually listening. Attentively. That gets rid of a lot of shit that's been eating them up inside. Spills it."

He pushed his glasses back. "That's only the start, though. Because the other person has to listen. A lot of people find that very difficult. But if they want to tell the story back, they've *got* to listen; there's no other way."

Here Ruth MacIver cut in. "It also lets you *hear* your own story for the first time. How it sounds coming from someone else. That can make a lot of difference. I remember when my story was told back to me, I thought: 'Who was that stupid creature living that life?' It's a way of gaining a new perspective."

If the Transition Institute does nothing but broaden the perspective of its members, it is accomplishing a great deal. Although the broadening may occur in some unforeseen areas.

One of the youngest workshop divorcees was a fellow of twenty-three. According to his own confession, he had enrolled mainly "to meet some broads." But after the weekend he approached Ruth, a strange new look of enlightenment in his eyes. "You know," he said, "I've really learned something here. All these women in their forties—why, they're still *women!* And they can be—well, charming!" He left then, still slightly bemused by his discovery.

eight

SWINGERS AND SWAPPERS

Once there were "key clubs," and they figured almost as prominently in America's suburban genre as amateur theatricals. Their role, however, was largely conversational. Somebody knew somebody who knew somebody who belonged to one, but that person was somehow never present when the subject cropped up. Thus nearly all the stories circulating about them were third- or fourth-hand and at least partly fictitious. Which, if anything, heightened their fascination.

Key clubs were clandestine gatherings with only couples participating. The men would drop their car keys or house keys into a hat, their wives fished them out blindly, then went off to bed with the owner of whichever key they had garnered.

These clubs were not altogether legendary. A handful actually existed, and some showed quite amazing durability. But the number of participants they mustered was minute enough to make them pretty exotic. The overwhelming majority of suburbanites preferred to practice their adultery in the traditional manner—on the sly.

Historically, the trading—or rather lending—of spouses is probably as old as the institution of marriage. As a form of hospitality it is still going on among Eskimos, certain tribes of Australian aborigines and the Hairy Ainus of Japan. The host will bestow his wife on an honored guest for the night and—incidentally—will regard refusal as a premeditated insult.

Americans never accepted wife-sharing as a custom—although the early settlers and frontier pioneers practiced it occasionally. But officially, at least, marriage was always governed by a single standard of sexual behavior, which forbade extramarital activities for either partner. The fact that these occurred with great frequency didn't alter the condemnation they evoked.

In practice, society imposed a double standard, allowing the husband considerable leeway (providing he was discreet about it) while refusing any such liberty to the wife. The unique feature of the key clubs was that they extended the single standard into extramarital realms. They permitted *both* partners to have sex with outsiders and—what's more—by mutual consent and approval. *That* was the revolutionary concept that added the spice to the gossip about them.

Key clubs and the associated term "wife-swapping" faded out during the 1960s. They were replaced by a fully fledged social phenomenon called "swinging," which developed from an underground fad into something resembling a national pastime. The word "swinging," in its specifically erotic connotation, is one of the most recent additions to the American dictionary. In its broadest colloquial sense it denotes all forms of sexual promiscuity. But to its organized adherents it means copulation within a selected circle, and under prearranged conditions of full equality. Free-lancing by only one party is taboo. I remember witnessing an outburst of incongruous but nevertheless sincere rage on the part of a swinging wife, who accused her husband of "cheating"—viz., sleeping with someone not belonging to their group.

Today, swinging has reached the dimensions of a subculture, with its own communications system, specialized magazines, newsletters, badges, handshakes and even bumper stickers. Four highly successful Hollywood feature films have dealt with the subject (one of them, *Bob and Carol and Ted and Alice*, became synonymous with it), and at least one scholarly treatise—Professor Gilbert Bartell's *Group Sex*—has given it an in-depth academic profile.

It would be an overstatement to claim that swinging is now generally accepted. But it has been socially recognized to about the same degree as, say, nudism. There are still some risks involved. In 1971 the Orange County, California, school board withdrew the credentials of a fifty-one-year-old teacher who had admitted making love to two other men in the presence of her husband. I also know of a Midwestern insurance adjuster who was fired when his company learned that he belonged to a local swingers club. But such instances are becoming rarer all the time. Most citizens, while not exactly approving of swingers, seem willing enough to live next door to or do business with them.

The reasons for this tolerance lie in both the numbers and the social characteristics of the swingers. An accurate body count of our swinging populace has yet to be made, but the lowest estimates put them at around 3,000,000; the highest, at above 14,000,000. A single Chicago organization I encountered had 3200 active members on its rolls, and is growing rapidly. On the East Coast and in California the individual groups tend to be smaller but more numerous.

Apart from being statistically formidable, swingers also blend in well with their bourgeois surroundings. They are predominantly white, middle-class and suburban, with only a token sprinkling of racial minorities and blue-collar workers. They keep their houses in good repair, mow their lawns, pay their bills and join the P.T.A. Professor Bartell noted that the majority were politically conservative; 40 percent of those he interviewed had voted for Wallace, most of the remainder were Republicans. They feel highly antagonistic toward hippies, radicals and student demonstrators, favor stricter law enforcement and keep their children well-isolated from their sex activities.

Their liquor consumption, I noticed, was on a par with the normal social intake, but very few of them were into drugs of any kind. Several, in fact, waxed indignant about "those damned Hollywood dope fiends who give swinging a bad name." By and large, swinging appeared to be their *only* deviation from a rather stodgy norm. Some seemed to epitomize Ambrose Bierce's definition of a debauchee as "One who has so earnestly pursued pleasure that he has had the misfortune to overtake it."

Swingers use three distinct methods of establishing contact with each other; through organized bodies, via magazine ads, and by proselytizing acquaintances. The last, however, is the least common route and looked upon with a certain amount of disapproval.

Swingers organizations have a great natural advantage over all other mating conclaves. Since only couples may join them, the numerical balance between the sexes is always even. And providing you have a partner, the enlisting process couldn't be easier.

For my first exploration venture in this field I teamed up with a petite, wide-eyed Texan girl named Daphne, whose Confederate "hisugarpie" approach camouflaged an astute and cool PR mentality. We went to a swingers club known as Inner Sanctum, which functioned in the backroom of Captain Kidd's restaurant in Lower Manhattan.

The club regions formed an enclosed zone, but admission was delightfully uncomplicated. I put our names down as Mr. and Mrs., purchased membership tickets for two dollars each, paid for four drinks at a dollar and a half a nip, and—*voilà*—we were in.

The dance floor was flanked by two rows of tightly packed tables, which gave couples the opportunity of leaning back and talking to the people behind them. Others simply walked up to table occupants, recited greetings and sat down. For the more timid, a permanently radiant hostess performed introductions as she tripped along. By about midnight, all the couples present had conglomerated into foursomes and sixsomes. Some had already left in group formation.

Our idea had been to play uninvolved spectators for a while. But within minutes of arrival we were joined by another couple. The man said, "Hallo, you two. My name is Joseph and this is Mary; but I'm not a saint and she's no virgin." He laughed uproariously.

Joseph was large, hawk-nosed and graying and could have passed for the Godfather disguised in a ready-made suit. His wife was blonde and billowing, with bare milkmaid's arms and adoring violet eyes that smiled constant approval.

The Godfather reached out and pinched Daphne's cheek. "We love swinging," he announced. "Both of us."

I felt slightly taken aback. I had expected at least a modicum of preliminary small talk. But Daphne showed herself mistress of the situation. She returned Joseph's pinch so hard his eyes watered and cooed: "Tell us about it, honey. We're kinda new around here."

The Godfather double-stroked his mustache. "Well, we've been doing it for five years, Mary and me. And we've met some real nice folks that way. Now me, I'm really good at it. I mean *good!* What I mean is, I'm not selfish. I like the *woman* to have pleasure. And I can carry on for—oh, five, six hours easy. Can't I dear?"

He turned to Mary for affirmation. She nodded enthusiastically.

"Also, I'm built for it," said Joseph. "What I mean is, I'm *big,* if you know what I mean. Not like some guys who've got nothin', so the woman can't feel nothin', if you get my meaning. And also, I'm gentle. I mean, I don't ever hurt a woman." He made as if to pinch Daphne again, but thought better of it.

"Yeah, and also I have the technique," said the Godfather. "Like, I know the right buttons to press to get your li'l ole motor going and *keep* it going. Now, my wife here, she don't know much about the scientific part of it, you see. What I mean is, she's a romantic. She likes the romance of it. Don't you, dear."

Mary accepted this as her cue and placed a plumply maternal hand on my arm. "I do think it's romantic, don't you? You *look* like you might. And, of course, it's very good for you. Spiritually and physically. I haven't had any of my asthma attacks for years now. And look what it's done for my skin." She slipped off a fair portion of blouse and revealed milky-white expanses.

"Whose idea was this—swinging?" I asked.

"My husband's." She threw a worshipful glance in Joseph's direction. He was engrossed in counting Daphne's fingers. "Whatever he does, he does well," she continued. "Swinging too. When he first suggested it, I said like I always say when he starts something new:

'Joe, are you sure you want to do that? Search your mind, now—are you *sure?*' And when he said he was sure, then *I knew* it would be all right. It always is. In his business too."

"Er—what's his business?"

"He's a building contractor. Oh, and wait till you see our house. It's adorable. Joseph designed it—well, mostly. He has his den and I have mine, and we each have color TV. My den is all in pink. Pink fluffy rugs and a pink bed. Joseph always says it goes with my complexion—pink rose. He's such a kidder. And I wear pink negligees— you'll see."

She flicked a playful finger at my wrist. "It's *very* private. And I have pink lighting over the bed. Romantic. You'll just love it. That's the wonderful part about meeting people like you. We can communicate. We can love. Oh, and talk too. I'm quite a talker once you get to know me. Not at first so much. I'm a bit shy. But after a while I kind of open up." She took two of my fingers and spread them. "*Open up*—you understand?"

At the other end of the table Joseph was making preparations to depart. "Okay, kids, what say we go, huh? You got a car or d'you want to come in ours?"

I hadn't reckoned with such a speedy procedure. "Well, if you don't mind," I said lamely, "I think we'd like to—er—stick around for a bit longer. You know, sample the scenery, ha, ha."

The Godfather looked slightly disappointed but quite unabashed. "Gee, I'm sorry about that, folks," he said. "Maybe another time, eh? Here's my card." He emptied his glass with one hand and collected his wife with the other. "Come along, Mary. Let's find some swinging."

They marched off toward the row of tables opposite.

In due course I learned that such blitz tactics are by no means unusual in swinging circles. As a rule the soundings are taken somewhat more leisurely—but not *much* more. After meeting in a club for the first time, couples will either fix a definite rendezvous date or go into action the same night. Any further procrastination is considered distinctly *de trop.*

Swingers take very few safety precautions, either legally or medically. They know that their activities fall into that shadowy border-land between the almost-legal and the near-illicit, which the police have preferred to leave alone in recent years. Theoretically, all of them could probably be charged under various ordinances pertaining to "lewd and lascivious practices" or "conspiracy to commit immoral acts." But the chances of making such archaic charges stick in a courtroom are almost zero, unless they involve minors.

Legal considerations are undoubtedly the main reason why most swingers steer clear of dope. Judges may shrug off mass copulation, but they *will* sentence you for a drag from a marijuana joint. Why add unnecessary risks?

Despite our current epidemic of venereal diseases, swingers don't worry much about VD, and the rate of infection among them is remarkably low.

This is due less to caution on their part than to the fact that the principal carriers happen to be teen-agers and hippies—two groups virtually excluded from organized swinging. True to their cultural background, most swingers also get frequent medical checkups, usually from doctors belonging to their clubs. As one member informed me proudly: "We've very hot on the hygiene angle."

If you were to mark the geographical density of swingers with colored pins on a map, you would notice the thickest concentrations in four distinct regions: the New York–Boston axis; Chicago; the San Francisco Bay area; and the Los Angeles vicinity from Ventura to Newport Beach. These are the swingdom capitals, but the organization matrix varies from place to place.

As stated earlier, Chicago boasts the largest networks. Only one or two, however, have anything like a headquarters. The weekly sex socials shift from one member's home to another, and the only printed material handed out are lists of telephone numbers. On the East Coast, action centers around the type of restaurant club I described. The clubs feature monthly news bulletins announcing forthcoming dances, dinners and special events, and charge between two and six dollars membership fees.

California, as might be expected, has the most numerous, most elaborate and most expensive swinging facilities in the country. Here the clubs bear registered titles like The Group, Rendezvous, "C" Club, The Duo, The Compatibles, Pace Setters, Jet Age Club, The Utopians, etc., and supply their members not only with lapel buttons, secret handshakes and bumper stickers but also, in some cases, with the premises to swing in (small chambers for those who like privacy, larger rooms for group action).

Application fees average twenty-five dollars, the monthly dues from twenty to sixty dollars per couple. Since some clubs demand a half-yearly payment in advance, the initial plunge into organized swinging may come to a lump sum of two hundred dollars or more.

The financial stake has the effect of weeding out window shoppers on the one hand and the impecunious on the other. Members can take it for granted that anyone they meet in the club is ready for more or less instant action. And because time spent there is money, they display very little tolerance toward the timid or gauche. The overture chord of a conversation may be: "Do you like your swinging closet or open?" Which immediately separates the players from the tourists, since very few greenhorns know that "closet" means segregated fornication, "open" denotes communal fun.

Swinging on club premises also has another, purely psychological, advantage. "In a private home," one enthusiast told me, "there's always that awkward vacuum period until *somebody* says 'Let's go' or starts peeling off. In a club, where you're on neutral ground, you seem to slide into action naturally—everybody at once."

The bumper stickers handed out by some organizations enable swingers to spot each other on the road. One outfit, the West Hollywood Utopians, has its triangular stickers numbered and coded and a description of the owners filed at headquarters. If two likely looking couples pass each other and phone in the appropriate serial number, the club switchboard service will get them in touch quick enough to spend the next night as a foursome.

What actually happened at a quartet arranged in that fashion was told to me by the only husband involved—the second pair turned out to be unmarried. Her boy friend, he said, was quite handsome in a conventional way, but the girl was a raving beauty—"a redhead with slanted green eyes and dazzling white teeth and those long legs that go all the way up to her crotch."

They went to the couple's apartment and—after one cursory drink—retired to separate rooms. The redhead was as stunning undressed as she had been in tennis shorts, and her naked body had a sharp, peppery young animal smell that worked like an aphrodisiac. But once the preliminaries were over, the husband suffered a peculiarly frustrating disappointment. In his own words: "There must have been something malformed about her vagina. I mean there was nothing *inside* her—like empty air. Very little warmth and just about no friction." He guessed that her womb was so large and slack that it would have needed "a pair of giants to fill it." They spent a rather unsatisfactory hour together. In the end, the girl obligingly masturbated him until he ejaculated. She herself had no orgasm, but didn't seem at all disturbed by their failure. Perhaps she was used to it.

Meanwhile the wife and boy friend appeared to have hit it off splendidly in the marriage bed. Their eyes were shining and they kept fondling and kissing each other even during the communal farewell drink—which bothered the husband no end. "I think," he concluded acidulously, "that guy was using his doll as a kind of decoy to get at normally shaped women. I sure as hell wasn't going to swing with *them* again, even though my wife was all in favor."

This was an example of what you might call "frivolous" swinging. There is another kind that participants treat with ceremonial earnestness, an act of social significance that permits no levity. The most dedicated exponents of that type, I discovered, were Morton and Hester.

Morton was an industrial chemist, given to endless well-meaning monologues that made you aware of the hardness of the chair you were sitting on. Hester, formerly a bookkeeper, wore pebble glasses and "sensible" clothes that didn't quite match. They had two small children and lived in a neo-Scandinavian apartment in Wheaton, Illinois. Their couches and armchairs were fitted with plastic protective coverings which—to the best of my knowledge—never came off. Both were in their early thirties and looked forty. They referred to swinging as "comarital sex." The telephone arrangements for their get-togethers were made as if delivering the message to Garcia.

"Sexual exclusivity," said Morton, "is one of the basic evils of our society. It is unnatural and inhuman and lies at the root of materialism, violence, insecurity and possessive greed. Only by the selective sharing of our mates can we hope to establish true and meaningful bonds with our fellow man . . ." He went on for circa ten minutes until Hester broke in:

"I'm sure that comarital sex has preserved our marriage. And many others. But you have to be selective."

"Of course," Morton nodded. "Highly selective. Otherwise it becomes animalistic."

Their group, I learned, consisted of four or five couples, but changed every few weeks. They made a point of never swinging with anyone until their second meeting, and then only "if we feel a spiritual kinship exists beyond mere carnality."

Such kinship, apparently, could not ripen with people displaying what Hester called "sordid streaks." One couple was promptly frozen out of the circle because the husband had recited a classic A. P. Herbert ditty that starts:

> The portions of the female that excite a man's depravity
> Are fashioned with considerable care,
> And what at first appears to be a simple little cavity
> Is really an elaborate affair . . .

Swinging took place every second Saturday when, by arrangement, the children spent the night with their grandparents. Both Morton and Hester assured me that they would be delighted to have me watch the ritual, providing I brought a partner. "Participation," declared Morton, "is entirely optional. We don't believe in compulsion. Some couples have observed us several times before deciding to join in." Hester added: "You won't embarrass us in the least. What we do is perfectly natural."

We were three couples that Saturday. Morton served us one drink each (nobody got a refill) and put Ravel's Bolero on the record player. Then proceedings began as if the host had fired a starter's pistol.

Hester purposefully approached a mesomorphic young accountant seated on the couch, kissed him on the lips, caressed his chin and ears with her tongue, reached down and unzipped his fly and groped around with a dreamy expression. Morton hauled a tall and thin legal secretary onto his lap and began to stroke her inner thighs, without breaking his steady flow of words. The custom, as had been explained to me, was "to become aroused communally, but seek fulfillment in private."

There was plenty of light from a standard lamp, although the thundering *Bolero* drowned out the sound effects. The whole scene resembled an amateurish porno movie with musical accompaniment. Morton's mouth kept forming inaudible words while his fingers were trying to unhook his lady's bra. She finally did it herself.

Hester, surprisingly, became completely abandoned within a few minutes. She was the last person you would have suspected of voluptuousness, but having shed her mismatched skirt and blouse, she revealed Junoesque proportions and an Aspasian temperament, quite unhandicapped by her glasses. Her accountant didn't have much to do except sprawl. Once I heard him give a sharp yelp that cut right through the Ravel pandemonium. Hester must have bitten him.

They were the first couple to seek private fulfillment. Hester, still in her white panties, led him out through the door by his hand, like a bespectacled Amazon dragging off a captive. Her husband took considerably longer. Eventually he escorted the secretary out of the second door, but more decorously.

About fifty minutes later, the entire company had gathered in the lounge again. Hester was still wearing her glasses, but nothing else. She had a smug, introspective look and kept very quiet. Her accountant appeared slightly battered. He stealthily felt an angry red mark on his shoulder. Morton, fully clothed again, was still talking fluently, but in my direction for a change:

"You must understand that among civilized, intelligent adults sexual jealousies and rivalry shouldn't exist at all. We extirpate them by the roots through the frankness of our behavior. Unlike those who sneak around corners to escape the pressures of monogamy . . ."

Regardless of what ecstatic heights swingers achieve in private, their public performances always appear rather wooden, as if the participants were wearing invisible stays. It may be that Anglo-Saxons, particularly middle-class Anglo-Saxons, simply lack talent for orgies. If you read what went on at the Aphrodisian Festivals, at the parties thrown by Alcibiades, at the Roman Saturnalias, the revels of the Borgia Pope Alexander VI, the Feast of Fools in the French Midi, the cave gatherings of Sir Francis Dashwood, the religious services of Rasputin's Khlysty monks, or the entertainments sponsored by the late King Farouk, you realize that our attempts at the business of concerted salacity come off like a high-school dance class trying to imitate the Bolshoi Ballet.

The trouble may be that we have no orgiastic tradition—at least not a recent one. Ours was cut off around the time of Hogarth, and even then it had been largely reserved for the aristocracy. The English-speaking bourgeoisie became too busy making money and improving the plumbing to retain much orgiastic finesse. It had become an almost-lost knack, like roof-thatching or coracle steering.

We also lacked reasonably graphic models. The books and pictures that could have served the purpose were universally banned for a couple of centuries. Hollywood, our foremost educational medium, was terribly handicapped by the Hays Office in matters of eroticism. Cecil B. De Mille, who probably staged more orgies than Crassus, got around the censorship bit by substituting grapes for venery. It grew into a formula. If the actors were feeding each other grapes and laughing shrilly, audiences knew they were having an orgy and would come to a bad end before the movie finished. Highly ingenious, but not really instructive.

Perhaps for this reason group swingers play a large variety of parlor games that don't require much erotic know-how, but generate tremendous activity. The more sophisticated involve all sorts of costuming. The women may dress up as harlots, the men pretend to be customers and sometimes actually pay their partners. The money collected is invariably donated to some worthy charity, thus adding a touch of philanthropy to the sport.

Some games feature timing devices and seem closer to endurance contests than frolics. The men sit on chairs in a circle and a timer is fixed to ring every half minute or so. The ladies then straddle them and start grinding. Every time the bell goes they disengage and move on to the next partner, and so on until—one by one—the men become *hors de combat* through ejaculation. Whichever male lasts longest is the winner. Another version assigns a male partner to each woman and requires her to make him come—by any means she fancies—within a given time span. Also popular is a naked variation of "Blind Man's buff" in which the blindfolded "it" has to guess the identity of his or her catches by feeling them all over.

Strangely enough, I could never verify a single instance of that classic American standby, strip poker, being played at these soirées. Either the game is too slow, or it went out with unfiltered cigarettes and garter belts.

But among the mass of swingers the number of habitual group activists seems to be fairly small. Of those I interviewed, only about one in every four or five. The great majority favored the "closet" style—doors shut and no kibitzers—although they didn't mind a brief social gathering in the raw afterwards.

This preference is only partly based on our conditioning to regard sexual privacy as akin to bathroom privacy. At least equally important is the fact that many men perform sexually very poorly in public and often can't perform at all. According to Dr. Albert Ellis, the popular psychotherapist, men tend to fail at the start of their swapping activities. "Practically no man is as virile as he imagines he would be in such a situation." The fear of failure alone may be sufficient to induce most males to shun the risk.

The women have no such worries. Once their indoctrinated reserve has been overcome, an amazing proportion turn into rampant exhibitionists, tirelessly inventing new forms of display. And here we come to one of the most striking aspects of swingdom.

In every case I heard of, it was the husband or boy friend who instigated the swapping experience, sometimes virtually dragging his mate along. Again and again the wives in question confided: "I only got into this because I thought it would save our marriage—stop my husband from chasing skirts on his own." But after a period "on the swing," women often grow far more enthusiastic than men, insisting on weekly sessions when their spouses might have been content with biweekly or monthly events, taking over the social arrangements and leading the way into action.

This is not due to any perverse streak on their part. They have simply discovered that in a group scene women have decided advantages over men. Some of these are purely physical. A man's climax puts him—at least temporarily—out of the running. A woman can have several orgasms and still continue in the fray, often with increased fervor. She can therefore handle more partners than her mate and will outlast him almost every time.

On top of that, she may gain great emotional satisfaction from her ability to arouse every man in the room. This confirmation of her attractiveness can play an important part, particularly for the not-so-young and especially since it takes place under controlled—and therefore safe—circumstances. As Dr. L. James Grold, Assistant Clinical Professor of Psychiatry at U.S.C., explained: "I think on the part of most women there is a feeling that, even for a moment, they are being wanted, desired and cared about."

Personally, I noticed that objections to spectators—such as myself—nearly always came from the husbands. The wives were more often willing to let an uninvolved couple watch, and sometimes helped overcome the men's reluctance. Their strongest argument was one that appeals to all addicts: "Let them see how much fun it is. They'll end up getting into the action." The craving for converts seems equally powerful among acid-droppers, evangelists, health-food fanatics and swingers.

In one respect, though, women appear to be at a disadvantage. "Let's face it," the female portion of a New York photographer's team told me, "some men are just totally unattractive, even in the dark. In a large group there are usually one or two real losers. If they approach you, you're in a spot. The rule is that you can turn down anyone and they're not supposed to be insistent. But you hurt their feelings terribly. I've seen one fellow actually cry. So occasionally you just shut your eyes and get it over with. We call them 'charity cases.' A few of them can put you off the swinging scene for good."

Most of the couples I quizzed insisted that their prime reason for swinging was to "strengthen" their marriage—which might be a euphemism for rescuing it. They pictured the process as "open-ended wedlock," a kind of advanced form of togetherness. How many marriages have actually been saved in that fashion is impossible to ascertain, though I'm sure it circumvented an awful lot of old-fashioned hanky-panky.

But there is another powerful motive for joining, one of which most swingers appear blissfully unaware. Nearly half the men involved, I found, were salesmen of something or other, and they utilized their swinging connections to push everything from custom-made shoes and cosmetics to insurance and real estate.

I met only one who actually admitted that his incentive to swing had been chiefly economic, but he assured me that the same applied to a great many others. He is a young, athletic Philadelphian I'll call Mark, and he makes an excellent living selling stocks and bonds —mainly to fellow swingers.

"Take my word for it," said Mark, "it beats becoming an Elk or Mason or Buffalo or anything. There's nothing like having a man ball your wife—and balling his—for lowering sales resistance. Of course, I never talk business during socials. I just make the contacts. But you'd be amazed how approachable the fellows become afterwards when I meet them casually for a drink somewhere."

Mark rubbed his handsomely clefted chin and added thoughtfully: "Now get me right, I don't want to sound too damned cynical about this. But, hell, it goes on all around you. Swingers buy from swinging store owners, go to swinging doctors and dentists, consult swinging lawyers, get their homes decorated by swingers—the works.

"One thing is for sure: If it weren't for the business angle we wouldn't be associating with that bunch. No, not because of moral reasons; that's all baloney. But, Christ, you ought to listen to them talk! As a crowd those swingers are the worst bunch of *nouveau riche* bores in town."

He wasn't the only one I heard complain about the dismal level of swingers' conversation. According to the widely experienced wife of a San Francisco wine merchant, they're at their dreariest when discoursing on their special topic:

"The women, really, aren't too bad. I mean, they'll *occasionally* come out with something original. But the men"—she rolled her dark eyes in a mute appeal to heaven—"they've got one thing on their tiny minds, and that's the size of their sex organs. I'm telling you, it's like an obsession. You talk to a man, and within a minute —no lies—within a minute he'll describe how terrifically hung he is. That's all he can think of, his penis! Like it's a flag and you're supposed to salute it or something! Maybe they think if it's big it turns women on. Well, it doesn't—at least no women I know of. It's what you do with it that counts."

There may be reasons other than mental limitation for the total absence of sparkle at most swingers' socials. The participants, I noticed, don't *want* to establish bonds with their group colleagues. Affinity rarely extends beyond the bedroom. They seem to feel that genuine interpersonal involvements would threaten their marriages. That while it may be quite safe for a wife to share another man's passion, it would become risky if she shared his thoughts.

Sociologist Carolyn Symonds wrote a thesis in which she divided swingers into two groups: "Utopian" and "Recreational." The former idealists who treat spouse-trading as part of their philosophy, which favors communal living in all respects. The latter regard it as fun and relaxation, a few degrees more exciting than Canasta. While "Utopians" occasionally form friendships with their swinging peers, the "Recreationalists" almost never do. In fact, they will avoid swinging with the same couples more than four or five times just to prevent such a development. Their contacts *must* remain on an exclusively sexual level or cease altogether. And since the relaxers vastly outnumber the philosophers, genuine friendships among swingers are a scarce commodity.

This applies especially to those swingers who meet each other through newspaper ads. We now have at least a dozen national magazines catering to mate-swappers—some produced by swingers organizations, others by publishing companies. They have titles like *The Local Swinger, Personal Approach, National Registry, Choice* and *Select*, cost between three and eight dollars each and contain anything up to twenty-five hundred swingers ads per issue. And this dazzling selection does not include the multitude of swap advertisements in the classified sections of mating mags and the Underground press (see Chapter 6). A random run of samples—all appearing the same month—reads:

> Couple, 30s, attractive, have many swinging friends, wish to meet more. We enjoy Roman & French activities. Please send address and phone ✄ for quick reply.
>
> Couple, AC/DC, 40s, interested in discipline & bondage. Photo & phone a must.
>
> Attractive, white couple, 30s, slim, wife bi. Want to meet other couples for fun & sex.
>
> Japanese gal 32, & male friend 43, both new at swinging, desire to meet with AC/DC gals or couples with bi female. Age & race unimportant.
>
> Attractive couple seeking same. Also bi-girls & well-built guys. We are not prejudiced. He 50, she 36, enjoy French culture. Very warm. Please send photo.

A striking feature about these ads is the recurrent theme of female bisexuality, which permeates the entire swap scene. For while overt male homosexuality is exceedingly rare among swingers, the female variation is not only accepted but enthusiastically encouraged. On one occasion I saw two husbands literally goad their wives into it.

This happened *after* the couples had returned from their respective bedrooms. The men were obviously spent, the women obviously not. They began by admiring each other's figures—one was a young Rubensian blonde; the other, an older, lithe and suntanned Yoga fan. Their husbands, lying back and recovering, prodded them on for several minutes before the ladies began to explore and caress each other. Then a latent current seemed to take over, and they forgot all about the men present and indulged in one of the most rapturous bouts of lovemaking I have ever witnessed. I'm sure neither of their male partners measured up to it.

At first I believed this was an exceptional occurrence, but I quickly learned that it was almost routine. The manager of a Los Angeles swingers club—who should know—even maintained that some wives only participate because it gives them a chance at other women. "For some it's an acquired taste, like oysters," he said. "A lot of people live half their lives before trying one. But once they do—wow!"

The near-taboo on male inversion is more difficult to explain. In part it is due to the fact that, while men find the spectacle of women making love to each other highly stimulating, women get no such charge from seeing men perform. This, however, is secondary. The prime factor lies in the traumatic attitude most men have toward homosexuality—an omnipresent threat to their masculine role, all the more potent because it just *may* strike a responsive chord in their own psyches. Their reaction is an instant—often hysterical —recoil that may result in violence. A single, even joking, homosexual gesture can break up a swingers party.

So can other—less psychic—human weaknesses. In 1971, a Hollywood entrepreneur launched one of the most ambitious swinging enterprises on record. He chartered a 190-foot luxury schooner, fitted to carry sixty swapping couples on a ten-day cruise to the West Indies and back. The bunks were equipped with silk sheets, the hold with enough scotch and champagne to float a sister ship. Tickets sold at seven hundred dollars per person and were booked out six months in advance of what promised to be a mass marine orgy. Neptune decided otherwise. The ocean turned rough, and every couple on board spent the voyage either bent over the railing or prone on their silk sheets, trying not to die of seasickness.

I could locate only one person with something like a "historical" view of the swap phenomenon. He is the above-mentioned club owner, whose patrons know him by a sonorous Spanish label, but whose real name is Jack Hagen. He and his wife Belinda have been operating their club in the Los Angeles area since 1963, though they've changed premises and titles several times.

At the moment, their organization has 304 dues-paying members and is based in a charming, palm-fringed house containing five bedrooms, a bar, an indoor pool, a gym, an enormous tropical-fish aquarium, a sauna bath, and not a single nude picture. The Hagens run four club nights a week. Wednesday is get-acquainted night, when—by communal consent—no action takes place. Friday, Saturday and Sunday nights are reserved for swinging, and no nonmember is allowed inside. The Hagens themselves don't participate any more. ("We used to, very enthusiastically, when we were both eight or nine years younger. Now we seem to have outgrown it.") They patrol the premises, arrange introductions, put newcomers at their ease, locate items of clothing lost in the shuffle, mix drinks, smooth out arguments, attend the stereo and—incidentally—keep their nostrils aquiver for the faintest whiff of marijuana.

Jack, whose swarthy Latin appearance belies his thoroughly Celtic ancestry, is an encyclopedia of swingers' lore. He has observed every nuance of the movement since it began spreading on a large scale and is more than willing to share his conclusions. ("I've thought of writing a book on the subject, but I reckon I missed the bus. Now all those professor types are getting ahead of me.")

There was a faintly ironic undertone in his vodka-flavored voice when he discussed the personality profile of his members.

"Swingers have an image of themselves as real cool, with-it cats," he rumbled gently. "They'll say 'fuck' and 'screw you,' and the women talk nonchalantly about balling and think they're all Isadora Duncans. You know—avant-garde and liberated and all that. But when it comes right down to it, they're pretty square. More concerned about their jobs and homes and cars and taxes and front lawns than about any amount of liberation. And that's not a bad way to be, really. My wife and I, we're a bit that way ourselves. Only we don't put on all that bullshit."

"Is this the wave of the future?" He shrugged with a half-smile. "I don't know. But I don't think so, somehow. I think most people will stick to having affairs. On the quiet. It seems more in accordance with human nature. We're a sneaky lot, at heart. No fun if it isn't *forbidden*. The old thing with Adam and Eve and the apple."

He tapped me on the shoulder. "You know, I've heard of a couple of real funny cases. Illustrate my point. There were two families and they both ran 'swinging households.' Like their children knew about it and the parents made no secret about what went on Friday nights. All aboveboard—all 'beautiful and natural,' nothing dirty about sex.

"And d'you know what happened?" His grin spread over his face. "Those kids turned into the most godawful little puritans you can imagine. One of the girls had to see a shrink after she got married—she was frigid. And one of the boys became a street-corner preacher here in L.A. Yelling about the sin of fornication . . . every blessed Sunday."

nine

ENCOUNTER MATING

About a thousand of us—all ages and sexes—were standing in the
grand ballroom of the Statler-Hilton in Washington, D.C., listening
to the guttural but mesmerizing instructions coming over the loudspeaker:

"Look around the room at the mass of people. Take it in. Now
focus on just one person . . . close-up . . . got that person? Now
walk toward that person . . . slowly. Take a head trip. Fantasize
about the feelings that person is arousing in you—*feel* them! In your
body . . . your *whole* body. Now fantasize about doing something
to that person . . ."

A thousand people were shambling toward each other, some with
arms outstretched, like sleepwalkers. The loudspeaker voice droned
on:

"Close your eyes . . . close them tight. With your hands describe
the outlines of your space . . . your territory. Think of taking a trip
into your past—now into your future—think of the year 2001. *Feel*
time moving . . . the world moving . . . *feel* it! Feel a poem
growing inside you . . . let it grow . . . shape it . . . let it come

out. Open your eyes now. Look around if you see someone to tell the poem to. Found someone? Now *tell* the poem—tell it!"

A thousand men and women milling around—moving, jerking, talking, squatting, embracing, laughing, waving their hands in accordance with the loudspeaker commands. A few seemed to have lost their bearings and shuffled in zigzags, muttering to themselves.

The date was September 1971, and the occasion the opening of the Association for Humanistic Psychology. The trancelike mélange of square dance, pantomime and close-order drill we were performing was, according to the program, a "Sensitivity Awareness Session." It was also—though quite unofficially—America's latest, chicest and fastest-growing approach formula between the sexes.

I could watch it working all around me the moment we adjourned. Men and women who had contacted each other briefly during the session now gravitated together, breathing hard and smiling shakily through layers of perspiration . . . "You really came through to me, you know that. I mean—I could *feel* you reaching out." . . . "Yeah, I felt you too. You were *here*—really *with* me. For gut-level real. By the way, how about going for a drink somewhere?" . . .

Their verbal exchanges were intellectually on a par with the more traditional predrink dialogues. But what sparked them was a wave of nationwide dimensions, a movement of such scope and potential that at least one prominent sociologist has gone on record stating, "We are on the threshold of the Encounter Age."

The movement he referred to is largely undirected, strangely formless, and so eclectic in its methods that it goes by at least a dozen different labels. Generically, it is known as the Human Potential Movement, a title meaningless enough to embrace such divergent manifestations as *Gestalt*, psychodrama, WILL, Fusion Groups, Guided Fantasy, Synanon, Bioenergetics, Rolfing, Alexander Technique, and various combinations of the above, such as Esalen. All of them are commonly, but not quite accurately, called Encounter Groups.

They share the basic concept that in order to reach the individual's potential resources, he or she has to achieve self-awareness and confidence within a group. The group represents a microcosm of society, and the idea is that by strengthening and widening interaction, both the individual and the group learn to function better and more fully in the outside world.

As a form of psychotherapy this method was practiced as far back as the 1920s, when Freud's former associate, Alfred Adler, established group guidance centers for his patients in Vienna. In America, where the term "group therapy" was coined, its pioneer exponents included Trigant Burrow, Harry Stack Sullivan and Karen Horney.

The great innovation came when the groups evolved to embrace "therapy for normals"—that is, with the creation of units whose primary purpose was to release and enhance the resources of ordinary people. The new bodies, titled "growth centers," began to operate alongside the older therapy groups and are frequently confused with them—which is not surprising, since participants often flit back and forth from one to the other.

Among the earliest growth centers was the Esalen Institute, founded in 1962. Two visionary psychology graduates, Michael Murphy and Richard Price, created it on a sixty-acre tract overlooking the Pacific Ocean at Big Sur, California. They had only a vague notion of what they intended to accomplish, but it was to be a forum for a whole spectrum of new ideas combining Western clinical psychology and Eastern meditational philosophy with such purely physical practices as men and women soaking naked in hot sulphur baths while gazing out at the sea.

Esalen enjoyed an almost explosive success. Within eight years some 107 other growth centers sprang up, purportedly in its image. But since this image was amorphous to start with—imposing no set curriculum—its imitators could practice pretty much what they fancied and still call themselves "Esalen-inspired."

The Esalen-type groups, however, constitute only a fraction of the encounter movement, which—according to recent estimates—now embraces over six million people. Mushrooming eastward from California, the wave has permeated every level of our educational system, from kindergarten to college. Human-potentials centers are flourishing in various churches, the armed forces and industry.

Business companies are holding encounter sessions called T- (Training) Groups for their employees, and local government agencies stage interracial encounters aimed at alleviating color friction. The Manhattan Board of Mental Health puts the number of groups functioning in New York City alone at five thousand.

The movement has become so multifaceted that it is difficult to make *any* generalization about it. This includes the fees involved, which range from fifteen dollars for a session at the New York loft headquarters of Anthos, to twenty-one hundred dollars for a seven-week program at the Maine retreat of the National Training Laboratories.

The one common denominator is the subjugation of the individual by the group. Participants are systematically stripped of all defensive shields—money, social status, education, manners, authority—and evaluated only by their naked psyches. The techniques by which this is accomplished vary from the gossamer gentle to the outright savage, but the purpose is the same: to take apart—to lay bare—to expose the member before the group.

It is this exposure effect that has made encounters the favored mate-hunting ground for an extraordinary number of people. Many, in fact, establish all their intimate associations within these groups and virtually come to ignore outsiders.

I learned the reasons from a woman who had actually met her current husband at a Gestalt workshop.[1] "You know," she said, "you can date a man for months—even sleep with him—without getting through his protective layers. But in just one or two group sessions you see the core of a person. Like having X-ray eyes, you see what's churning around way down deep. And then you can decide if you want to get close to him. And it works just as well the other way around."

The process can be—is meant to be—a searing experience for the participants. I attended a Personal Growth Lab where a cherubic, pink-cheeked young man named Robby was given a sofa cushion

---

[1] *Gestalt,* German for shape, form, is a branch of psychotherapy founded by the late Frederick S. Perls. It includes role playing, with the patient acting out different fragments of himself.

to hug, representing his mother. He began by holding it tenderly, but as the group kept shouting at him to show what he felt—stop faking—he started to pound it instead. As he struck he worked himself into a frenzy, his blows getting harder until he was flailing away with both fists, muttering, then screaming at the cushion: "You bitch, you lousy bitch—you only loved Arthur—only loved Arthur—never ME—ONLY Arthur . . . I hate you, you goddamned bitch . . . I'll kill you . . . !"

He was drooling and weeping, screeching in a terrible infant's voice, trying to tear the cushion with his teeth until he finally collapsed sobbing, rubbing his face against the cloth, moaning, "Love ME, love ME . . ."

Two girls ran up to him, tears running down their faces. They cradled him to their bosoms, stroking him, comforting him in voices shaking with genuine emotion: "It's all right, Robby—it's happened to all of us—you're loved—we all love you."

The rest of the group, men and women, crowded around, hugging Robby, hugging each other, sharing his anguish among them. Finally he stood in the middle, sheltered and supported by the group, his eyes still watering but radiant. "I love you," he said hoarsely, "I love all of you."

It was a classical encounter happening. First Robby had been mercilessly lashed into his outburst by the group. Then—having displayed "gut-level" feelings—he was consoled by the group, taken in by them, made to feel understood, cherished and protected. All this warm wave of approval in return for one minute of hysteria.

The bond between Robby and the girl-mother figures who had seen his raging despair and brought him relief would be a special one, almost impossible to duplicate in the outside world. It seemed only logical for him to date one of them, to utilize the special understanding between them as a form of protection against the coldly unconcerned rest of humanity. This, in a nutshell, is both the joy and the peril of the encounter movement.

But the group approach between the sexes is often far more direct. In the sensitivity workshops (S-groups) members spend much time stroking, fondling, caressing and exploring each other—not necessarily in a carnal fashion, but including enough erogenous territory to arouse each other fairly thoroughly.

A few groups encounter in the nude, their theory being that nakedness adds to intimacy, helps to eliminate self-consciousness, and makes members relate more honestly. In Escondido, California, psychologist Paul Bindrim has his unclothed flock dip into a luke-warm Jacuzzi bath he calls a "womb pool." At the Elysium Institute, in suburban Los Angeles, the program includes mutual massages and an innovation called "blind walk." The naked Adams and Eves are paired off and one of them is blindfolded. The other leads him or her around a garden area, touching trees, smelling flowers, climb-ing over logs, feeling and enjoying the growing confidence the blindfolded party has in the guide. At the end of the walk they switch roles.

Contrary to certain wishful rumors, few encounter groups ac-tually have sexual intercourse, although many go through the pre-liminary stages of what medical textbooks call "heavy petting." But the atmosphere is often so warmly sensual that it serves as a natural prelude to subsequent affairs. At one S-group in Washington, D.C., eight out of sixteen people present told me that they had gone to bed with each other at least once; two of them eventually married. This is a considerably higher proportion of matches than any singles club has ever achieved.

"Love is intimacy," one of the girls explained, "and we had reached such a deep level of intimacy that *making* love—after-wards—seemed only a kind of logical conclusion. Of course, the physical part can be an anticlimax after a head trip—it was in my case—but that might have been because I picked the wrong partner. I think our hangups were too similar."

Ever since the encounter movement began its triumphant march eastward it has drawn fire from such dissimilar opponents as ortho-dox Freudians and the John Birch Society (psychology doth strange bedfellows make). The Birchers charged the groups with "Communist brainwashing"—their blanket phrase for any activity they disapprove of. And it seems somewhat unlikely that enterprises like Federated Stores and Procter & Gamble—not to speak of the

Methodist and Episcopal churches—would organize Communist gatherings under their roofs.

The psychological establishment took the opposite tack. They branded encounter methods as "a form of fascist tyranny, imposing the will of the group on the individual." New York psychologist Emanuel Schwartz compared the advance publicity for Esalen to circus barnstorming, and his colleague Albert Neer stated that the sensitivity sessions at the Washington Hilton reminded him "of a collection of well-fed zombies prancing around to the commands of a witch doctor with a microphone."

To me the shadow side of the movement was epitomized by a leaflet which a chinless youth thrust at pedestrians on New York's lower Broadway. It listed nineteen assorted encounter groups and declared (in blurred print): "Interpersonal Liberation and Encounter Groups Belong to the People! Join One! Start One! Now! Group Power!"

The leaflet was telling the truth. Encounter groups do indeed "belong to the people," insofar as anyone can start and run one regardless of qualifications—or total lack of them. And here, in the leadership principle, lies the most ominous flaw of the entire human-potentials syndrome.

The more starry-eyed encounterers insist that the groups work without leaders, that all members are equal and that the people issuing orders merely act as "facilitators." This is not just semantic sophistry; it's deliberate self-delusion.

Encounter leaders, in fact, do more than lead—they *dictate* the entire atmosphere and procedure of the group, often following no other rules than their own whims and imagination, which frequently means imposing their own neurotic hangups on their flock. They also collect anything up to two thousand dollars per weekend for their trouble, a juicy reward for a little "facilitating." Most of them gleefully foster the egalitarian myth of the movement for the simple reason that this enables them to enjoy the power, the profits and the prestige of their position without being burdened by responsibility.

Some male leaders assume a kind of unwritten *droit du seigneur* over their female groupies, hauling them off to bed with the regal nonchalance of a medieval baron "honoring" peasant wenches. I watched one—he looked like a slightly gaga Old Testament prophet— whose every tactile gesture was aimed at the breasts or bottom of whatever woman happened to be within reach. Several tried to squirm away and were immediately accused of being "uptight." The group promptly echoed the accusation like a well-rehearsed chorus line, and the offending ladies had to offer long and squirming explanations of just why they didn't relish the touch of the Führer's chewed-off fingernails.

The fairy tale of group equality also serves as an excuse for the leaders' missing credentials. (As long as the word "therapy" doesn't appear in their literature they require no training whatsoever.)

One popular Chicago "facilitator"—a high-school dropout—was a door-to-door Bible salesman, Fuller Brush man, sports promoter, used-car dealer, and real-estate speculator, and went through two divorces, two bankruptcies and a stretch in jail for assault before hitting on sensitivity awareness, at which he currently nets around thirty thousand dollars a year.

Even those leaders with psychology degrees have not necessarily received *clinical* training. Their qualifications often turn out to belong in an entirely different branch. Letting them conduct groups is rather like permitting a dentist to extract tonsils.

But the real danger stems from the kind of inadequate personality for which the human-potentials movement seems to have an irresistible attraction. An appalling number of "facilitators" are emotional cripples, themselves in dire need of the help they claim to give others. They may use their groups primarily as ego crutches, leaning on their members for the respect and attention they are unable to gain from outsiders.

Among the most pathetic examples of this type is a Philadelphia group leader so desperate to be regarded as youthfully "with it" that he wears granny glasses and squeezes his middle-aged paunch into patched Levis. A compulsive womanizer, he invariably picks the more disturbed and unbalanced of his groupies for his one-night stands, sending several over the mental-breakdown edge they had been hovering on. An equally compulsive card player, he once borrowed three hundred dollars from a colleague for a special training course. He went through every cent during a single night at the poker table.

It doesn't take much imagination to realize the havoc such individuals can inflict on the exposed psyches of their adherents. Particularly as, in the case of laymen, there is no code of ethics, no book of rules, to restrain them. Like most quacks they are excellent at taking apart but quite incapable of putting together again. And although encounter techniques are usually harmless per se, they can be shattering when performed on fragile personalities. And it is precisely those personalities that are most apt to be drawn into the movement. They become what is known as "casualties"—participants who suffer varying degrees of psychological impairment in the process.

Bill Schutz, one of Esalen's sensory-awareness experts and author of the bestseller *Joy*, claims that "The so-called 'casualties' have been greatly exaggerated." But the figures tell a different story. A test group of two hundred Stanford University students, put through a wide range of personal growth experiences, showed a "casualty rate" of 8 percent—sixteen participants. Dr. Irving Yalom, who headed the American Psychiatric Association's research force on encounter groups, reported that after one Training Group session, between 10 and 15 percent of the members experienced a variety of adverse psychic effects that made them seek treatment.

The treatment required is not always psychic. In a frightening number of instances the damage is physical. This is the result of the infantile reasoning of certain group leaders, who figure that if free expression of feelings is good, then total expression—including violence—must be even better. And in some cases you can't escape the conclusion that the spectacle of violence gives them a great deal of pleasure.

There is no other explanation for the experience of Anne, a good-looking California commercial artist, who attended a series of six Esalen encounters in the hope that they would help her become less tense with strangers. The group leader, a former architect, was known to gross one hundred dollars a night for his "facilitations." Here is the story in Anne's words:

"During the second meeting our leader decided we were wasting time with verbal intercourse—he called it 'mind fucking'—and proceeded to get hostilities out into the open in the most elementary fashion. He had one person go around the room and tell what he disliked about every other person. One girl was told that her legs were too heavy; a man, that his eyebrows grew too close together. When the person in the middle decided whom he disliked most, the two were told to stand facing each other, let their hostilities build up, then to start hitting each other. Sometimes these fights got really vicious. One man suffered a broken rib.

"I was very often chosen as the most disliked person in the room (the reasons were always: hard, cold, ungiving), but my fighting spirit rarely came to the fore. They would take a few swipes at me, and I'd step back. But once a girl worker from the Free Clinic picked me, and for some reason I felt my emotional balance give way. I said, 'If you hurt me, by God I'll kill you.' Whereupon *she* stepped back. This was the first time I ever received support from the group. They all agreed that I had truly expressed my feelings.

"At the following meeting a middle-aged college professor singled me out. His reasons for disliking me were that I was unfeminine, aloof, haughty, and that I failed to arouse him sexually.

"The leader told us to square off in the middle of the room. By the way, this group would certainly have met with the approval of Women's Lib—there were no special rules about hitting women more gently than men. The professor landed a hard blow on my jaw. I became really infuriated and plowed into him. We had what can only be described as a knock-down-drag-out fight. My blouse was ripped right down my back, the crotch of my slacks was torn, my face throbbed with blows. He had a big bloodstain on his back, where I had bitten him. Right through the cloth—I can still remember the sensation.

"Finally, when we were panting so heavily we couldn't move, we fell down where we were. The professor took his shirt off to examine his wound, then walked back to his place with a look of great pride and accomplishment."

Sensitivity leaders also use several other means of violent self-expression. Groups are ordered to form a tight circle by linking arms, one person being left outside and told to force his or her way in "to show determination to join." If they fail they are informed that they just weren't determined enough. As a determination scale, this exercise is ludicrous. The decisive factor is simply weight. A heavy man can batter his way in quite easily; for male or female lightweights it means frustration.

But the favorite system seems to be the clownish variation of single combat described above, with the leader apparently relying on the participants' lack of fistic expertise to prevent injuries. In one New York encounter our head was an excitable stout woman in her fifties, with the vocal cords of a fishwife and every symptom of severe menopause disturbances.

The young man next to me—a weedy, ferret-faced fellow—was picked as "most disliked person" and positioned opposite his selector. The other man, about a foot taller, immediately began to pummel him, but my neighbor merely stood still, looking around with a vaguely embarrassed air.

Our leader became near-demented at the sight. "You're copping out," she shrieked, waving her arms. "Participate! Hit him back!"

Ferret-face blinked in a bewildered fashion and gave a perfect Gallic shrug of apology. Then he swung once and knocked his opponent cold. He was, it turned out, an amateur flyweight boxer. "First time I've ever hit anyone outside the ring," he told me afterwards. "She"—pointing at our harridan-in-charge—"ought to have her head examined."

There is no doubt that the potentials movement will run into serious trouble unless it sheds some of its more self-indulgent or plainly incompetent leaders. In 1972, an Ohio businessman filed a two-million-dollar suit against the Leadership Dynamics Institute, Inc., for a savage beating he allegedly received during a sensitivity session. The Ohioan, Richard E. Schaefer, charged that he was pounded to such an extent that he suffered ". . . bleeding from the rectum and urinary tract, injuries to the back, head, shoulders, arms and legs and extensive bruises over the body . . . sutures were required."

Schaefer claimed he paid one thousand dollars for a four-day session which, he was promised, "would change his whole life." He had informed the organizers that he had a shoulder injury, and "they promised him there would be no damage to the shoulder, when in fact, it was reinjured during the sessions." The suit declared the defendants "so carelessly and negligently controlled, organized, supervised and conducted [the program] . . . so as to cause those present to physically and emotionally beat, strike, harass, terrify, threaten and kick" Schaefer.

These so-called "Aggressive Stimulators" make up only a minority of leaders; although, in their own estimation, they represent the elite. For the most part, group leaders are fairly mild-mannered, and some at least exude genuine supportive warmth. (One of the best I watched in action was, curiously enough, a rather placid young woman conducting sessions on behalf of the Sexual Freedom League —of which more later.)

Most of the games played, too, are inoffensive, and several fulfill definite emotional needs of the players. An outburst of tears may be the signal to form a "cradle"—the crying member being rocked tenderly in the air on the arms of all the others. The "free fall" entails letting yourself drop backward and being caught by two fellow members until your confidence in them—and your serenity—becomes complete.

Body-awareness exercises really do make you become aware of parts of your body you otherwise rarely notice. They include writing your name in the air with your shoulder blades and learning to move each one of your toes independently. While they may not lead to any profound psychological insights, they help ease nervous tension and can give you a delightful sense of discovery. Other awareness techniques teach members to smell—really *smell*—things like fruit or flowers, utilizing a sense that in our civilization has almost atrophied.

Some groups go considerably further. Friends Inc., a sensitivity outfit meeting in a rural retreat in Pennsylvania, includes a course in "Oral Discovery." Seminarians are blindfolded, then told to explore *all* the cavities and orifices of each other's bodies.

The intensive preoccupation with the physical is an essential part of Gestalt therapy, devised by Fritz Perls and incorporated—among a vast collection of other techniques—in the Esalen curriculum. But whereas the late Mr. Perls was an innovative giant, many of his current apostles are imitative midgets, far more concerned with mouthing his slogans (such as "Lose your mind and come to your senses") than applying the meaning behind them. Their interpretation of his "here and now" principle, for instance, is a total shutdown of the thinking process. For any attempt at using reasoning powers they have devised the enchanting term "mind fucking"—considered to be among the gravest accusations that can be hurled at an encounterer.

Through them the entire movement has become tainted with a distinctly antiintellectual flavor that places feeling *über alles* and thinking nowhere. The greatest praise bestowable is to call something "gut-level," i.e., below the belt and well away from the cerebral centers. Hysteria, rudeness and ostentatious sewer language pass for sincerity. Novices soon learn that the use of correct grammar and clarity of expression earn them the immediate suspicion of copping out—dodging honest emotion. Even leaders with impeccable academic backgrounds do their damndest to convey an impression of illiteracy. One way of accomplishing this is by studding every sentence with the words "like" and "you know" and—whenever possible—leaving it unfinished.

This does not mean that encounterers are averse to speech. In fact, they talk—sorry, rap—interminably. Their oral defectiveness—real or pretended—merely assures that they don't understand each other too well. Most of their verbal communication sounds like a gathering of transistor radios, all playing simultaneously and slightly off-station. The following exchange, overheard at a Chicago encounter, is fairly indicative:

WOMAN: I see all these shapes. I'm aware of them. Everybody here is a shape. Something awful is going to happen.

MAN: I think you stink.

GIRL: You're beautiful.

MAN: I think you both stink.

LEADER: Now get in touch with yourself. Like really in touch. You know, let it all hang out. How does it feel—like now?

WOMAN: Everybody is a shape. You're all shapes.

MAN: You stink.

This kind of patter is apt to continue as long as the leader allows the drift to be general. It is only when he turns the spotlight on an individual—that is, manipulates the group's attention—that something revealing occurs. Without this stage direction every group loses itself in diffuse word shambles. This fact alone makes nonsense of the assertion that encounter works spontaneously "from within." The very opposite is true—the more authoritatively a group is conducted, the more positive (that is, revealing) are the results. Thus the peak of encounter experience, the marathon, has to be as skillfully managed as a formal dinner party to produce anything of consequence.

A marathon is the longest and most intensive degree of encounter, lasting from twenty-four to forty hours, usually stretched over a three-day weekend. Conditions vary, but they can be absolutely grueling, some groups going without sleep and talking uninterruptedly. These monster sessions are held in country retreats or hotels, and certain hostelries around New York have become so accustomed to them that they've worked out two standard rates: one for non-sleeping groups, the other for encounterers who need beds.

Gestalt marathons, which currently enjoy the greatest vogue, start off gently—at least under skilled leaders. Participants go through yoga breathing exercises, spend long periods gazing into each others eyes, walk around silently with eyes closed, hold hands, stroke, caress and embrace each other, then sit on the floor in back-to-back pairs, saying anything that comes into their minds at that moment—the "here and now" syndrome.

At intervals the leader inquires whether anyone wishes to "share an experience." If there is even a slight response from a member, the leader immediately focuses group attention on him or her. The group joins in—encouraging, querying, badgering, hammering the individual until a "gut-level" response occurs. In some ways it's like teasing and taunting a caged animal, continuing until the creature becomes momentarily frantic, then switching to petting and stroking to produce—likewise momentary—euphoria.

After twenty or so hours of this, the group may achieve an "altered state of consciousness." The atmosphere becomes dreamlike, reality recedes, outlines crumble; nothing exists except the nearness of the others, their hostility or their comfort. They and you are *all* that matter.

Participants have grown haggard from lack of sleep, hoarse from talking. Their features sag, make-up dissolves, men rub their beard stubbles and sweat through their shirts. Now, around seven in the morning, is the "magic hour," the time when human psyches erupt and gush lava streams of anguish.

A bank manager groans that the only woman he ever truly desired was his sister. No, not just desired. Enjoyed. The image grips him, shakes him. Somebody sneers: "Aw, come off it. You're just trying to sound interesting. Because you're such a drip." The bank manager shakes both fists at the sky, he bellows at the top of his voice: "I screwed my sister! I want to have her again. I want *only* her! Nobody else! Only her! And I can't have her—ever . . ." He buries his well-groomed graying head in his hands and sobs. The group gathers around him, strokes him, cries with him.

At one stage or another they all cry or scream—mostly both. The affluent suburban housewife with a successful executive husband and three well-behaved children, who doesn't love any of them— doesn't love anybody or anything—yells that her life has been nothing but play acting for twenty years. The young chemistry student who *knows* he's homosexual and can't stand the idea. "I want to puke on myself—I stand in front of a mirror and I wanna be sick! I'm a stinking faggot!" The dentist who simmers with continual suppressed rage—at his patients, at his parents, at everything he reads in the newspapers, at people he meets and at people he's never met.

His anger gnaws at him, terrifies him; he is sure he'll murder some-one someday.

And then there is Irma. Every marathon has at least one Irma, sometimes several, and frequently she is male. Irma is a nondescript person, competently filling a humdrum job, attracting minimum at-tention as a civilian. But at encounters she hogs the spotlight as much as the leader will let her. She has three weeping fits to every-body else's one. She screams more than the others, often for no dis-cernible reason. Or rather for a great many reasons, all of them vague. Irma produces gut-level emotion on a conveyor belt. In re-turn she is cradled, sandwiched, hugged and wept with.

Irma, in fact, is a "group bum"—an encounter nomad—roving the field from Aureon to Paragon and points in between, though she carefully steers clear of the more punishing routines like Synanon. Outside encounterdom she is a colorless nonentity, deprived of the attention she craves, largely ignored by people with other things on their minds. Only within the groups can she become a focal point— simply by throwing well-timed tantrums. Irma has rediscovered a childhood formula, together with a setting in which it still works. She—and her male equivalents—are hooked on encounters the way others are on liquor, drugs or promiscuity.

This may be the right point to ask the pertinent question put by Robert Southey's small listener after hearing the veteran's account of the Battle of Blenheim:

> "But what good came of it at last?"
> Quoth little Peterkin.
> "Why, that I cannot tell," said he;
> "But 'twas a famous victory."

During a three-day public hearing at New York University's Medical Center in May 1971, the experts locked horns over the threat or promise of the Human Potential Movement. They couldn't even agree on basic definitions. Is an encounterer a patient or a client? Are group sessions opportunities to interact with people or psy-chological experiments? Esalen, among others, regards itself as an educational body and calls its participants "seminarians."

Group leader Sarah Dowson claimed: "We are not doing therapy.

We don't claim to *treat* anyone. We merely provide an environment for people to meet, talk about life, their feelings and their immediate experiences."

Countered Dr. Daniel Casriel, a director of Group Dynamics: "Encounter therapy is an extremely strong psychological device to change people's values, attitudes and behavior . . . There is immediate need for the cessation of nontrained people opening up groups of their own, prying on unsuspecting, uninformed citizenry, overtly lying as to their credentials and training."

The movement's advertising methods came under attack. Dr. Magda Densee, of the State Psychological Association, condemned "untrained group leaders and trained leaders who advertise themselves as if they were selling shoes. There are self-styled charlatans who do anything or promise anything to bring people in."

J. Herbert Fill, the city's Commissioner of Mental Health, declared: "It's bad enough we know so little about the mind in the entire science, but when a layman comes along with his own ideas a client could have disastrous experiences."

Even to a layman-listener like myself it was obvious that part of the trouble stemmed from the hazy borderlines separating regular therapy groups from the ambiguous rest. Sometimes amateur leaders are responsible—for although they carefully avoid *calling* themselves therapists, they often bend over backward trying to convey the impression that they are. More often the fault lies with the clients. Tens of thousands of them have come to regard encounters as social functions, ideal pickup events at which to find bedmates, and simply don't give a damn about the exact brand of the occasion.

But the movement contains a more subtle form of danger, one that applies equally to encounters run by professionals or dilettantes. Rather than acting as a springboard to the outside world, it tends to become a world within itself. As a psychologist friend of mine phrased it: "For many of us, suspending all judgment and submitting to the will of a charismatic leader is a wonderful relief—almost a sexual pleasure. And it can be more habit-forming than tobacco."

The group can become *all*; gaining its approval and support, an end in itself. And once you have grasped the rules, it is an end only too easily attained. All you have to do is let go—emote, let the howling infant in you break out—and the group promptly rewards you with acceptance. It doesn't demand performance or applied effort, merely the baring of your soul. It understands everything, forgives everything. And if one should weary of your hangups, there are hundreds of others with new sympathies ready to welcome you.

The trouble is that the group does *not* resemble society. Its rules are artificial and don't apply to the world outside. As Jane Howard wrote in her report on the human-potentials movement, *Please Touch:* "Just as it is hard to be sober when nobody else is, I found what thousands of other veterans of groups have found: that it is hard to re-enter 'back-home' reality after the intoxicating communion of a successful encounter or T-group." Many participants put one toe on the chilly tiles of social reality and quickly slip back into the encounter steambath. The group may be a tyrant—and a harsh and capricious one at times—but it is a tyrant that *cares*.

Male-female relationships established at encounters are often nothing but attempts to carry a bit of group atmosphere home. To prolong total, gut-level intimacy into a permanent routine. Which is the reason why those liaisons formed at peak empathy usually slide downhill fastest. They die like hothouse flowers must die when transplanted into an open field.

ten

DATES FOR HIRE

"Good afternoon," said the trim young blonde from behind her desk. "Can I help you?"

Her voice blended well with her surroundings. Fresh, bright, winsome, and totally unerotic. The place was a converted apartment on Hollywood's Sunset Boulevard, with pink carpets, yellow drapes and a definite touch of homeyness. Even the miniature office desk looked like a mildly eccentric piece of living-room furniture.

"Is this 'Tiger Girls'?" I asked. I had expected a somewhat steamier décor.

"It sure is. Do you want a date?"

"Er—well, not right now. I actually wanted some information."

Her smile became a shade brighter. "My name is Elizabeth," she said. "I'm the manageress. Ask me anything you want."

"What kind of girls do you have available?" I ventured.

She flipped open a pile of index cards with the air of a cheerleader showing off the class of '68. "Take your pick. At the moment we've got—let's see—about seventy gals. Registered nurses, teachers, models, secretaries—whatever you like."

The girls, each one beaming from a glossy photograph, looked nearly as collegiate and wholesome as Elizabeth. She tapped one of the pictures. "That's Jenny. You'd love her. Sweetest gal you've ever met. You could go out with her tonight. I know she's free."

I glanced at Jenny. There was nothing remotely tigerish about her. Or even catlike. She could have gone on TV, advertising health food.

"Well, what's the procedure?" I asked. "I mean—what do I pay and how much date do I get?"

Elizabeth ticked it off on her fingers. "You pay five dollars registration fee. Then twenty-seven dollars for the introduction. And, of course, whatever you want to spend on your date. But that's up to you. You meet your gal right here in the office. After that, you're on your own. Nobody tells you when to bring her back. That's between you and her." She frowned cutely. "And that's all there is to it."

There was, I discovered, a bit more to it than that. The client's credentials are checked fairly thoroughly. He has to show his driver's license and Social Security card and give at least one reference name. If he's a stranger in town, he gives his hotel. And Elizabeth actually rings to find out whether he is registered there.

It seemed a rather cagey routine after following up an ad that read:

> Want an easy date? Hello, dear hunter. They call us tiger girls because we are sharp and attractive Hummm . . . but believe me, when we meet a man like you we become as tender as kittens, so we will wait for you to call us at Tiger Girls . . .

Elizabeth's flow of information never faltered. She answered every question with the brisk alacrity of an insurance promoter. What did the girls get out of the deal? "They get twelve dollars from the introduction fee." Tips? "Yes, tips are permitted, but not—uh—required."

Did the ladies ever get *involved* with their dates? "You mean, become their girl friends? It happens. Not very often, though. It just means that from then on they make their own dates between themselves, not through us. And she loses her twelve dollars."

It was hard to listen to her and keep remembering that we were, after all, dealing with the most exotic wrinkle of the entire mating trade. Exotic not so much in concept as in its application to the Western world. Even now, a remarkable number of Occidentals have no idea that it is going on right among them and react with slightly shocked dubiousness when told about it.

The basic formula of renting dates comes from Japan, where the geisha system originated. The geisha was—and is—a hired hostess-escort-entertainer, paid so much per hour of her company. The accent is on *company*, because the geisha is not a prostitute. Some of them *may* finish up on their clients' mats, but that's not part of the deal and is left entirely to her own predilection. She is essentially a highly trained social companion who sings, dances, chatters, plays instruments, tells jokes, and knows a fabulous number of innocuous and supposedly amusing little parlor games.

There has never been an actual Western equivalent of the geisha. The closest thing to her—the Playboy Bunny—is a club hostess who (at least theoretically) is not allowed to accompany clients off the premises. Her role is that of a glorified cocktail waitress.

The earliest escort bureaus, in the current sense of the label, were operating in London around 1960—roughly the period when that city first began to acquire its reputation for "swinging."

To the best of my knowledge, there were only three of them—two in Soho, the other in Mayfair—all depending on tourism for their clientele. The ladies on their books unanimously described themselves as "models," which in local parlance means anything from unemployed barmaids to underemployed call girls. But these bureaus were one step ahead of their Japanese predecessors: They had both male and female escorts for hire.

The transatlantic versions acted much more timidly at first. In 1963, for instance, the ultrarespectable San Francisco matchmaking agency of Ellinor Arnold added an escort service "to accommodate visitors." Their dates were hedged in by so many puritanical restrictions that patrons might just as well have stepped out with the inmates of a girls' boarding school.

But with proliferation came diversification. Today the hundred-plus outfits functioning in the United States provide most types of escorts for most purposes. You can rent dates for two-hour sightseeing tours or for week-long trips to Bermuda. You can hire them singly, in pairs, couples, or in troops, and stipulate that they play tennis, demonstrate gadgets, make scintillating conversation, wear bathing suits or hold large quantities of liquor. The only limitations (just about) lie in your wallet and in your knowledge of where to find them.

For America's escort services are oddly maldistributed. They have developed not so much according to local demand, but according to the varying tolerance levels of the authorities.

On the California landscape they sprouted like yuccas, with a dozen or more thriving in Los Angeles alone. There are perhaps six each in Florida and Texas and similar clusters in Hawaii, Nevada and Arizona. But they have barely penetrated the Midwest and Northeast. At the moment, the whole of New York City boasts only three or four of modest proportions, though this may have altered by the time these words are printed.

Unlike their British counterparts, the U.S. variations depend on genuine amateurs, escorts who hold more or less steady jobs elsewhere and use dating as an extra income. That income can be quite hefty. The Miami-based "Date-A-Supergirl" agency, for instance, offers lady companions for seventy-five dollars an evening or a hundred and fifty dollars a day. If clients wish to take the girls for a gambling weekend in the Bahamas, they must provide separate hotel rooms. And, as in other agencies, there is no limit on tipping.

The newspaper advertising put out by these bureaus tends to be uninformative, and deliberately so. They give you little idea as to the extent of their services. The reason for this is the dark-hued suspicion with which they are regarded by the police—a rather puzzling attitude considering the almost boundless latitude granted to other types of ads. It is also the reason why most escort agencies cultivate fronts of such wholesome plastic blandness, with not even a girlie calendar in view.

The "Tomata-Patch" (*their* spelling) is a case in point. Headquartered in a quiet, painstakingly neat suite of offices near Hollywood's famous Chinese Theatre, the only note of levity displayed is a shining wax "tomata" on the reception desk.

Linda Tangeman, half-owner of the Patch, used to be an employment agent and has retained the air of unflappable optimism that went with her former calling. A frosted-haired lady speaking in a softly reassuring voice, she has the kind of low-key aplomb that goes with years of trying to fit square pegs into round holes.

"We charge a ten-dollar consultation fee, thirty dollars per single date and forty dollars for two days." She smiled serenely. "Our escorts get ten dollars of the fee. Plus tips, of course. Yes," she nodded, "the tips can be very good. But we check our escorts out pretty thoroughly before we take them on. They're all fingerprinted by the police, the prints matched with the files to see whether there's a criminal record. That applies to both women and men. And here's the form they have to fill out."

There were two application forms: pink for the girls, blue for boys. Both asked whether the candidate had ever been convicted of a felony, how well they knew Los Angeles, their racial prejudices (if any), languages spoken and skills acquired, and contained an intriguing self-rating system by which applicants could describe themselves with a large selection of adjectives ranging from "naïve" to "experienced," from "square" to "hip" and "magic."

"Our clients," said Mrs. Tangeman, "make their selections from these sheets here"—she handed me one. It had a photo on one side, personal particulars on the other, including the escort's education, zodiac sign, smoking and drinking habits, special talents and general characteristics . . . "Warm personality, very sweet and outgoing."

She pointed at the carpet. "Everybody gets introduced in this office, but clients only by their first names. That's because we get a lot of married people, you understand."

"Married men or women?"

"Both. Of course, they don't always tell us."

"What's the sex ratio of your clients?" I wanted to know.

"Oh, about 80 percent men, 20 percent women. And they pay the same rates. Sex equality." She chuckled politely. "Only with lady clients we have a special procedure to save them—well, embarrassment. She hands over whatever she intends to spend on her date to her escort right here. We note down the amount. So wherever they go, the man will do the paying. Next day he has to account for what he's spent. And if there's anything left over, she gets it back."

I asked her who was harder to please—men or women clients? Mrs. Tangeman didn't have to think about that one. "Women," she shot back. "Definitely. But not the way you might assume. Most of our lady clients are over thirty, so you'd guess they'd want handsome young boys." She shook her head. "Actually, very few of them do. Most of them want escorts who look and dress like successful businessmen. Executive types, you know. Distinguished. Our male escorts range from about twenty-two to sixty, and the guys over forty are the most in demand."

It took considerable digging before I began to get an idea of the impressive variety of reasons that make people hire their dates. The escorts I hired myself didn't prove very helpful. Their looks, morals and intelligence fluctuated immensely, but all of them shared one trait: They wanted to let *me* talk, whereas my aim was the opposite. Most of my rented rendezvous ended in a distinct atmosphere of stalemate.

I realized that I would have to change my *modus operandi* to get results. I began to follow up the notices advertising for escorts—not, to be sure, to apply for the jobs, but to make contact with those who did. A typical ad might read:

> Smart, attractive girls wanted to dine, dance and sightsee with visiting executives. 21–30. Knowledge of languages an advantage. Looks and grooming a MUST. Apply . . .

There were always half a dozen applicants for each vacancy; sometimes the waiting rooms were packed with them. After they emerged from their interviews you could see on their faces whether they had gotten the job or the "don't-ring-us-we'll-ring-you" routine. Either way, most of them were ready for a drink and a sympathetic shoulder to bitch on. With this method I struck pay dirt. I learned more in an hour with an applicant than in the course of an entire evening with a paid escort. After several repetitions, the jigsaw picture of the escort industry assembled before my eyes.

The various agencies, I learned, aimed at different levels of clients, though you wouldn't guess it by reading their publicity. A handful at the top concentrate entirely on the "executive trade," leaving tourists, conventioneers and dateless locals to their competitors lower down on the scale.

The cut for the escorts is fairly uniform—between ten and fifteen dollars per date, regardless of the size of the fee charged by the agency. The vital difference lies in the tips—they are what distinguish the escort aristocrats from the proles. Some outfits, in fact, could get their escorts to work without cuts and depend on tipping alone.

At the peak of the gratuities ladder stand the so-called "contract clinchers." These are occasions when a businessman takes a potential customer for a night on the town, hoping to mellow him sufficiently to sign on the dotted line. He'll rent two girls, ostensibly as an escort for each of them. Actually, both ladies are intended for the customer's enjoyment.

"That's where you have to use your brains," a green-eyed beauty named Paulette informed me. "Some business types are smart enough to tell you beforehand, 'Never mind about me—concentrate on *him*.' But not all of 'em do. So you have to dope out the situation yourself . . . Who's trying to sell whom! Because that's where the lettuce grows.

"I have a girl friend, name's Ella, and she's mostly my partner on these dates. Sometimes we put on real little comedies. Like, we start as a regular one-to-one foursome, right? But during the evening we both go for that one guy. Like, he's irresistible, you follow? The other fellow—the one who hired us—he gets kinda left out in the cold. He can't understand it. And when they go to the washroom together he might say something like, 'How the hell do you do it, Harry? D'you put something in their drinks?' Well, of course, it's all arranged beforehand—Ella and me even rehearse a bit. But it makes the one guy—the customer—feel like a billion. Like he's Paul Newman. And so, mostly, he'll come through on that contract."

She wrinkled her snub nose in a truly delightful grin. "And the man who hired us, he'll come through with the tips. Christ, I've made a hundred bucks out of one of those comedy deals. And it didn't involve climbing into bed with anybody. Just a bit of brain-work."

A wholesaler or manufacturer wanting to entertain an important female buyer may suggest that they go on a tour of the fleshpots "with another couple." The other couple, though the lady buyer will never know it, are rented escorts; and the male partner will certainly be an excellent dancer. In the course of festivities he will gravitate more and more toward the lady, dancing with her exclusively and courting her as strenuously as propriety permits. His partner may even put on a mild jealousy huff to make it convincing. The buyer, particularly if she is past her prime, gets an ego rejuvenation. And the wholesaler gets her order.

These occasions are costly, but rarely to the organizers, since they either figure as tax deductions or as items on an expense account. Some services obligingly hand out receipts marked "Gratuities"—it looks better than a bill from So-and-So's Escort Agency.

One notch down on the scale range executives on a business-cum-pleasure jaunt. Likewise good tippers, but not nearly as lavish as the above category. They may also want more for their money.

"Well, yes, quite a number of them want a bedroom finale," said Paulette, "but not as many as you'd expect. And fewer still are really persistent about it. It's mostly kind of casual. The catch is, though, that when you have to say 'No' (if you're smart you make it sound a bit regretful) it always brings down your tip. What's the average? Well, on a straight date like that—no strings—about twenty or thirty dollars."

"That bit in the ad about foreign languages," I asked. "Are they really an advantage?"

"Only for steady work. Like, the big-big agencies will have a few Japanese girls, and some that speak French or German or Spanish. They get all the visitors from those countries and it keeps them busy, but it doesn't exactly make them rich. Oh, the Japanese tip pretty well as a rule, and the Germans not too bad. But the French and Latin Americans—forget it! All you get from them is flowers and a hand kiss."

Neither Paulette nor her friend Ella bothered with the third and least prestigious category of clients—the tourists and lone natives who make up the majority of customers. They may be very well heeled, but their tipping standards—at least for straight escort duties —put them into economy class.

The men on the agency's books are mostly confined to that bottom bracket, and at least one of them complained bitterly about the scarceness of female executives. "Me for Women's Lib," he proclaimed. "What this country needs—what *I* need, anyway—is a few thousand more dames in top management. Boy, I'd clean up!"

His name is Chris, and his leonine, affably creased features are quite familiar to watchers of video commercials. ("I'm that banker guy who's always trying to loan people money.") Chris could pass for the ambassador of a slightly down-at-heel nation, and indeed possesses one of the chief requisites for a diplomatic career: an immense capacity for absorbing liquor. He must be near fifty and told me with great seriousness that he couldn't remember a day during the past twelve years when he was *completely* sober. On the other hand, I am certain that he never gets *completely* drunk.

Apart from his frequent television spots, Chris works with one of the largest escort bureaus in Los Angeles and is much in demand. He dresses conservatively, dances well enough to have been an instructor, and has the God-given talent of maintaining a conversation without listening to a word.

But he feels genuinely disadvantaged because few expense-account clients come his way, whereas his female colleagues get them in batches. "Now and again a buyer or somebody in fashion or cosmetics or market research. But mostly it's just lady tourists. Sure some of them are loaded—stocks and alimony and stuff—but they don't have that—uh—freewheeling attitude of the corporation crowd."

He produced a silver cigarette case from the pocket of his double-knit yachting jacket. "You know how many of these I got? About a dozen. All with my initials engraved, so I can't hock 'em. Because a lot of those dolls would sooner spend fifty bucks on a present than give you twenty as a tip. They think it's more *personal*." He spread his hands in a gesture of supplication, palms up. "So who wants to get personal? Not me!"

Chris emptied his glass, and the waitress brought him another vodka and tonic without being told. Apparently she knew him. "The sex angle? I knew you'd ask that." He gave me an amiably conspiratorial smirk. "Well, it comes up, but maybe not as regularly as you think. I mean, I used to get propositioned more when I worked for the dance studio. Of course, I was fifteen years younger then." He yawned like the MGM lion and rubbed his face. He sniffed at his glass in an oddly suspicious manner—as if suspecting arsenic—before tossing off the contents.

"It's quite delicate, really. You'd be surprised how many of the clients just want me for company. Just to dance and drive them around and listen to 'em talk about their ex-husbands. Listening— *that's* the important bit. Because nobody else does. Mostly I don't either, but on me it doesn't show.

"Now, in this line you've got to remember that you never make a pass unless you're sure the client wants it. Not just sure—*dead cer-tain!*" He rapped the table for emphasis. "Otherwise you get complaints and the agency drops you. Or worse—the lady figures she's *given* you something and forgets about tipping. So the way I play it, they just about have to take my hand and *lead* me to bed, goddammit. Some do, of course, but—like I said—quite a lot don't."

Another vodka appeared miraculously before him, and Chris repeated his sniffing ritual. Somebody, sometime, must have slipped him a Mickey. "All the while, though," he went on, "you've got to look as if you'd just adore to ravish her on the spot. You only barely restrain yourself because you *respect* her so much. That makes it romantic, see? So it's important to have the right facial expression, particularly when you're dancing—that's when their scent is supposed to grab you. I make a point of thinking about my mortgage. Makes me look suitably desperate."

He glanced at his watch. "And now, if you'll excuse me, I have to meet a dear soul from Vevay, Indiana. Owns a flour mill, I think."

He exited superbly. Erect, with a mere soupçon of swagger. Leaving me with the check.

Very few escorts in America make dating their livelihood. The majority hold steady and quite mundane jobs and restrict their outings to three or four a week. The bureaus, in fact, are rather wary of taking full-timers, since these frequently turn out to be prostitutes. Nor are models and TV actresses as much in demand as I assumed, though for different reasons.

Spectacular good looks are apt to intimidate clients, especially if the girls are taller than average. The less-than-devastating beauties get chosen more often, except in the contract-clinching line, where the client wants to impress a customer. The best draws, it appears, are college girls with impish grins and just a trace of freckles.

In recent years some agencies have grown large enough to open branches. Escorts by Suzanne now operates both in Dallas, Texas, and San Diego, California, and is contemplating further extensions. In 1968 the Waikiki Date and Escort Co. spread into downtown San Francisco under the label of Dial-A-Date. The firm's Hawaiian headquarters is a luxurious complex with its own massage parlor, where clients can get a quick body tune-up while waiting for their dates, unless they prefer to use the pool table, which is likewise on the premises.

The mainland offshoot, by comparison, was rather Spartan. It consisted of one desk and one chair in a mezzanine corner of a smallish hotel in Powell Street. The trappings, however, were not indicative of the company's popularity. That mezzanine nook was a very busy corner, the telephone line almost permanently engaged. When I dropped by, both were temporarily in charge of Karen Lewis, a pony-tailed blonde with octagonal glasses, the body of a track sprinter and the knowledgeable cool of a lady croupier. Karen began at the escorting end of the business, but was swiftly promoted to managerial level, although she still took on occasional dates after working hours . . . "when there's pressure and if I feel like it."

She was an unusual find, insofar as she knew both sides of the service. Most escorts, I discovered, have no idea of what goes on at the administrative end.

Dial-A-Date, at that time, had a hundred and forty girls and five men on its books. The girls were chosen roughly according to the specifications laid down by American Airlines for flight hostesses.

The men, whose ages ranged considerably higher, looked clean-cut and average, at least in their pictures.

"We have a variety of dates," said Karen. "One is daytime, from midday to six P.M.—that's for sightseeing—and another from six till two A.M. They both cost thirty-one dollars and ten cents. The ten cents? That's tax. Then we have out-of-town dates. Anywhere—but mostly they go to Las Vegas. Those cost a hundred and sixty dollars a day. The client, of course, has to pay the fares both ways and all other expenses. No, there's no limit on the number of days." She thought for a moment. "Oh, and there's the night special. Starts at six and goes till four in the morning. That one comes to one hundred dollars."

"Now, wait a moment," I put in. "If your two A.M. date is thirty-one dollars, how come the man has to pay sixty-nine dollars more for just two hours extra?"

Karen didn't reply. She glanced at me octagonally, the way an algebra tutor might view an outstandingly imbecilic student. It took me several silent seconds to catch on. California bars close at two in the morning. Those last two hours would have to be spent somewhere else.

"Er—about your female clients," I came back. "Are most of them tourists?"

This time she answered promptly. "Mostly—not all. We had a couple who wanted to hire men to make their husbands jealous."

I sat for a while, listening to Karen handle telephone inquiries. She was minutely informative about times, rates and available escorts, and superbly noncommittal when asked what *else* might come with a date. "That, sir," was one of her standard retorts, "depends entirely on your charm and the lady's good will."

In an oblique way, she was telling the truth. Sex in the escort business is—in practice—a purely private arrangement between client and date, unconnected with the original contract. Nearly all bureaus have an application clause declaring that "Reports of immoral behavior, if verified, will result in instant dismissal." The key word, of course, is "reports." If nobody complains, the company can plead ignorance of almost anything. Some—a very few—agencies enforce regulations that render extracurricular activities, difficult, if not impossible. The majority leave the matter to the discretion of their escorts.

The degree of that discretion varies as much as the escorts' daytime occupations. At one extreme are the professional hookers who utilize dating services merely to meet prospective customers—often without the management's knowledge. At the opposite pole you find those who follow a cast-iron rule *never* to sleep with a client. The great majority fall somewhere in the middle. Meaning that their behavior is governed by the attractiveness of the client, their own mood, and the current state of their finances. Girls who are temporarily unemployed and rely on dating for rent money tend to be rather flexible in their moral dicta.

But regardless of motivation, erotic interludes always count as extras and are definitely not included in the dating fee.

(The same intriguing unpredictability exists in another Oriental import—massage parlors. The services they provide differ from one establishment to the next, so that visiting them entails a distinct element of pot-luck. A friend of mine, the sales director of a San Francisco engineering firm, was asked by a customer from Oregon to recommend a "real hot one" among the city's famous massage dens. Not knowing any of them firsthand, he mentioned the name of one using the most blatantly lascivious advertising. Here is the Oregonian's subsequent report:

"I walked into this wild waiting room—it looked like a harem—and there were all these big, gorgeous blondes. They asked me a lot of questions—what my tastes were and what I *really* enjoyed and like that—and the whole swarm took me into the massage room. They told me to take off my clothes and put on a little towel. Then they left me, and I waited, lying on that table with just the towel draped over my middle. And then this big heavyweight Swedish guy came in, and he beat the shit out of me!"

My friend's firm lost a sale to Oregon.)

The nature of escort services can be particularly confusing when the service is run in conjunction with—or as part of—another establishment. In New York, for instance, an outfit called Tennyson

Hostesses shares premises with Theatre Erotica in a peeling block on West Forty-eighth Street. The theater, combining a variety of sensory sensations, features "adult" movies, live burlesque, nude photography and art sketching, body painting, massages and free snacks for an admission price of seven dollars and fifty cents, and invites patrons to "come and stay as long as you like."

Yet the Tennyson Hostesses service, located in this supermarket of salaciousness, requires clients to sign a form solemnly promising not to demand sex from their escorts or to make sexual advances to them.

One of the plushest escort bureaus in America likewise functions as part of a conglomerate, though on a drastically different level. This is Aangel, whose ads sport a halo over the second *a*, plus the slogan, "Aangels Are for VIP's!" Aangel is a smallish cog of the National Sociological Institute, a group of companies dealing with computer matchmaking, employment selection, career guidance and executive assessment programs. The Institute is housed in Los Angeles' palatially Gargantuan Beneficial Plaza block, guarded at night by an electronized security force that could just as well be protecting the Pentagon.

Dating duties (at forty dollars per Aangel per date) make up only a minor part of their services. Long-legged platoons of them march forth for civic functions requiring massed pulchritude, form reception committees, act as convention hostesses, run hospitality suites, and take charge of product display booths. Individually, they can be hired to welcome a heavy account at the airport, take him to his hotel, arrange a car for him, help him shop, and usher him around every attraction the town offers—from celebrity-spotting centers to those little "in" dens tourists rarely discover.

Apart from looking like movie hopefuls, Aangels are better briefed for their tasks than any similar line-up.

"Before we send girls out on a company assignment," said Lou Ross, who is in charge of them, "we make them study a pamphlet about the nature and product of that particular corporation, so that they can talk about it intelligently. And we pick the kind of girls who *can* talk intelligently."

Lou Ross, manager of Aangel, is a round-faced young executive who takes pride in his intense gregariousness. ("If I had to spend much time on my own, I'd be climbing up the walls.") Currently he has forty girls on his list—a small retinue for an escort bureau, but a hand-picked one.

"Beauty we take for granted," he said, "but we need a lot of other attributes. Good knowledge of the city is one of them. And from these forms which the girls fill in we assess the rest." The form he showed me listed fifty questions, mapping out the applicant's temperament, conformity ("Shouldn't be *too* conforming"), sexual attitudes ("Not for bed, just for the vibrations"), and religious views ("Mustn't be too strict").

Aangel vets its clients almost as carefully as its crews. The company does not accept local residents for single dates—the only outfit I found that followed this rule. And the girls are given not more than one date a week. "Otherwise," Ross explained, "they lose some of their freshness and become too professional.

"And," he added, "we tell the girls that if we catch them going to bed with anyone, they're out."

"How," I inquired, "do you catch them?"

Mr. Ross shrugged. "That's difficult," he admitted. "But it's the principle that counts."

Aangel would never have hired Audrey, although when I met her she rated among the most popular escorts in Miami Beach. They would have objected to her previous employment—she was a "taxi dancer" at Roseland in downtown Los Angeles.

Audrey hails from Coolangatta, in the Australian tropics, and looks as if she had been wheeled on a surfboard instead of a baby carriage during infancy. Her hair is sunbleached to a whitish shade of yellow, her permanent tan might have come from a Florida tourist poster, and she has a bustline firm enough to crack a flea against. She took the job at Roseland because the ads promised two hundred dollars a week and she needed money for her one abiding passion—traveling.

Audrey was supposed to have been my rented date in Miami, but on discovering our common background we decided to make friends instead. I remembered the tinseled decrepitude of Roseland, where you paid the girls fifteen cents for one minute's dancing. Or rather for those rhythmic calisthenics that have given those establishments the names of "rubbing academies" or "friction factories." "How the hell," I asked, "did you become a taxi dancer?"

"They don't call 'em that," said Audrey. "We were hostesses. And getting the job was easy. Sticking it was the hard part. Especially on my bloody feet." She worked her toes reminiscently. "Those men —they were the biggest drongos[1] I've seen in my life."

The remuneration involved turned out to be somewhat more complicated than she had expected, arithmetic not being her strongest subject. The hostesses had to punch each ticket given to them by a customer and were paid a sliding scale per ticket, according to the number of nights per week she worked. Eight cents per ticket if she worked six nights, seven cents for five nights, six cents for four nights a week. The guaranteed minimum wage was only seventy-two dollars weekly—the unlimited rest depended on how frequently and how long she danced and the tips she collected.

"I reckon I'm a pretty fair dancer, but they don't give you a chance to show it. They just grab you tight and want you to rub up against them. The harder you rub, the better they like it, the more tickets you get, the more money you make. That's how it goes." Audrey waggled her ironing board-flat stomach in an imitation of the "grind." "And they get so busy upstairs, they can't watch their feet. And you get your toes squashed."

"What were the patrons like?" I asked.

She drew an expressive finger across her throat. "Pretty bloody sad. Two kinds, mostly. Young ones who couldn't speak English— not enough to chat up a bird, anyway. So they come to the dance hall, where all they have to do is buy a ticket. Some of them were nice-looking blokes, all right, but that rub-a-dub stuff gets on your nerves after a while.

"The old ones—they had better manners. But, Christ, they were depressing. Most of them wanted to talk. You can sit down at those

[1] *Drongo,* an almost untranslatable Australian slang term signifying—together with Alf, dill, ning nong, galah—a sap or sad sack.

little tables and talk. That costs them nine dollars an hour and it's easy on your feet. But sometimes I'd sooner have danced instead of listen to them.

"They were lonely, but with the kind of loneliness nobody can do anything about. Some of them had families, too. Either they couldn't stand their families or the other way around. You had to treat them like eggshells. They had these awful inferiority what-you-call-its —complexes. They felt like they were—oh, bits of nothing. And you know," Audrey added thoughtfully, "a lot of them were right."

Audrey stuck the job for three months before heading east, going Greyhound all the way to Florida. In Miami she landed a position with a deluxe beach hotel whose architectural design reminded her of home—a cross between the Taj Mahal and Hamburger Heaven. At the time of our meeting she was teaching hotel residents scuba diving in the daytime and doing escort work three nights a week. She had also acquired a low-slung green MG racer, which she drove with maniacal panache and tremendous grinding of gears. She had christened it George.

"George comes in pretty handy on dates," she confided. "He saves me a lot of good-night trouble, you understand?"

I didn't, quite.

"Well, the way they work it with my agency is that you never escort a fellow back to his hotel. He is either supposed to drive you home or take you to where your car is parked. Get it?"

It still hadn't sunk in.

Audrey sounded patient. "Well, look—if I want to get away from someone, there's George waiting in the moonlight. I just drive off. But if I like a fellow—that's not often—he can drive me home. I just don't *have* a car then."

Understanding dawned. "And how are the clients here?"

Audrey mused before delivering judgment. "Most are from New York and they all have dough. Otherwise, they couldn't afford to pay sixty dollars for a date. So it's mostly visiting businessmen. They can't swim for a bet, and they think my accent's funny. I met a lawyer I liked. And a dental surgeon took me game fishing. That was great, only he talked my ear off all the time. About how he has a daughter my age and why she hates him. And how he can't stand his son because he won't wash. Like that."

She shook her head slowly, wrestling with an image. "It sounds nutty, but a lot of these clients—the way they talk in a streak—the way they talk *at* you all the time—they're like those old men we used to get at the dance hall. Only richer."

eleven

THE GAY CROWD

On the sweltering night of June 28, 1969, when the New York air felt like a hot and smelly dishrag on your face, I walked into a historic event. I was crossing Sheridan Square in Greenwich Village on my way home and suddenly found myself in the midst of a screaming, waving, scurrying mob of young men. They banged garbage-can lids, they yelled "Gay Power!", they vaulted park railings, they marched round and round chanting: "Two, four, six, eight—gay is just as good as straight."

A small troop of cops stood observing the commotion from the other side of the street. They wore faintly bemused looks, like householders witnessing their Chihuahua savage a postman. As I passed, I heard one of them say, "Holy Jesus, now the fairies are starting, too."

They were indeed. For what had erupted over Sheridan Square was the first homosexual protest demonstration in world annals. Like most such outbreaks, it had been sparked by a totally insignificant occurrence. Earlier that night, according to hallowed pre-election custom, the police had raided a gay bar, a basement hostelry called Stonewall Inn.

But this time the patrons did not—as hitherto—scatter as fast as they could manage. Instead, they "took to the streets," noisily proclaiming their right to assemble and mingle with their own kind. They flung leaflets announcing, "Do you think homosexuals are revolting? You bet your sweet a— we are."

In the months that followed, it certainly looked that way. All over the country, homosexuals were marching, demonstrating, picketing government offices, appearing on TV talk shows, passing out handbills, even fighting back when the police tried to stop them. In New York, Washington D.C., San Francisco and Los Angeles they were joined by their female counterparts—organized lesbians— and the marches took on a genuine mass aspect. On Gay Pride Day of 1970, some twenty thousand homophile men and women gathered in New York's Central Park for a "Gay-In" of speeches, songs, sign-waving and chanting, with the slogans reflecting an increasingly militant temper:

> Say it loud! Gay and proud!
> Better blatant than latent!
> Ho-Ho-Homosexual!

Within another year, over two hundred homophile organizations had sprung up in fifty-three cities throughout the nation, local politicians were openly courting gay voters, priests were establishing all-gay congregations, and enraged inverts had crashed the Washington meeting of the American Psychiatric Association, confronting the two thousand gathered mind specialists with the demand that, "Homosexuality should be removed from the psychiatric list of diseases."

Another American pressure group had been born, complete with political factions ranging from the conservative Mattachine Society to the middle-of-the-road Gay Activists Alliance and the far-left Gay Liberation Front.

The Stonewall Inn raid was, of course, no more the reason for this eruption than the shots at Sarajevo were the *reason* for World

War I. The combustive elements had been piling up for a long time. It is nevertheless significant that a routine "bar bust" triggered them off.

It was precisely the routine nature of the pounce that proved the ultimate irritant. In New York, as in other U.S. cities, swoops on gay establishments are standard ingredients of mayoral campaigns. Headlines like "Cops Close Homo Hangouts" make splendid reading for voters, simultaneously demonstrating the moral fiber of the administration and the zealousness of the police. (This is by no means a uniquely American practice. It happens just as frequently in Canadian, Australian and New Zealand cities.)

For homophiles these raids represent a nerve-grinding disruption of the very center of their social lives, more corroding than other forms of harassment. The shadow of a "bust" looms over every tavern, club and ballroom frequented by inverts and accounts for the peculiar undercurrent of hysteria that permeates them. It also accounts for the regular payoffs their owners have to render to precinct officers if they wish to remain unraided for reasonable periods.

From the victims' viewpoint, the most infuriating feature of these casual swoops is their doubtful legality. For although at the moment all states except Illinois, Idaho, Connecticut and Colorado possess legislation against homosexuality, this legislation is directed against the acts as such, not at potential perpetrators.

Thus in order to raid a hostelry the police have to see "lewd and offensive behavior" taking place on the premises. This is accomplished by sending in plainclothesmen, who can be relied upon either to observe such behavior or—failing that—to provoke it. Every vice squad in the country boasts a few officers of a type attractive to gay males, who specialize in overtures guaranteed to get response.

Furthermore, while there is no such thing as an anti-lesbian statute (as far as the law is concerned, female homosexuals don't exist), their gathering spots are raided and closed down almost as often. The police use undercover ladies and the same blanket formula.

Homophiles are more dependent on bars and clubs for their social pleasures than is the straight community. The badgering and shutting of their recognized hunting grounds strike at their life pattern (as it is meant to do), depriving them of the chance to relax among themselves, to dance, flirt, make contacts and assignations—in short, to find their particular brand of bedmates. And the fact that this may happen merely as a vote-catching stunt enrages them more than any other measure.

Very few of those I interviewed had ever asked themselves *why* these raids should be so pleasing to so many voters. The question wasn't put, for the good reason that the answer is too frightening. A 1970 Harris poll revealed that 63 percent of the population considers homosexuality per se as "harmful to American life." And my own inquiries showed a strain of virulent, deeply rooted antagonism among ordinary citizens that is both disturbing in its intensity and astonishing in our alleged age of tolerance and permissiveness.

One branch root of this hostility was laid bare during a 1972 debate in the California Assembly, when legislators rejected, by forty-one to twenty-five votes, a bill proposing to legalize homosexuality in the state. Opposing the bill, Assemblyman Robert H. Burke declared, "I'm mighty ashamed of this body today. We're saying, 'Let's elevate ourselves above God.'" His fellow Republican Frank Lanterman observed, "The capital of this state is Sacramento— not Sodom and Gomorrah." And Assemblyman E. Richard Barnes even read the appropriate passage from the Bible, citing Leviticus, eighteenth chapter, twenty-second verse:

"Thou shalt not lie with a man as with a woman. It is an abomination."

This was a sample of the religious basis of antihomophile sentiment. (Though it should be noted that politicians borrowing Old Testament thunder in support of their moral stance always ignore another portion of Leviticus, 25:36, where it says something equally unequivocal against charging interest on loans to the poor.)

But another argument, based on a historical view, is even more widespread. It stems from the assumption that homosexuality has a softening effect on men, degenerates a nation's martial fiber and undermines its willingness to fight, thus causing its ultimate down-

fall. I found a typical specimen of this line in Louis Berg's fore-
word to the popular paperback *The Velvet Underground Revisited*.
Dr. Berg tells his readers:

> History has shown that the decay of a culture is invariably the
> effect of the debasing of sexual mores that results from the domi-
> nation of the deviate. In ancient Greece and in the days of the
> Roman Empire deviation flourished. Degeneracy was at the core of
> Nazi Germany and reached such heights that Hitler was forced to
> liquidate men of rank and stature within his own movement.

It is quite a feat to compress so many fallacies into such a limited
space. Let it be said in defense of the author that he is, after all,
a medical man and not a historian. But in order to unravel this
coil we'll have to pick the knots one by one.

The ancient Greeks were primarily bisexual, not homosexual,
since they refused social status to any male who failed to father
children. Among the "deviates" who dominated them were such
degenerate weaklings as Themistocles, Plato, Socrates, Aristides and
Solon. Their downfall was caused not by enervation but by *Hubris*
excessive muscle-flexing that resulted in the twenty-nine-year-long
Peloponnesian War between Athens and Sparta and turned their
city states into ash heaps. Both sides in that conflict were about
equally bisexual, but the victorious Spartans leaned slightly more
to the homo position.

The Roman Empire fell from a variety of ailments, none of them
even remotely connected with morality: the ruin of small farmers
through large estates worked by slave labor; the elimination of the
artisan class through factories also manned by slaves; the monopoliza-
tion of trade by a few giant companies; and the state's inability to
figure out a system of imperial succession other than civil war. The
Empire disintegrated ultimately because a mere handful of people
owned most of its wealth, leaving the vast majority with no stake
in its survival.

The reference to Hitler being "forced to liquidate men of rank
and stature" because of their degeneracy is the essence of black
humor. It's akin to saying that Stalin had Trotsky assassinated because he was Jewish.

Hitler did indeed perpetrate history's greatest massacre of homosexuals during the June 1934 "Blood Purge" that wiped out Chief of Staff Ernst Roehm and seventy-two of his top S.T. (Storm Troop) commanders. Their inversion, however, hadn't bothered the Führer one iota while they were backing him in his struggle for power. On dozens of occasions he declared that "Roehm's sexual tastes are his private business." And to prove that he meant it, he made Roehm the *only* man of his entourage permitted to address him with the familiar German *"Du"* instead of the formal *"Sie."* He unleashed the purge because the tightly knit S.T. leaders formed a rival power bloc within his movement, not because they habitually slept with each other and their brown-shirted bully boys.

Which brings us to the general theme of homosexuality as an enfeebling influence. It so happens that inversion is one of the chief manifestations of overmilitarized, aggressive, and rigidly disciplined societies. This tendency can be traced from the Spartans—who practiced it as a martial tradition and combed their locks in preparation for death in battle—to the Kaiser's Prussian Guards, whose mutual amours were a national joke in Germany, which didn't prevent them from ranking among the finest combat troops in Europe. The same proclivity shows up in every elite fighting force in history, from the "Immortals" of the Persian conqueror-kings to the French Foreign Legion.

It also applies to so-called savage societies living close to nature, barely touched by the mellowing effects of civilization. Inversion among them seems to stand in direct relation to their warlike tendencies. Homosexuality was most common among the fierce plains tribes of American Indians (who saw nothing either detrimental or shameful about being a "squaw man"), but much rarer among the gentler, less scalp-hungry forest Indians. The same goes—or went—for the desert Bedouin, the African Zulu and Massai tribes, the Berbers of the Atlas Mountains, the Danakils of Ethiopia and the perpetually warring headhunters of the New Guinea highlands.

The most graphic cases in point are probably the Pathans, an incredibly tough bunch of mountaineers inhabiting the northwestern frontier between Afghanistan and Pakistan. The Pathans live mainly by armed robbery, use sharp stones for toilet paper, carry rifles in place of walking sticks, and kept entire divisions of the British-Indian army at bay for seventy years. Yet Pathan youths rim their eyes with kohl, wear blossoms in their long greasy hair, and traditionally indulge in sodomy with their older instructors. A much-quoted Pathan proverb says, "A woman for heirs, a boy for pleasure." And the opening lines of their favorite love ballad, "Injured Heart," go: "Across the river there's a lad, with a bottom like a peach, but I have no boat . . ."

So much for the supposedly emasculating impact of homosexuality, which appears strangely absent in those societies most prone to it. If we go by historical examples, it should, in fact, be branded as symptomatic of a dangerously belligerent trait.

What causes the opposite impression is a tiny minority of mincing, giggling, limp-wristed effeminates who, in trying desperately to imitate the other sex, become caricatures of their own. As Dick Leitsch, Director of the Mattachine Society of New York, explained: "They were taught that there are only two roles: John Wayne and Doris Day. If you can't be one, you must be the other."

Together with this urge for biological role-switching in some homosexuals, goes a bitter self-derogatory streak in others. No other group parodies itself so scathingly, particularly when under the eyes of straight observers. I have seen homosexuals who were behaving in a perfectly normal fashion suddenly go into "raving faggot" acts when they felt themselves being watched. There is an element of both exhibitionism and despair in these performances, tragically similar to the old-time southern "darkie" acting out the image he knew the white men had of him. Homophiles even delight in telling slightly reconditioned Negro jokes against themselves: "A faggot—that's a homosexual gentleman who has just left the room."

Such constant displays, both in manners and clothes, make for overvisibility and create the illusion of much larger numbers of them than actually exist. Homosexuals tend to derive a great deal of comfort from numerical strength and will go to ludicrous lengths to bolster it. An acquaintance of mine, a highly educated member of the Chicago Gay Activists Alliance, automatically ascribes inversion to every celebrity, living or dead, who happens to crop up in conversation.

It isn't enough to have Alexander the Great, Julius Caesar, Michelangelo, Tchaikovsky, Oscar Wilde, and half of all contemporary stage and screen stars; he wants *everybody,* including Einstein and Fidel Castro. The same endeavor is present among lesbians. Because in recent years several prominent females have revealed themselves to be disciples of Sappho, they are convinced that sapphism lies latent in the breast of every housewife. The most relentless crusader in this cause is Jill Johnston, who devotes most of her columns in the *Village Voice* to the weekly uncovering of fellow-lesbians-at-heart. Her most triumphant find to date was the late Janis Joplin, whom her friends and associates believed to have been rather rampantly the other way.

These omnivorous calculations are based on the undoubtedly vast number of "closet queers," who pass for heterosexuals except for occasional, stealthy and often guilt-ridden slips. The closet category is frequently married and the father of children (remember that Oscar Wilde had two sons) and is often the loudest and most violent denigrator of overt homophiles. Every party-goer is familiar with the type of male guest who, the moment he has a couple of drinks under his belt, bursts into anti-fag harangues and proclaims his own sterling normality, blithely unaware that he "protesteth too much."

Of late, coming-out-of-the-closet has become a fashionable public ceremony. It was started by author Merle Miller, who wrote a piece entitled "What It Means To Be a Homosexual" for the magazine section of the New York *Times* in January 1971. Since then a lengthy array of men and women have followed in his footsteps into the public eye. But, as Miller observed, "The closets are far from emptied; there are more in hiding than out of hiding."

The question is, How many more? The National Institute of Mental Health describes between three and four million Americans of both genders as "predominantly homosexual." Nobody doubts that this is merely a chunk of the iceberg. But how large a chunk? And how do you define the rest? Because all statistics depend ultimately on definitions, the answer depends on whom you define as homosexual. If you include everyone who has ever experimented with inversion, then the homophiles' own estimate is probably correct—one out of every six adult males. That, however, is like classifying every person who has taken a drag from a reefer as a "drug addict."

According to this form of reckoning, New York City would have a homosexual population of around 400,000 (out of some 7,750,-000 inhabitants), and San Francisco—America's unchallenged homophile capital—50,000 out of 700,000 citizens.

While these strenuously inflated figures may fascinate sociologists, they don't come within the scope of this book. The mating trade is concerned only with those homophiles who need regular facilities to meet their peers. The major proportion of those included in the above compilations never set foot in a gay establishment. San Francisco, for instance, has only fifty-five recognized gay bars and clubs (fifty for males, five for females), and these appear quite sufficient to fill local requirements. They do not, however, reflect the numerical proportion of male and female homosexuals. Lesbians tend to congregate less than male gays; they are more accepted in ordinary circles, and also prefer private parties to socializing in public. As far as anyone can tell, the number of men and women deviates is about even.

The hostility encountered by obviously gay males in workingmen's taverns frequented by hard-hat types is not only real but occasionally violent. Proprietors, faced with the risk of a brawl or the loss of their straight customers, sometimes take the easy way out and simply refuse to serve blatantly homosexual patrons.

In recent years the militant Gay Activists Alliance has taken to "liberating" such establishments by staging noisy demonstrations and sit-ins along the lines pioneered by the NAACP. The risks involved in these methods are just as genuine as they were for the Black Liberationists. I have seen bar patrons turn apoplectic with rage at the mere entrance of a pair of "swishes"—a fury as unbridled as it is incoherent. I once asked a longshoreman, over our fourth beer, why, exactly, he felt that way.

Instantly he exploded. "Why?" he barked, "why? Because the sight of 'em makes me sick. That's why!"

Which was probably a truer summation of sentiment than all the religious-historical arguments put forward more eruditely by others. A large number of people can't stand the sight of gays—at least of the ostentatiously effeminate kind. They feel themselves mocked—their own masculinity impaired—by the mere presence of gays. Subconsciously they identify with them, not necessarily as latent homosexuals but as fellow males. You often get a parallel reaction from women faced with strip dancers or prostitutes. Something of what they do and stand for rubs off on *them* by the mere fact that they, too, are females.

This reaction is among the chief reasons why gays prefer to cluster in segregated areas. So much so that certain resorts have become homosexual ghetto communities.

The most publicized of these is Cherry Grove on Fire Island, a thin sliver of beaches and boardwalks about forty miles from Manhattan. At first glance The Grove appears like an overacted, ham-humored stage satire on fagdom. Boys with purple hair and green toenails; boys in hotpants and bikinis screeching at each other across the dunes; boys walking with fingers intertwined, stopping every few yards to peck each other's cheeks; boys in stamp-sized, leopard-spotted swimming trunks endlessly, ceaselessly performing body-building gymnastics in the sand. Chintzy little cottages with curlicued names like *Les Boys, Pin Puff,* and *Queen for a Day*; couples melting in hot and hairy embraces on doorsteps before proceeding inside; couples dancing rouged cheek to rouged cheek, bracelets jingling, at the bar called The Place.

The first snatch of conversation I overheard had the same script-dialogue quality, as if carefully rehearsed and recited for my benefit: "Daaarling, did you hear about that fabulous blond fag pro who got arrested by the fuzz on Fifty-fourth and Broadway? No? Well, dear, it seems the pigs got so excited over their catch it took them *one hour* to drive to the station house. One hour! Yes, and blondie was back on the beat shortly afterwards. Richer by thirty dollars and grinning from one chewed ear to the other . . ."

It took me a while to catch on that all this represented the homosexual equivalent of a singles weekend in the Catskills, and that it made many inverts as uncomfortable as it made me: "The Grove is definitely not everyone's dish," one of them told me. "It's for the bitch fringe, the screamers, the way-outs. I went there for two weeks and—well, never again."

I learned that the homosexual world has a distinct class and taste structure, and that the blatant transvestites occupy a lowly position in it. The more fashionable homophile resorts, in fact, try to freeze them out. Also, that my impression of their theatricality was correct. "The one thing those camp queens want," my informant added, "is attention. They literally wither without it. Ignore them, and they evaporate like bad smells."

The number of "drag queens" is actually diminishing at the same rate the unisex look is growing among both heteros and homos. Transvestism is becoming more and more the trademark of male prostitutes; costuming as a whole is increasingly confined to a few specialized hangouts. San Francisco's Gay Switchboard, an information service operated round the clock by the Metropolitan Community Churches, offers an up-to-the-moment guide list of what to expect where on the deviate social scene. The same stratification applies to most of America's large cities.

On the Switchboard's list, "O" stands for "older crowd," meaning conventional dressers; "C"—"collegiate"—short-haired, fraternity types; "H," meaning "heads," signifies the drug scene; "U"—for "under-age"—cafés that cater to teen-agers and serve no liquor; and "L" —short for "leather"—a category that requires some elucidation.

The so-called "leather cult" is the rock bottom of the deviate social scale, a mélange of motorcycle and cowboy mystique with strong overtones of sadomasochism. It has its own prop shops, periodicals and movies, a whole range of specialized pornography, and a large number of bars conducted in its image.

These bars are invariably situated in a proletarian section of town, away from the plush watering holes of the sophisticates. In San Francisco this means south of Market Street. Walk into one and you're entering the Melody Saloon, Dodge City, circa 1875.

Winchesters and buffalo heads on the walls, sawdust on the floor, cuspidors in the corners. Behind the counter a serving trio, each of whom can close his fist over a tennis ball and ask, "Guess what I've got here?"

The patrons stand in packed rows, holding subdued, menacing conversations ("Where I come from, stranger, we keep our voice low.") So everyone talks softly and presumably carries a big stick. They wear denim shirts decolletaged down to the navel; brass-studded belts, jangling boots, black leather jackets decorated with flags, slogans, insignia, and anatomically incorrect skulls.

Now and again they encounter each other in the sawdust arena. Hands hanging loose, slapping leather, or thumbs hooked defiantly in chain belts. Bodies bent forward at slight angles, eyes riveted on the man opposite. It's Doc Holliday facing-down Bat Masterson. Or vice versa. Any second now the Colts will be spitting orange muzzle flames and the spectators diving for cover. Instead, however, arms are flung out and clasped manfully. "Hi there, Dave." "How's it goin', Joe?" Bloodshed, it seems, has been averted.

Not only are the cowboy outfits deceptive, so are the biking garbs. Some of the black-jacketed, braceleted patrons actually own motorcycles. Most don't. They can't afford them. All their money goes into their uniforms. Outside a bar bursting with bikers' costumes, you'll find maybe six machines parked. The rest of the easy riders and bronco busters came by taxi.

The leather cult may serve one good purpose in demolishing the stereotype image of powderpuff homosexuality held by so many outsiders. Motorcycle mobs and the merchant marine are at least as saturated with "gayety" as the entertainment world; a construction worker or cab driver is as liable to be homophile as an architect.

Most gay hangouts, therefore, have no characteristic décor. They reflect the neighborhood in which they are located. In New York this ranges from the encrusted grime of the West Twenties to the gleaming mahogany of the East Seventies. In Greenwich Village the "gay oases" for a time consisted of nine after-hours hostelries, all dispensing hard dope along with liquor, all controlled and protected by a certain underworld syndicate whose heads bear Sicilian names.

The drinking habits of the patrons vary according to pocket and have no connection with their erotic tastes. It's beer for some, daiquiris for others.

The only part that remains standardized is the pickup. It hardly differs from Lower Westside to Upper Eastside. One example from mid-Manhattan can illustrate the whole syndrome:

A man in his forties, wearing horn-rimmed glasses and a Cashmere sports coat, is sitting at the bar. A younger man in a white turtleneck sweater steps up beside him and orders a whiskey sour. While he waits for his drink the two make eye contact. The Cashmere man breaks into a wide grin. Turtleneck remains grave. Then, slowly, he unfolds a slightly mysterious half-smile, holds it for an instant, then lowers his eyes. His drink comes and he toys with it, ignoring the other, looking diffidently at the impaled cherry in his glass. The ball is, so to speak, at Cashmere's feet. It's up to him to kick off.

For three, four minutes the game is in doubt. Will he or won't he? He will! He takes off his horn rims, slides them into his breast pocket, and leans over to turtleneck. "You here by yourself?" he inquires.

The younger man nods. "Yes, I'm just having a quick one."

"Well, have one with me. My name's Robert."

"Yeah, okay. I'm Lanny."

They talk for perhaps an hour. Then they depart. As they walk through the door Cashmere nonchalantly—almost accidentally—guides turtleneck's elbow. It was, as Lanny indicated, "a quick one."

This procedure is known as "eyeball cruising," the most common variation of the cruise. The conversation that follows the initial contact gets briefer as the evening progresses—just before closing time it has usually shrunk to a few hurried exchanges. The main thing is to get a partner to go home with. The later the hour the greater the hurry to find one—selectivity be hanged. For although most inverts will earnestly assure you that they're looking for "lasting relationships," variety is not merely the spice of their life—in most cases it *is* their life. Their promiscuity is far greater than that of either straights or lesbians, their friendships much more ephemeral.

This, of course, does not preclude lifetime "marriages" among inverts; it merely makes them exceptional.

Bar cruising is inextricably bound up with the homosexual life style, yet a surprising number of gays are fully aware of the sordidness it involves.

"It can be downright sickening," a Los Angeles hairdresser confided to me. "Often I say to myself, 'This is the last time,' but I know I'll be out again the next night or the one after.

"Even when you've made contact with someone, he's looking over your shoulder to see if somebody better, younger, handsomer hasn't just walked in. And the worst part is . . . you're probably doing the same over *his* shoulder."

One explanation for this pattern was offered by Les Morgan, a sociologist working with the Scientific Analysis Corporation:

"Being forced to meet in furtive, unpleasant environments such as bars, public restrooms or bathhouses makes it difficult for a person to develop a positive image of his sexual behavior. Successive failures in love relationships . . . can lead to depressive reactions or compulsive promiscuity, which further reduce the individual's self-esteem."

Among the people trying to break this mold are a handful of the clergy, who perform marriage ceremonies for both male and female couples in gay churches throughout the United States. These nuptials, of course, are recognized by neither canon nor civil law and actually constitute illegal acts. But they may help to alleviate the guilt obsession that lies at the core of much gay behavior.

As the Reverend Troy Perry put it: "What I'm saying to my congregation is, 'God really does love you. You can be His child without changing your homosexuality.'"

Perry's congregation at his Metropolitan Community Church in Los Angeles averages around nine hundred every Sunday—more than at the city's Episcopal Cathedral. The Reverend, a cherubic, bushy-browed man of thirty-two with a lilting southern accent, received his training in the rural Pentecostal Church of Florida. He married a pastor's daughter from Alabama and had two children. But when he realized his own inversion, he left both his family and his church.

In 1968, he began holding services for gays in his living room. Today his religious organization has its own large church in central Los Angeles, plus a total of twenty churches and missions in other parts of the country. Perry's marriage ceremonies follow the orthodox lines in most respects, except that he refers to "spouse" instead of "wife."

As yet these attempts to regularize homosexual liaisons are mere curiosities—in the eyes of most gays as well as heteros. Homosexual life continues to center around bar and club cruising, despite the risks involved. The risks come mainly in the form of plainclothes cops, who use entrapment as a routine method of making arrests. Vice-squad officers play the roles of *agents provocateurs* wherever inverts may gather—parks, alleys, beaches and restrooms—but bars are most favored because they enable detectives to combine a few drinks with their official functions. The consequences of arrest can be manifold—from a shakedown by the arresting officer to a stretch in prison—but the indirect results are often worse. Newspaper publicity means exposure, often followed by the loss of a job, the ruin of a career, family breakups or eviction notices.

Few of these risks are shared by female homosexuals, and for reasons that nobody is quite clear about.

Lesbians[1] enjoy a curiously privileged—almost normal—position among deviates. They were left out of the various legislative acts that penalize their male equivalents. Why this happened remains one of the mysteries of modern jurisprudence. The answer probably lies in the fact that legislators either didn't consider their behavior offensive or didn't know about it. Whatever the reason, this oversight has rendered lesbians immune to the arrest and blackmail threats that still hang over gay males—although, as mentioned earlier, this doesn't prevent the police from frequently closing their gathering spots, sometimes for permitting "unlicensed dancing."

In researching this portion of my book I became extremely grateful for an early part of my training, from which I have

---

[1] Derived from the Greek island of Lesbos, where this practice was particularly common. The most famous lesbian of antiquity was the poetess Sappho; hence, the term sapphist for its adherents.

benefited ever since. The first writing job I held was with a magazine in Sydney, Australia, whose editor was a lady named Beryl. She was a smart efficient, completely dedicated yet healthily cynical woman, who knocked most of the purple prose out of me, taught me the fundamentals of descriptive reporting, plus the art of *hearing* people talk instead of just listening to them. She was possibly the best boss I ever had. She was also a lesbian, and made no bones about it, even to the point of occasionally seducing her young secretaries.

What I learned through association with her was acceptance. The kind of attitude sensible people bestow on, say, left-handers or vegetarians.

It stood me in good stead later in my career, while working alongside large numbers of journalists and photographers who were wholly or partially sapphist. I got on splendidly with them because I didn't regard them as either challenges or exotics, simply as colleagues.

I also learned that very few of them were anxious to appear masculine. The swaggering bull-dike types constitute as small a faction among them as the mincing bottom-wrigglers among male homophiles. A large proportion look upon themselves as a genuine third or fourth sex. The majority, however, follow the classical Greek view of mankind as essentially bisexual—they are "double-sexed" in the true meaning of the term—with only a slight preference for their own gender.

Lesbian establishments fall into three general categories: mixed bars, catering equally to male and female homosexuals; open bars, which allow men inside with a female escort; and clubs—often in name only—which exclude men completely. For my visits to the second variety I took along a fairly well-known authoress on the subject (I'll call her Melissa), who also filled in my information gaps about the third.

I noticed two outstanding features about these hostelries. There is far less casual cruising than in the male hangouts—more girls arrived in pairs and left together, rarely even changing dance partners. Also there is an unmistakable atmosphere of latent violence —what Jack London called a "knuckle aroma"—which reminded me of Liverpool, the harbor front of Marseille and portions of Red Hook, Brooklyn.

In one Greenwich Village spot I witnessed two scuffles within three hours, in mid-Manhattan I walked into a full-fledged fist fight, and there were corresponding numbers of near-collisions flaring up at regular intervals. All of them emanated from and around a handful of "butches" or "diesel dikes" or "bull daggers," but what these cartoon types lacked in numbers they more than made up in truculence.

I struck no trouble myself, but Melissa was less fortunate. We were standing near a pool table where a sinewy young chick with a Marine Corps haircut was making her shots, admired by her long-haired and doe-eyed girl friend. Crewcut drew back her cue, poking my escort forcefully in the stomach. Melissa let out an irritated, "Hey, watch it," and the effect was instantaneously explosive. The girl whirled around, spat on the floor, and grabbed her cue like a war club. Luckily, the femme rushed over and soothed her ruffled Amazon, while I firmly led Melissa away, remarking, "Listen— it's *my* life you're trifling with."

On another occasion I was sitting in a Chicago homosexual haven, when six "baby butches"—teen-agers—charged in and, pursuing heaven knows what feud, began to wreck the joint with bike chains. They caused a fantastic amount of destruction in record time, but respected my neutrality. One even grinned, "Excuse me," while she smashed a framed ballet poster hanging next to my head.

Most of the clashes, however, involved femmes or "dolls," and I avoided those by adopting a strict "hands off" policy. There was something insanely desperate—almost suicidal—about the aggressiveness of these lady stompers I didn't care to explore.

Generally the girls were gentler and dressed in a sleek, tight-panted unisex style that could pass anywhere without attracting attention. A few wore minidresses and were disturbingly pretty. Some turned out to be amazingly communicative.

"I'm not really interested in anyone here," said a tense and sallow photographer named Sharon. "I only come here to get out of my stinking studio. I've been going nuts by myself since Silvie left."

"Who's Silvie?" I asked.

"The girl I was living with. For three years. The warmest, most giving person you can imagine . . . ," she swallowed and faded out.

"Did you have a fight?"

Sharon shook her head. "She left me for some stinking fat bitch who has a house in Cape Cod." Her voice sounded dry with defeat. "After three years . . . for a lousy weekend cottage . . ."

Melissa turned to me. "She ought to take a walk to the ladies' room," she said, obviously unmoved. "They've got about a million telephone numbers there, scribbled all over the walls. She's bound to click with *one* of them."

The jukebox was always playing and couples always dancing. The girls didn't drink much, but they cuddled a lot—on the dance floor, at the tables, in every corner—caresses ranging from tender hairstroking to extensive breast and thigh explorations. Now and again a pair went into a deep movie-style clinch, emerging minutes later looking flushed and breathless. Occasionally they were greeted with applause from other tables.

Male gays behave much more circumspectly in their establishments. There's always the chance of a visitor from the vice squad.

Although gay life centers largely around bars, it doesn't exclude other spheres. There are several exclusively homosexual swingers organizations, and a vast number of contacts established through advertising and specialized dating clubs. Some of the sexual liberation movements (see Chapter 13) embrace separate branches for gay members and look upon them with considerable pride, as proofs of their true erotic libertarianism.

One trend, however, is beginning to appear in both deviate camps, and it points to some rather grim future developments. It is a rising note of paranoia, feeding not only on genuine grievances (of which there are quite enough) but creating phantom additions. And while this may be the natural reaction of long-oppressed minorities, it is nevertheless a fairly dangerous one.

On the lesbian side it manifests itself in the infiltration of the

Women's Liberation movement by hard-core sapphists who utilize the organization's platform for the most vicious forms of antimale, antistraight propaganda. At the Conference on Prostitution, held in New York in 1972, lesbian speakers—supported by a noisy claque—hurled torrents of abuse at masculinity in general and indicated that *they* were the only true feminists in the hall, since the others all fraternized with the "enemy." Later, one of the speakers, a lady named Pamela Kearon, wrote an article declaring that the distinction between prostitutes and noncommercial normals was that the latter were "unpaid vaginas."

Note how the debate was turned away from the very real issue in question and transformed into a diatribe against straight sex—i.e., against normal society.

The far-out fringe of male homosexuals have chosen psychiatrists as their whipping boys. During the Washington, D.C., convention of the APA (American Psychiatric Association), veteran Gay Militant Dr. Franklin Kameny forcibly seized the rostrum and proclaimed: "Psychiatry is waging a war of extermination against homosexuals. The psychiatric profession is the major enemy of the American gay community." In conclusion, he informed the convention members: "This is a declaration of war against *you!*"

This outburst was largely the consequence of the view held by some psychiatrists that homosexuality is a disease, perhaps even a curable one. According to recent findings it *may* be due to an endocrinological imbalance, an excess of male hormones, and might therefore be treated with drugs at a future stage.

This highly speculative theory touched homophiles at their most sensitive point. Most of them will argue calmly against accusations of perversion or even degeneracy. But call them "sick" and you've made real enemies. It arouses a vision of enforced hospitalization and mind-altering medication that evokes the nightmarish sequences from *A Clockwork Orange*.

In some it conjures up an even more sinister spectacle. In July 1971, one Don Jackson wrote an article for the Los Angeles *Free Press* concerning a "monstrous conspiracy for the genocide of homosexuals." He claimed that "Gay Liberation has exposed antihomosexual psychiatry as a hoax—nothing more than a semantic device to veil the religious beliefs of shrinks with the respectability of scientific terms."

The main instigators of this plot, according to Mr. Jackson, are neo-eugenicists, and their motivation is based on religious doctrine. He stated: "The fact that the neo-eugenicists are almost unanymously [sic] Jewish is relevant. The antihomosexual taboo can be traced to the ancient Jews. . . . Antihomosexualism became the patriotic attitude connected with the territorial ambitions of the Jewish kings. It became an obsession of the Jews and permeated every aspect of their culture. It was carried into Christianity by Saul of Tarsus [St. Paul], who spews forth antihomosexual venom in the 'Epistles of Paul,' more than half of the New Testament."

It would be futile to point out to Mr. Jackson that eugenicists are neither unanimously nor even predominantly Jewish. Nor would it serve any purpose to reveal to him that Jewish psychotherapists were among the first and staunchest advocates of the legalization of homosexuality. It would be useless because, as Oliver Wendell Holmes, Jr., once wrote: "The mind of the bigot is like the pupil of the eye; the more light you pour upon it, the more it will contract."

But it is interesting to note that professional anti-Semites have consistently accused Jewish psychologists of *favoring* homosexuality. In the United States as well as in England, Canada and Australia, neo-Fascist publications scream about a "Jew-Homo plot" to undermine the moral strength of the Western world by removing the stigma from acts of inversion. In pre-Hitler Germany, Nazi propagandists directed their most vicious attacks against Dr. Mangus Hirschfeld, then head of the Berlin Institute for Sexual Science, for his fight to abolish Paragraph 175 of the German Criminal Code, which made homosexual relations between men punishable by up to fifteen years imprisonment.

The conspiratorial view—that is, the simplistic attitude toward problems, beloved by mental Neanderthalers of all shades—makes for some strangely assorted kinships.

From the straight side this is frequently expressed in remarks like, "The fags are taking over everything." The "everything," in this case, being certain specialized kinds of work—particularly interior decorating, window display, ladies' hairdressing and fashion design.

The concentration of homosexuals in certain fields is a matter of affinity, not conspiracy. On occasions, though, it does tend to give you a vague feeling of being surrounded.

I remember sitting in a New Orleans night spot in the early-morning hours, idly chatting to the lady pianist. She was a friendly soul who looked like somebody's runaway grandmother in sequins. Because we were virtually alone in the place, she had time to tell me about the woes of the establishment. The bar, it appeared, was a welter of unrequited passions: The manager was in love with the Belgian chef; the chef was in love with the Mexican busboy; and the busboy, in turn, was hopelessly enamored of the Negro doorman.

At this stage my native simplicity broke surface. "Tell me," I asked, "doesn't *anybody* in this joint like girls?"

The lady pianist smiled. "Well, as a matter of fact," she said dreamily, "I do."

twelve

THE IMPORT TRAFFIC

Peter Dvorak stood at the customs gate of Kennedy International Airport, New York, smoking his umpteenth cigarette while waiting for his bride-to-be. She was due from Sprendlingen, West Germany, within a few minutes. In his right hand Peter clutched a bunch of roses, in his left a small photograph. The first item was a romantic touch, the second a necessary one. He had never seen the girl before in his life.

Replicas of the above scene, which reads like the somewhat contrived opening of a mystery thriller, have been enacted hundreds of times before and since. In this particular case the date was October 1968, and the ending happy. The Dvoraks now live in Idaho, have two daughters, and what might be called a splendid marriage.

"I guess we were pretty lucky," Peter told me. "An awful lot of things could have gone wrong. If I'd known just how many, I mightn't have written to Irene at all. I'm glad I took the chance, though."

It is a chance that a surprising number of people seem willing to take. For every year droves of young women—nobody knows the exact figure—are imported to the United States to marry men they have either met very briefly or never met at all. Their courtship is conducted—sometimes entirely—through the mail.

Most of my acquaintances, I discovered, found this practice more distasteful than any other aspect of the mating trade. This is rather curious, because the arrangements concerned are neither illicit nor immoral nor in the least coercive. They merely offend against certain ingrained notions of romantic egalitarianism.

For a start the traffic is exclusively one-way, in every sense. The woman always comes to the man, never vice versa. It is she who has to do all the adjusting, since her mate stays in his native environment. And as this environment is usually on a much higher material level than hers, she may approach it in a spirit of humility that her American sisters find quite obnoxious.

But the most offensive part of the deal is that the man operates in a buyer's market of colossal dimensions. He enters a world where eligible males with decent incomes are at a premium, and the choice of females at his disposal is infinitely greater than it would be at home. He can attract girls of a caliber who—in his own backyard—wouldn't bestow a second glance on him.

These last details don't apply to men like Dvorak, who obtain their mail-order brides from Western countries. But they go for the majority of wife importers, who turn to the less-developed, sexually more lopsided nations by preference.

The process involves several international introduction bureaus and specialized magazines with titles like *Glamor World, Oriental Beauty, Gina's Bulletin* and *Your Sweet Heart.* They cater to two separate sets of readers and patons. Those abroad are women who pay to have their particulars circulated in the U.S.A. The local clientele consists of men who claim to be interested in marrying them. The role of the bureaus and publications is to establish contact between them—nothing else.

In order to catch the eyes of American males, however, they resort to a pernicious brand of propaganda, aimed at psychologically very sore spots. Strategically placed in male-slanted periodicals, you'll find ads proclaiming:

Tired of Pampered, Cold, Uptight Yank Females?
Then try our Beautiful, Passionate Señoritas!
Women reared to OBEY their Man joyfully,
To cater only to his happiness and comfort.
We have hundreds of lovely and pure ladies,
All eager to love you! Send $3 for list.

Those three dollars, as a rule, get you more than just señoritas. The replies frequently encompass young women waiting in Hong Kong, Taiwan, the Philippines, Japan, South Korea, Thailand and Singapore, as well as Mexico and all of Latin America. The one feature all of them have in common is *serious* intentions. You can go through half a hundred of these returns without catching even a whiff of frivolity.

They consist of six to eight pages of photographs accompanied by brief but descriptive captions: "This cute young lady wants to marry soon, she is very serious. Age 22, very light complexion, 108 lbs., 35-24-35." . . . "My name is Doña Alicia, I live in Quito, Ecuador. I am tall, 5 ft. 9 in., my weight is 132 lbs., age 23. I wish to marry a gentleman who is serious." . . . "Unkissed Chinese girl of 17 years, 99 lbs., 5 ft. 2 in. tall. Likes to cook and take care of the home." . . . "Beautiful voluptuous girl of 26 from Venezuela. Private school teacher, 5 ft. 4 in., 115 lbs. Interested in marriage."

On unwary males these photographs can have a dizzying impact—rather like getting sales brochures from an exceptionally well-stocked harem. The girls are nearly all young and mostly very attractive. Compared to the line-ups featured in the Stateside lonely-hearts press, they look like so many candidates for a beauty contest. (Nor, incidently, are these portraits outdated or overglamorized. Every man I questioned after he had actually met his choice commented on the realism of her picture.)

But the headiest part are the ladies' exceedingly modest demands. Respectable wedlock is the Alpha and Omega of their desires; everything else ranks as jam on the bread—nice to get, but not essential. The age brackets they stipulate are much wider than those that American girls would consider. A reasonably well-off bachelor or widower of, say, forty-eight can take his pick of fillies in their early twenties or even late 'teens. A man of fifty is a long way from passé in this corner of the field. Numbers of girls, in fact, state their preference for a "kindly gentleman over forty." Looks, height and education hardly figure at all, though a "fair income" is frequently demanded.

Here, however, the law of relativity works in the man's favor. A living standard rated as just passable in his home state often means the lap of luxury for a lass from Bolivia. In his own eyes he may be just another blue-collar Joe. In hers he may appear as a minor-league Croesus who drives an automobile and watches color TV. As Miss Zsa Zsa Gabor once observed on the subject of money: "What I call loaded I'm not. What other people call loaded I am."

The basic situation thus appears deceptively rosy for the questing male. The difficulties emerge gradually and pile up as his quest proceeds. For although the ladies are certainly willing, eager and able, they are also tucked away behind barriers that only materialize as the converging movements begin.

One of the most popular countries for mail-order romance has long been Mexico. Too popular, as far as the Mexican authorities were concerned. Five years ago the Mexican Government forbade all newspaper and magazine advertising mentioning the word "matrimony," thus depriving the postal matchmakers of their chief outlet. Several promptly moved from Guadalajara to Texas and continued publishing on this side of the border.

The initial perplexities, however, have nothing to do with official disapproval. They are financial and lingual. For a Mexican office girl or shop assistant, earning perhaps the equivalent of three dollars a day, airmail replies constitute a fair expense. Most American men realize this and thoughtfully enclose a couple of dollar bills in their first letter. This results in the girl getting neither the letter nor the cash. Since it is illegal to send money through the Mexican mails, postal clerks hold all envelopes under a strong light and confiscate those containing currency. The correct thing to do is to purchase Mexican airmail stamps in this country and put a supply of them into the first communication.

The language barrier may be tougher to crack. While a large proportion of ads announce that the lady pictured possesses "some English" or is "learning English," these are pretty nebulous concepts. The "some" frequently indicates a the-cat-sat-on-the-mat stage of proficiency.

The experience of a factory foreman from Omaha is by no means unusual. He had a three-month correspondence with a girl in Durango, during which she sent him lengthy and fluent epistles couched in almost Gothically stilted prose, invariably beginning with, "In reply to yours of the 4/17th . . ."

Eventually he flew to Durango during his vacation. "She was just as pretty as her picture," he told me, "but you could have put all her English on a postage stamp. Those letters were written for her by a girl friend who worked for an export company. And all *she'd* ever handled was business mail."

This particular romance ended there and then. But an engineer working in the same Omaha plant contacted another Durango girl via the same matrimonial magazine. Noel is a tall, slightly stooped man in his late forties with a shock of gray-peppered hair and a diffidently nervous blink. He had been living at home as a confirmed bachelor until his mother died. Then he frankly began looking around for a woman to take care of his creature comforts without making too many demands.

"I kinda liked the idea of a Latin gal because they're supposed to be real domesticated," he drawled. "To be honest, ah didn't care a hoot about the language bit. Long as she'd cook for me and look after me. I'm not much of a talker."

Noel exchanged only two very rudimentary letters with Agustina before he traveled to Mexico to meet her and her family. There was a quarter-century age difference between them, and the girl had never worked, never left her home state, and never been alone with a man who wasn't a relative.

And, despite the fact that he was accepted as her *novio*, she wasn't left alone with him either. "Leastwise not for more than five minutes. Those folks of hers didn't trust nobody in pants." He gave a brief reminiscent chuckle. "There was always somebody trailin' us—her aunt, her kid sister—some kinda chaperone. Ah didn't mind, really, that's just their custom. They hadn't a thing against me. They liked the idea that I was Catholic too. So we had a proper church wedding and everything."

"How did it work out from there?" I asked.

Noel grinned slowly and complacently. "I ain't complainin'. And ah don't think my wife is either. She got herself a washing machine, new vacuum cleaner, a whole pile of new clothes. And I'm teachin' her driving. She still don't parley zee Eenglish so good, but . . . we get along okay."

I heard an entirely different angle of the situation from another type of señora. Francisca works for a Chicano social organization in Los Angeles to support herself and her small son. She looks rather like Liza Minnelli in an off-diet year and talks like Bernadette Deylin with a Spanish accent. She had placed an ad in a Marriage Club bulletin which did not—to put it mildly—reflect her personality. Among other things, it described her as "gentle and eager to worship a loving man."

"Why did I place such an ad?" She tossed her black page-boy fringe like a fractious pony. "Because I didn't want to marry a Mexican man. Because for a woman with—with spirit, married life in Mexico is life in prison. No, worse—because prisoners don't have to pretend they are happy all the time."

Francisca clenched her fists and shook them in a perfect gesture of frustration she uses when the words won't come fast enough. "All this talk about liberation. For girls in Mexico this is a lot of" —her fists shook faster as she groped for the right expression— "a lot of crap."

"Before marriage a middle-class woman she is allowed to work for a little while. After marriage—never. Her place must be at home with the children. Lots of children. One after the other. And she hardly sees her husband except for meals. Sometimes not even then. Oh yes, for the *comida*—that is the midday meal—but not in the evenings. At night he is always out with his—his friends, his buddies. They go to cafés, to parties, to dinners, but without their wives. The women must stay at home. Alone. And if the husband goes to his little girl friend in her *casita*—that's his business."

She stood up. She needed movement to give vent to her feelings. "Did you ever see Mexican television commercials?" Francisca asked, then added without waiting for an answer: "There is one that used to drive me crazy. The woman screams she wants to be liberated, like the Swedish girls. 'From what?' the husband asks. 'From this dirty house,' she yells. So he gives her an Electrolux vacuum cleaner. And she is happy. '*Now* I am liberated,' she says. That is what they mean by liberty! No, thank you. Not for me!"

Francisca's ad, with accompanying photo, got her five replies from American men, a tribute to her talents as a copywriter. She selected one from an electrical contractor in Denver. The correspondence flourished, thanks to her excellent English. The couple finally met in El Paso, Texas.

On the exact whys and wherefores of this encounter she was as reticent as a British historian discussing the Opium War. Why El Paso? "Well, I only had a border-crossing card. It didn't allow me to travel further inland." Did her parents know she was meeting a man there? "Er—no, not really . . ."

Here Francisca lapsed into totally uncharacteristic silence. All I could elucidate was that she—somehow—married her contractor in El Paso. His name was Cliff, and the marriage staggered along for four bumpy years en route to the divorce court. But her comments on Cliff were astonishingly mild:

"He was a good fellow in his own style. Only he married me for the wrong reasons. He had heard about Mexican women—what they say in magazines. And maybe I perhaps misled him a little bit. He thought I was that kind of little pigeon—we say *mamacita*—I would just adore him and pamper him and ask nothing else. But I'm not like that." She tapped her forehead. "I think maybe the trouble was that I am brighter than him. He read nothing, he had no—no ideas. Just his work and, yes, baseball. Still, in many ways he was a good man. Only not good for me."

Francisca's marriage obviously foundered on the mountain of misconceptions a great many American men harbor about foreign women. The volume of ignorance is certainly mutual, but seems to matter less on the other side, since women are usually more adaptable. Many of these delusions are assiduously fostered by popular literature tailored for masculine appeal, and the truth—once it dawns—can be dismal.

The truth, of course, is that women are individuals with attributes that vary as much in Yokohama as in Yonkers. They are often *forced* to conform to a certain national mold, which will appear the more uniform the stronger the social pressures brought to bear upon them. But once these conforming pressures are removed by a change of environment, their individualism will emerge—for better or for worse.

Some masculine notions concerning foreign females are based chiefly on resentment against the American prototype. U.S. women are thus; therefore the overseas breed *must* be different. The difference, however, is not necessarily in their favor.

The magazine ad I quoted earlier played upon one of the most widespread locker-room legends by referring to American women as "cold" and "uptight." This, it indicated, was in contrast to those "passionate" señoritas available in the Latin latitudes. It must have come as a considerable shock for any number of importers to discover that frigidity is not only common but even considered laudable among *limpia* (clean, pure) ladies south of the border.

In the same vein, American women are constantly accused of being materialistic, dollar-dedicated and compulsively acquisitive. Their attitude, nevertheless, is positively Bohemian compared to the average French or Swiss girl, some of whom make a religion out of counting their centimes. It is true that this trait usually makes them excellent housekeepers on a tight budget. But it can also stifle every generous impulse on the part of their husbands and turn their lives into an endless routine of penny-pinching.

The list of legendry circles the entire globe, ranging from the purported sexual prowess of Swedish girls to the alleged handicraft skills of the Peruvians. It is reinforced year by year by tourist tales and impressions brought back by military personnel—two groups who only come in contact with a minuscule fringe element of the local populace, which resembles the whole about as much as airline hostesses resemble the gross of Americans.

The most fabled species are probably Japanese women, who have managed to preserve their Madame Butterfly image more or less intact, despite Pearl Harbor, Beatle spouse Yoko Ono, and the transistor revolution. Which is undoubtedly why Americans are marrying them at the rate of about two hundred a month.

A large proportion of these liaisons is arranged by an outfit called Japan International Social (JIS), which operates both in Tokyo and in Newport Beach, California. This is more than merely an introduction bureau. With the initial registration fee of twenty-five dollars comes a guide service for visitors to Japan and a gift-exporting feature through which patrons can obtain specified goods at the lowest shopping rates. They also get the most effective propaganda blasts on behalf of Nipponese maidenhood since Puccini. A few samples from publicity pamphlets put out by JIS will give you an idea of the tone:

> Although women are born with a natural inclination to please and serve men, this desire has been smothered and stamped out in the United States and other Western countries by ambitious and self-centered women. In Japan and Eastern countries, this trait has been developed and refined.
> While many husbands want to send their American wives to Lower Slobovia (and their wives, for the most part, are anxious to go), it is indeed a rare case to find any domestic discord in a marriage where the wife is a happy, cheerful homemaker, as the majority of girls are in Japan.
> In Japan women are taught from childhood that their place is in the home, to be obedient and faithful. They are taught the skills and shown the duties necessary to please a man and keep him contented. If you've been to Japan you know what we mean. If you haven't, ask someone who's been there, or any of the great number of American males who are happily married to one of those wonderful, adorable creatures . . .

Along with this siren song comes a gallery of snapshots (top-quality glossies) depicting some of the most exquisite chicks extant. The girls are not so much conventionally beautiful as piquant, very young looking and tremendously appealing. If anything, they demand even fewer qualifications in a prospective husband than their Latin rivals. Income is hardly ever mentioned and stipulations rarely go beyond the desire that he should be "nice and honest" —and eligible.

The comments of Miss Michiko H. indicate the standard:

> I am 24 years old, five feet four inches tall, and play the Koto (harp). I work as a secretary and make my own dresses. I would like to correspond with a well-mannered gentleman who is interested in marriage. I would like age around 35 up to 45. I would not mind if the gentleman was around 55 or so.

Marrying via an introduction service is a much easier step for a Japanese girl than for a Westerner. As a whole, Orientals have few notions of "romantic love" in our sense of the term. Even today most Japanese marriages are still arranged either by relatives or professional marriage brokers, with bride and groom frequently not meeting until shortly before the nuptials. A man's appearance hardly matters at all, his age very little. Family background and character are almost the only considerations. Love is regarded as something of a luxury plant—it may or may not sprout in the course of marital involvement, but this needn't affect the happiness of the match in the least. Loyalty—a sense of belonging—is what counts, together with the creation of an honorable family and household. The frequent mention of "honesty" in the girls' ads is not meant in the literal English connotation. It stands for "uprightness, rectitude."

If the Japanese ladies have a strike against them, it's distance. A trip to Japan is a long hop, even in the jet age. But a surprising number of them are willing to travel to the U.S., providing their airmail suitor pays the fare. In this respect, Japanese women seem to be far more venturesome than Latin Americans. This is one of the numerous paradoxes that can't really be explained in terms of their upbringing, but may be due to the fact that the Japanese are somewhat less obsessed with female virginity.

Reg Kenney was one of the fair number of American men who courted his Japanese wife by mail, sent her an engagement ring the same way, and met her for the first time after she had flown nine thousand miles for the rendezvous.

"The funny thing was that I'd actually been to Japan," said Kenney. "But that was eight years earlier, with the Navy. I thought then that Japanese gals were the sweetest dolls I'd ever seen and that I'd fancy marrying one. Only, well, the kind you meet when you're in the service—on liberty—well, they're whores mostly. I mean, you couldn't marry them. But the idea stuck with me."

He saw Hiroka's photo—peach-faced, snub-nosed, with breast-length black hair and a wistful gamin smile—in the selection forwarded by Japan International. Her dossier announced that she was a telephone operator in Nagoya, spoke good English, liked cooking, hiking, rock music and gardening, and wished to marry "a good-hearted U.S. gentleman, not with beard."

After a couple of letters, Kenney became completely enchanted with her. Hiroka wrote with tremendous earnestness ("You could just about see the tongue sticking out of her mouth over her work.") in an argot that was entirely her own. Once she warned him against going out in the rain without an umbrella: "You may become engrossed with moisture."

Even after sending her the engagement ring, Kenney didn't know how she would react to his suggestion of coming over for a visit. He was then working as a television repairman in Minneapolis, trying to build up business, with no hope of holidays in the near future. "Besides, I wanted to find out if she liked this town."

Hiroka's response was quite matter-of-fact. She inquired about money, visas and climate. Not a word about his intentions, honorable or otherwise.

It was this absence of concern that made him determined "to do the right thing by her." Her trust in him was total. "I'd have felt like a rat if I'd taken advantage of her—you know what I mean."

The Kenneys were married after two weeks of explorative—but entirely chaste—contact. She lived in the local YWCA, Reg in his bachelor studio. Every night he drove her back to the Y, and returned to his single bed. Hiroka went along with this procedure with the same unquestioning *sang-froid*. It was what *he*—apparently —wanted; *ergo* it was right. They went through a certain amount of immigration hassle; Hiroka had to leave the country and re-enter with a different visa. A year later they moved to Wisconsin, where Kenney now runs a TV repair service. Hiroka adapted to her surroundings with uncanny speed. She even stopped sucking in her breath (the Japanese indication of respect) when she noticed that it irritated her husband. Her cooking has become sufficiently tasteless to please his Midwest palate. She doesn't drink herself, but knows her husband's favorite cocktail mixes and has one ready for him the moment he gets home from work.

"She made a rock garden in our yard—you ought to see it. Made all the neighbors jealous." There was a lot of pride in Kenney's voice. "And she treats me like I was royalty, no kidding. Difficulties?" He scratched his receding hairline. "Yeah, some. Like she won't come out with it if something's bugging her. Just withdraws, kind of. I always have to try and guess if I did something wrong. She'll never tell me. Makes me nervous sometimes. Doesn't happen too often, though. As a whole"—he pointed at my notebook—"you can put me down as a happy man."

There is no real Western equivalent of JIS. The closest facsimile may be the Cameo (Anglo-American Friendship Club) in London. This is something like the overseas department of the Ivy Gibson Bureau, one of the oldest and staidest matrimonial agencies in the world. The Cameo Club offers the same service for Americans and Canadians—or anyway attempts it, albeit handicapped by distance. It has to forego the close personal scrutiny the mother firm bestows on prospects, but does its best by avoiding anything resembling glamor treatment or high-pressure persuasion.

The ten-dollar fee for a half-year membership gets you no glossy prints of desirable damsels. In fact, it gets you no pictures at all. Instead, you receive demure little white booklets listing the attributes and desires of available ladies in considerable detail and minus any superfluous frills or adjectives. They are, bar none, the most confidence-inspiring brochures of their kind. You get the feeling that they were checked by a sternly benevolent British matron with a red pencil, who occasionally strikes out an entry, murmuring, "We're not having *her* sort."

The supply of English candidates is vast, but the girls are considerably more demanding than either Latins or Orientals. Nearly all of them want men with secure jobs (not necessarily well-paid), some set educational standards, and a few even stipulate sense of humor. Their age brackets, though generally wider than those of American girls, are sharply defined. "Must be under 48," is a common clause. A sprinkling insist on Protestants or Catholics, or disqualify divorcees.

Some of the listings, however, are quite astonishing. I came across a London trio—one Mrs. and two Misses, all living at the same address and obviously a mother and two daughters—who wished to correspond with and eventually marry three almost identical Americans, though in different age groups. Now, *there* was a plot for a sex comedy if ever I saw one.

Since the names and descriptions of transatlantic Cameo members are automatically circulated in Britain, you may receive responses without having written to anyone first. I got a remarkable communication from a widow in Manchester, who described herself as a professional medium and was obviously smitten by my biographical statistics. Her tea leaves had revealed, she informed me, that she was destined to marry a man with my exact date of birth and physical appearance, and we'd better not try and defy destiny, as this was apt to have unpleasant consequences all around. So what was the earliest I could come to Manchester, or—better yet— when would I want her to come to America?

The actual dangers involved in this traffic are much smaller than might be assumed. Since the man importing a girl invariably has to send her a return ticket, the process doesn't lend itself to white-slave schemes. Unless she loses or cashes in her ticket, the girl isn't going to find herself stranded in a foreign land. And the mechanics are really too lengthy and expensive to attract anyone with only seduction in mind. If anything, it is the male who runs the greater risks. He may find that he has bitten off more than he can chew—and sometimes of a different substance than he expected.

A New York insurance promoter, who shall remain anonymous,

introduced me to a very pretty brownette he had imported from London. She was, he explained proudly, an actress and graduate of the Royal Academy of Dramatic Arts (RADA), who would—after their marriage—pursue her career in the United States.

I heard about three sentences of the lady's adenoidal Cockney and knew that if she was a RADA graduate I was Howard Hughes. I asked her what kind of acting she had done and she answered "in pictures." I inquired which studio.

"Oh, Parade Productions," she said brightly. "It's in Old Compton Street."

The company in question figures prominently in London police blotters. Its output is restricted to hard-core pornography, and the casts are drawn entirely from the C.O.D. ladies and their pimps who inhabit Old Compton Street, Soho, en masse. I would have wagered my front teeth that our lass had been of that fraternity. True, the evidence was purely circumstantial. But as Thoreau observed: "Some circumstantial evidence is very strong, as when you find a trout in the milk."

The German-born wife of a friend in Chicago supplied me with another example. She met the imported bride of her husband's barber, a curly-locked Berliner who—on discovering their common background—gave vent to warm demonstrations of kinship. She showed her compatriot her entire—very extensive—collection of jewelry, appraising each piece and finally remarking casually: *"Ja, und Alles auf dem Rücken verdient."* ("Yeah, and I earned it all on my back.")

One of the best-established contact services for European women is run by Frau Zimmer-Hartman of Hamburg. Mrs. Hartman has been advertising in U.S. matrimonial publications for twenty years and offers selections not only from Western Europe but also from various Communist countries, including Russia. For a fee of twenty-two dollars you can get introductions to ladies residing in the Ukraine, Poland, Czechoslovakia and Romania. Applicants are mostly American men from the same ethnic backgrounds, who are willing to go through the maddening rigmarole of Soviet red tape in order to acquire a mate who can cook like Momma used to. For them the chief requisite is determination. Exit permits take up to three years to come through and frequently require forms to be filled in quadruplicate.

But the majority of prospects are German, though the numbers have dwindled considerably since the postwar era, when Germany—having lost around three million men in battle—was suffering from the most lopsided sex ratio on earth. For some years the situation was so desperate that lonely females sought partners via vending machines. These gadgets could be found near any metropolitan railroad station. You fed them a small coin and received a card with a girl's photo and address printed on it. The women concerned were definitely not "scarlet"—most of them held ordinary, respectable jobs. They were war widows or young girls deprived of the usual social contacts by the manpower shortage they owed to the late Adolf Schickelgruber.

Ever since then, German girls have been possibly the most enterprising of all when it comes to matrimony. They are not only willing to travel and to take chances, but also show a remarkable facility for learning languages, quite apart from their well-known domestic talents.

Their *Hausfrau* qualities, in fact, seem to be more frequently exploited than their genders. After an exchange of suitably romantic letters, girls are persuaded to come over for indeterminate periods, to "see how they like America." For the benefit of the Immigration authorities they come *au pair*—that is, as language students who do light housework in return for their meals and lodging. Since they receive no wages they require no working permits.

The household may consist of their "fiancé" and his aging parents, possibly children from a previous marriage. And the girl discovers that she has been recruited as an unpaid but virtually full-time cook/housekeeper. Theoretically, of course, there is nothing to stop her from flying home immediately. But this is rarely how it works in practice. In all likelihood she will want to prove her worth to her prospective family by becoming a model skivvy. Somehow the wedding date gets postponed month after month, but is always referred to as being just around the corner. By the time she awakens to the fact that she is being played for a sucker, she may have toiled along for a year or more. When she finally does pack her bags she will have rendered services worth several times the cost of her air fare. And there is nothing to prevent the "fiancé" from repeating the game with another import. I know of at least one wifeless New York family that has kept itself supplied with gratis maids in this fashion for the past four years.

Outright sexual entrapment is much rarer. When it happens it usually involves a psychotic rather than a Casanova figure. Normal wolves can get all the intrigues they can handle at home without sending overseas for them.

I learned of one particularly nauseating case concerning, of all people, a highly esteemed San Francisco medico. Dr. X came to California from Germany as a young man and not only built up a flourishing practice but also made a reputation as a lecturer. In 1970 he began to correspond with a divorcée living in the small Rhineland town of Braubach. Armgard is a softly rounded blonde in her mid-thirties who was then working as secretary for a pharmaceutical firm. There were few eligible local men in her age group, and the doctor's letters sounded like trumpet calls of romance from across the sea.

"What good is my house, my convertible, my fortune, without a loving someone to share them with?" wrote the doctor. "What good is life without a sweetheart?" (He used the German expression *Herzliebchen*, which is several degrees gooeyer.) "My roots, alas, are still in the land of my birth, and I cannot find the right soulmate here."

He accompanied his epistles with color snaps showing him in his house, his garden and his convertible: a corpulent, dough-faced but passable gent, only slightly marred by a supercilious smirk. Like most romantics, Armgard has a blotting-paper capacity for absorbing treacle, and those letters were the most thrilling things in her life. When Dr. X suggested that she spend the next summer as his guest, her "Yes" went out by return mail.

The *Herr Doktor's* actual appearance came as rather a shock. He was at least a decade older than he had claimed, wore pancake make-up to hide his wrinkles and a toupee to cover his baldness. The house and fortune were real enough, but he had no inclination to share either.

One of his first actions was to confiscate Armgard's passport and return ticket "for safe keeping." During the following weeks he managed to persuade her that by cohabiting with a man not her husband she had committed an offense against U.S. alien laws and was liable to deportation—possibly imprisonment—if caught. This frightened her so thoroughly that she hardly dared to venture out of the house for over a month.

In that month she became a kind of sexual toy for Dr. X. The good doctor was virtually impotent, but owned a large selection of errotic gadgetry to overcome this handicap. This included an artificial penis stiffener, electrical masturbators, whips, gags, leather harnesses, plastic dildos, a cushioned chair that could be transformed into a flagellation bench, and an alphabetically ordered library of pornographic pictures and films.

He forced Armgard into activities that were not so much painful as unspeakably degrading and of almost macabre obscenity. One of his more printable diversions was to dress her up as a pony—with bit, bridle, leather eyeflaps, and a horsehair tail stuck in her rectum—and have her perform circus stances while he cracked a whip.

During the day she was left alone while he went to his surgery. On one such occasion she rummaged through his desk and found letters indicating that he had brought over at least two other women under the same circumstances and was corresponding with several more. This, apparently, hurt Armgard worse than the doc's sexual eccentricities. It stung her sufficiently to overcome her fears and seek help.

She went to a local German restaurant, where she confided to the proprietor and his wife. They first of all put her straight on the legal angle, then contacted the doctor.

Dr. X was outraged over Armgard's perfidiousness. Was this, he demanded emotionally, the gratitude for his hospitality? He only simmered down when the restaurateur threatened to call the police. Armgard got her travel documents back the same evening, together with a pained note indicating that she had destroyed the doctor's faith in humanity. Also that she owed him fifty-seven dollars and forty cents "for meals and laundry expenses."

She flew home to Braubach the following day. Her rescuers haven't heard from her since. Dr. X has retired from the medical scene and now devotes his time to the enjoyment of his house, fortune and convertible. Presumably, he is still corresponding with *Herzliebchens* in the land of his birth.

thirteen

FREEDOM FOR ALL!

The table in the assembly room of San Francisco's Unitarian Church center seated seventeen people, including myself. The fourteen men and three girls talked softly and with some of the apprehensive good-fellowship that characterizes draft-board inductees. Through the thin walls came the plinking of a bouzouki from the Greek folk-dancing class proceeding next door.

A statuesque blonde, long-haired and wearing glasses, walked to the head of the table. She cleared her throat, nodded curtly, and began: "Welcome to the open meeting of the Sexual Freedom League [SFL]. My name is Margo. I am the coordinator of the San Francisco chapter." Her voice was dryly matter-of-fact, almost gruff. "Now—are there any questions?"

I raised my hand. "Could you tell us something about the aims of your organization?"

"Our aim," she said flatly, "is to become unnecessary. To get everybody so liberated that society in general will live as we do now."

I remember wishing that more chairmen were as brief and incisive with their answers. She kept it up through the confused barrage of questions that followed, most of them inquiring how—precisely—League members *were* living.

The queries sounded positive and interested, though a little nervous at times. Every few minutes a balding man, who had described himself as a psychologist, leaped up and shouted, "That's a hostile question! Why are you hostile?" As far as I could make out, the only hostility in the room emanated from him.

Margo fielded the balls as fast as they came, leaning back and rapping replies through the smoke clouds of her cigarettes: "What's that? Why did I join the League? To meet men. Liberated men. I had enough of the other kind. Did I meet any? Well, I met my husband, Frank . . ."

Margo Esposito's husband edits the League's monthly publication, *Sexual Freedom.* She herself sits on the board of directors and works as a full-time officer of the movement. "Full-time" means exactly that, because the SFL now has fifteen hundred members in seven national chapters and runs an extensive range of activities.

"We call them Changes, and they cover every day of the week—including Sundays," said Margo, sounding like an engineer explaining a blueprint to a junior apprentice. "There are different kinds of Encounters: Psycholib, Movement, Acceptance and Couples Encounters. Then we have the Sensorium—that's hard to explain; you'd better attend one. Aphrodisiac cookery classes. Massage sessions. The More Than Two Circle—that's a breakaway from the traditional pairing—you know, three or four. And then the regular Saturday parties."

"What are they like?"

"Sex parties. You'd call them orgies." She lit another cigarette and added: "We used to make them open houses, but then we had about fifty men and five girls turn up. So now it's couples only."

For the more philosophical aspects of the movement she referred me to the codirectors. Tom Palmer and Virginia Miller. I left Margo with a bundle of pamphlets, brochures and magazines from which to glean background material.

The SFL, it appeared, was founded in 1963 by a radical young

New Yorker named John Jefferson Poland, Jr. Since Mr. Poland lacked both the desire and the ability to head an expanding organization, he eventually relinquished leadership to concentrate on other matters. One of them concerned his name. As a gesture of defiance against the bourgeoisie, he decided to drop the Jefferson part and replace it with a semiforbidden four-letter word starting with F. His purpose, he claimed, was to give the word legal status. This he achieved insofar as his bank accepted checks signed with it. But in January 1971, he went a step further. On that date he inserted an official advertisement declaring that he wished to shorten his name by deleting "Poland." He would, henceforth, be known simply as John F . . . From what I have gathered, he has no trouble cashing checks and getting his mail delivered. But the California government has so far refused to list his new appellation on the electoral rolls.

With Mr. Poland gone from the leadership, the SFL became a somewhat less flamboyant but more effective outfit. It gained enough status to have the California Assembly Judiciary Committee listen to its views on the qualifications for marriage. These included the legalization of homosexual unions, multiple marriages for either sex, and the abolition of incest strictures, which would enable members of an immediate family to marry—"in a relationship not intended for procreation."

Despite their different surnames, Tom Palmer and Virginia Miller are a married couple with a delightful small son. They live in a comfortable old house in Oakland, strewn with papers and automobile parts (Tom's *other* interest is motor racing), decorated chiefly by a glass cage with gerbils that spend most of their time eating or sleeping.

Although their directoral status is equal, Tom is decidedly the spokesman of the pair. Bearded, gentle-voiced and graying, he has the air of an unusually affable mathematics professor.

I asked him why the League attracted so many more men than women.

"Because we say that sex is good and should be indulged in. And because in a society where the great double standard says that women should be passive—shouldn't really enjoy sex—they're reluctant to join an organization in which sex is a focal point."

At the moment, about two thirds of all members are couples, the rest mostly single men. "Some of them—let's face it—are what you might call socially inept types who simply can't talk a woman into bed with them." He gave a slight shrug. "I tell them quite frankly that if their purpose in joining the League is just to get laid—it probably won't happen. But things are changing." He raised a professorial finger. "The tide is starting to run our way."

Tom, undoubtedly, is a strong contributing factor to that tide-turning. "Yes, I lecture quite extensively. I *like* public speaking. Television shows, colleges, high schools . . ."

"Did you say high schools?"

He nodded, relishing my surprise. "Sure. Mostly sponsored by student organizations. They can get anybody they want."

To him the keynote of the SFL is the "Freedom" part. "What we're after, fundamentally, is a country where sex is a part of your life that you aren't hung up about at all. Where no one has to feel guilty or afraid about his or her sex life."

Did he encounter much hostility for his views?

"Not at public meetings. Sometimes on television. But"—he grinned amiably—"I'm good at handling that. Once, on the Les Crane Show in Los Angeles, they'd invited the head of a Fundamentalist Bible College to debate us. He was *very* hostile. He accused us of trying to destroy the family structure and intimated that we were Communists. Then Les Crane kind of warned him that we might sue him for that. So he backed down on that point. Obviously," Tom chuckled, "he'd never been to Russia—the most dourly puritan of countries."

While Tom and Virginia share their basic philosophy, they are by no means unanimous in expressing it. Tom likes to walk around the house in the nude, Virginia prefers to stay dressed.

"Why?" She hesitated for a moment. "I just find that I'm more comfortable with my clothes on. To me there's a time and place for everything. When the right time comes to take my clothes off . . . I take them off."

"What about another sexual-freedom aspect," I asked: "Would you, for instance, proposition a man?"

This time the answer came quickly. "Yes, I would."

"Would you ask a man to marry you?"

"Yes. Certainly." Then she smiled. "But, you know, I wouldn't open a door for a man. *That* I just wouldn't feel comfortable doing."

The SFL may not have developed an original philosophy, but it does offer at least one unique form of entertainment. The Sensorium could be described as a happening with optional orgasm, and I rather suspect that any day now some commercial entrepreneur will get hold of it. In which case patrons should expect to pay considerably more than the six dollars (and no tips) currently changed.

The Sensorium is a biggish apartment, draped in velvets and satins and liberally sprinkled with low couches and cushions to produce a seraglio atmosphere. At the door participants are blindfolded and assigned a guide. A male guide for women, a girl for men. They are then led individually through the apartment. It takes a few minutes before the patron discovers, by feel, that his or her guide is stark naked.

After the exploratory stroll, patrons are laid down on pillows and slowly undressed by their guides. They are massaged—feet, fingers, scalp, stomach, thighs, back, shoulders—every square inch of body, including the intimate inches. Grapes are popped into their mouths, slices of apple and sips of sweet cranberry juice. The guide strokes them with feathers, strips of velvet and soft fur. They are given a rose to sniff and have a body-warmed alabaster egg rolled over their bellies. Soft tassles are vibrated over their skins. Then comes a massage with warm oil, which is carefully, lovingly applied to their skin before their hands and feet are soaked in it.

The guide kisses them, caresses them, and they are free to kiss and fondle back—or not, according to mood. Also according to mood is the finale. They either make love there and then or are dried off, dressed and unblindfolded. I didn't notice anyone take the second alternative.

The SFL is only one of half a dozen similar bodies in the United States, all flying the motto of "sexual freedom" on their mastheads. At first glance their very existence seems paradoxical. Sexual freedom—license, if you will—has come to be taken pretty much for granted in our time.

But there is a vital difference between enjoying liberty on loan, so to speak, and having it codified and constitutionalized. The current era of permissiveness is based on nothing more than a few Supreme Court rulings and a certain degree of public tolerance. Court compositions change, so does popular sentiment; and often as not it changes backward. The current situation is rather as if Prohibition had never been abolished but merely suspended: the Volstead Act not amended, only kept in abeyance—to be enforced whenever it appears propitious.

The sexual equivalents of Prohibition are still on the statute books of most states. They can be dusted off and applied as and when the authorities deem fit to do so. The fact that some of them date back to the colonial Puritans, and others were passed to humor legislators from hillbilly constituencies, does not diminish their potential weight. They remain *laws,* and perusing them means getting powerful whiffs of *1984.*

In every state except Illinois, for instance, oral-genital contact is punishable by fines and jail terms of not less than a year—regardless of whether or not the couple concerned are married. Adultery laws, preserved from the days of the Massachusetts Bay Colony, stipulate up to ten years imprisonment for both offenders.

Rectal intercourse, still labeled "the detestable and abominable sin among Christians not to be named," carries from one to thirty years in prison, according to the state. In California the penal code was framed in 1870, a period when medical opinion held masturbation responsible for a fabulous array of ailments, including vertigo, consumption, epilepsy, impotence, insanity, amnesia and myopia. Apparently anxious to prevent the pastime from spreading, the legislators affixed a penalty of one year to life on the act, if performed within sight of others. Most of New England officially retains the concept that fornication outside wedlock is a crime per se, punishable by law. The ancient penalty of "twenty stripes sharply layd on" has merely been transmuted into fines and/or jail terms. Other regulations forbid men to don women's clothes or make-up, even in the privacy of their homes, and prohibit the telling of "lascivious stories, jokes or anecdotes" within the listening range of ladies.

To us these hoary scraps of dormant jurisprudence may resemble comic museum pieces; some of them certainly read like extracts from Part III of *Gulliver's Travels*.[1] But just as Swift's satire had very real bearing on eighteenth-century England, so does the mentality behind these legal relics cast its shadow over our momentary spell of *laissez faire*. The ideology that created all of them is rooted in the refusal to distinguish between crime and sin, the notion that governments can and should legislate people's private morality.

This can become dangerous to any form of freedom when coupled with the view that something should be proscribed because a number of folks consider it offensive. To illustrate just what may fall under that heading, here is the tail end of a letter sent to the Los Angeles *Times* in 1971 by the Reverend Walter K. Pifer on the subject of masculine hair styles:

> When a man wilfully persists in having flowing locks, he defies God, and by his insistence, offends many people. While he may not always have this in mind, it nevertheless does so.

Since shoulder-length tresses were worn by men ranging from Dante to Buffalo Bill (to say nothing of the popular portrayals of Jesus), I can't guess how the Reverend arrived at his conclusion. But I do know that for approximately sixty years his particular outlook virtually barred long-haired males from appearing in public in most of America's smaller communities, just as it prevented women

---

[1] Gulliver's third voyage was to the "Kingdom of Tribnia, by the Natives called Langdon," where the greater part of the population consisted of spies and informers. Learned professors had perfected the science of discovering people's secret thoughts by examining their excrements.

from wearing pants. The significant point is that it may do so again at any time in the future. The local ordinances designed to keep the Reverend Pifers from being offended are still around.

There is, of course, no question of most of these anachronisms being enforced en masse. This would result in the incarceration of a goodly percentage of our adult citizenry. As Judge Morris Ploscowe phrased it: "Most men and women copulate in sovereign disregard of penal statutes." But they could and would be used to eliminate individuals who—for one reason or another—have made themselves distasteful to the authorities.

These are bound to include the free enterprisers now operating so-called "sex boutiques" in a number of U.S. cities. They deal in lubricious merchandise, mostly overpriced (though not nearly as much so as certain "organic" foods), on small, smart premises with a youngish clientele. Shops like New York's Pleasure Chest and Chicago's Dr. Feelgood stock erotic incense, perfumed body oils, imitation Spanish fly, allegedly aphrodisiacal herbs and bizarre rubber condoms alongside waterbeds, bubble pipes and velvet poofs.

They do not sell hard-core smut and cultivate a semifashionable image, contrasting with the leering sordidness of the conventional porno stores. Which is precisely what's bothering the watchdogs of public purity.

One New York anticarnality crusader told me bitterly: "Those boutiques are ten times worse. Why? Because they attract a class of customers who wouldn't go near an ordinary pornography den. They get young housewives, college girls—kids who could be our daughters. They just wouldn't be tolerated in other countries."

He had, I discovered, never heard of the Beate Uhse stores. Mrs. Uhse is a middle-aged German lady who became a mark millionairess by starting a chain of sex supermarkets now encircling West Germany and the Netherlands. Her shops resemble streamlined Woolworth branches, and retail bargain-rate erotica to the strains of Muzak interspersed with loudspeaker eulogies of the variegated frenzies induced by her products. Their prevailing atmosphere is nearly as debauched as a hardware department.

I told my crusading acquaintance about this, but didn't cut much ice. "Well, that's there," he argued logically. "We're here. That's entirely different."

He was a true disciple of John S. Sumner, former head of the Society for the Suppression of Vice (SSV), who died in 1971 aged ninety-four. Mr. Sumner, whose name is virtually unknown today, wielded considerable power in his time, largely by nudging the authorities into applying the suppressive ordinances at their disposal. As one journalist phrased it, "He almost succeeded in making morality a dirty word."

Sumner's efforts were mainly directed against the publishing industry. He kept James Joyce's *Ulysses* and Theodore Dreiser's *The Genius* off the American market for a decade, and very nearly managed to do the same for the works of James T. Farrell and Erskine Caldwell. To the SSV vice meant sex, and any expression thereof. Above all, it meant the *enjoyment* of such expression. When Sumner was asked why his Society had made no moves against the Kinsey Report, he replied: "Well, it was mostly statistics—not the sort of thing a person could read and enjoy."

The influence of the SSV went far beyond the realms of salaciousness. It imposed a pattern of Bowdlerism on public bodies that could be called antilife. In 1953, for instance, the New York State Censorship Board actually banned the screening of Walt Disney's nature study *The Vanishing Prairie*. The reason: a two-minute sequence showing the birth of a buffalo calf. Respectable buffaloes, as everyone knew, were hatched in incubators.

While such a step is unlikely to occur today, the legal levers that made it possible are still part of the machine and have become only slightly rusty from disuse. Twenty years are a very brief span, judicially speaking.

The aim shared by the various sexual liberation groups is to bring about in letter what currently exists only in spirit—that is, the scrapping of the arsenal of statutes dangling over their heads like so many swords of Damocles. This has already occurred in Scandinavia, Holland and—partially—England. In America, however, the task is rendered more difficult by the fact that most of them are state laws, thus requiring not one amendment but fifty.

The liberators themselves are as mixed a bag as their opponents. Some, at least, have managed to combine idealism with profit-making to the point of inextricability.

John Raymond, for example, presides over a trio of organizations that have made him a budding tycoon at the age of twenty-four. He is executive director of the American Sexual Freedom Movement (ASFM), Gay Sexual Freedom (GSF) and a social-educational outfit called Top of the World Clubs International (TWC). Each of these loosely interlocked bodies has its own program of parties, encounters, lectures, outings, picnics, hikes and tours, and the combined fees and admission charges add up to a very handsome flow of revenue.

In 1971, Raymond opened a one-hundred-thousand-dollar "pleasure palace" for his members, which also doubles as his home. The house, high above Los Angeles in the Hollywood Hills, was the property of the late Lenny Bruce and has been fitted as a swinger's dream castle. It contains—among other amenities—the world's largest water bed, a heated swimming pool, a bar, dance floor, programed stereo sound, and a panoramic view of the city below through a picture window taking up the entire wall of the block-sized living room.

You somehow expect the host to receive you in a Mandarin silk dressing gown à la Noel Coward, champagne glass in one hand, ivory cigarette holder in the other. But Raymond wears a battered pair of shorts around the house, doesn't smoke, drinks very little, and drives an old Volkswagen with flower emblems. He is a tall, muscular Svengali type, black-bearded, black-browed, black-haired, with an oddly contrasting high rapid-fire voice and gestures that are volatile rather than mesmeric.

"All this"—he swept an arm around the pleasure palace—"grew out of a starting budget of four hundred dollars. That's all I had. Just four hundred. Will you excuse me—I've got to eat something. Been a long day at the office."

He unwrapped a container of frozen Italian gourmet food and

continued his discourse while watching the water boil around his dinner. "We have an essential philosophy—a guiding theme or whatever you want to call it—and it's harmonious with what America was meant to be. It's the belief that all people should be free to do what they want as long as they don't infringe on the rights of others.

"I was at my print shop recently and I made this point to one of the printers there. And he stepped back and said, 'Gee, John— like 1776!' Well, he was trying to be cute, but he'd built my case for me. He was right. We're not devising anything new—we are based on the essence of the American spirit. Excuse me . . ."

He fished the container out of the water and began digging into the contents. "Will you have some?" He held his fork up like a question mark. "It's excellent. No? Well, as I was saying . . . we're trying to get people involved in what I'd call a free experience—where they're not being legislated in their behavior."

"When did you start this?"

"In 1968," Raymond said, chewing. "I was going to radio school then with the idea of pursuing a broadcasting career. But then I hit on this thought of expanding my social life and perhaps improving my standard of living as well. I had four hundred dollars, so I rented a house and put an ad in the paper announcing, 'Sexual Freedom Movement Now Open in Southern California!' Well, the following day I was on the phone till eleven at night. The response was—just unbelievable." He smiled around a mouthful. "And that's how we got started."

What emerged from this modest kernel is not so much an organization as an environment. Raymond's "pleasure palace" forms the stage setting, his advertising brings in the participants, his ingenuity supplies the movement. In return for their fees the three segments of club members gain admission to a ready-made, exciting and luxurious libertarian world they could never create on their own. The fees run from thirty dollars per weekly membership to a hundred and fifty dollars a year, gatherings are restricted to sixty people at a time, and the current lists of active members total more than a thousand.

"I sell it like an investment. They invest in an idea—also in their trust in me. They trust that I can attract the kind of people they want to meet and give them the kind of background they enjoy. The people who come in *believe* in our project, they *want* to see it work—it's not just a practical business deal; a lot of idealism goes with it."

"But what do they get—in practical terms?"

Raymond's gesture embraced the entire house. "They get involvement. With this as well as with each other.

"They come here for group dynamics—that's when people talk out their problems—or for the Sunday open house or for the parties. They may get leads—introductions—from me, or they may meet someone here by themselves. The important point is"—he raised his fork for emphasis—"they're in on a scene; they're part of the action."

Raymond's parties (gay on Fridays, hetero on Saturdays) have acquired an almost legendary aura of concupiscence, vastly more purple than they actually are. Their real theme is *libertinage* in the widest sense—meaning that the participants are equally free *not* to participate, but to talk, wander around, watch others make love, swim, listen to music or get drunk as the fancy takes them. This theme of perfectly relaxed license, the absence of any pressure to perform, may possibly attract more members than any number of strenuously regimented orgies.

"The difference," he explained, "is that at swingers parties you are more or less compelled to swing. Here you *may* swing, if you feel like it. But I honestly believe that a lot—maybe most—of the members come here for sociability, friendship, rather than to find lovers or even trade partners. I never promise a sex partner to anyone. I merely offer people an opportunity to mingle with kindred spirits. In a conducive setting. They have the run of the house— the only room I keep locked is my private bedroom."

He rose and tipped the remaining scraps of his dinner in the garbage. Then he walked to the picture window and stood for a moment in rapt contemplation of the glowworm splendor below. His voice became mellow.

"You know," he said slowly, "I relate to this very much." He was not, I felt, merely referring to the view.

Most of the liberation movements profess some political tinge, either broadly reformist or anarchistic. But several have gone back to a much older form of erotic group expression—the concept of sexuality as a religious function. They represent a link with pre-Christian cults such as the Greek worship of Aphrodite Kallipygos or the Roman devotions to the god Liber. The rituals they involved were completely orgiastic, though the deities themselves were assumed to be merely approving spectators.

At least one American cult, however, has gone a large step further. Their object of worship actually participates in the proceedings. He is a heavily bearded and highly charismatic black man known as OM, the "Eternal Self-renewing Spirit," whose followers call themselves the United World Community. The tracts they pass out depict a swan-winged male angel copulating with a female angel on a bed of clouds, their halos remaining firmly in place.

OM is best described in his own words, as quoted in his group's periodical *The Winged Envisioner*:

> I Am OM, the Greatest of the Possible Great, the Highest of the Possible High, God of gods, the Longest Awaited Beloved, the Almightiest Champion of the Needy, Whose Most Exalted NAME even the One whom you call God must rely on as the Eternal Source of Strength . . .

On another page we get a little background information:

> Before Time, while holding The Sun in His Right Hand, looking across to His Left, OM spat, and That Created the total world which men and women know . . .

According to OMsian theology, intercourse was originally meant to be a sacred function but was defaced by the "corrupt practices" of mankind. The main task of the United World Community, therefore, is to restore the act to its sacramental place. As their sacred scriptures, *The Song of OM*, phrase it:

> But marrieds as well as unmarrieds who enter enthusiastically into the opportunity of this New Provision wherein all fucking is done

in order to celebrate My Eternal Majesty alone, I prize beyond all other mortals, I watch their act, and I bless it. I enter into it with them, and I make it outstanding in Ecstasy, Divine beyond all description, and most-abundantly fruitful.

The correct procedure is taught at "sacred erotic classes" aimed at "bringing back to maximum life the spirit inherent in the initiates within the class." The reward of the faithful is the Perfect Orgasm . . . "Once experienced, the Perfect Orgasm never diminishes or fades; but rather continues, day after day inundating the recipient in Ecstasy."

Since the United World Community does not divulge statistical information, I can't quote any figures as to the number of OM Lovers at present enrolled. At the time of writing, the movement has chapters and regular services in Chicago, New York, Oakland and Los Angeles. It has also had at least one brush with the law.

This happened at L.A. airport, where OM and three of his adherents (Lovers) were arrested while lying down in the rear of their parked truck. The ostensible charge, burglary, was dropped by the police without any of the accused ever appearing in court. The reason for the swoop seems to have been chiefly an excuse for searching the truck.

Only one freedom group espouses no political or religious cause whatsoever and expresses its philosophy solely in its life style. It had the unlikeliest of founding fathers—a former Trappist monk, who exchanged his vow of silence for a remarkable flow of erudition.

At thirty-seven, Mike Steele is an institution among southern California swingers, although few of them can tell his Sexual Freedom Alliance (SFA) from all the other bodies with similar initials. But the SFA follows an essentially different course. It acts as a clearinghouse and screening device for scores of erotic activities while organizing none of its own. Steele's reputation is based on the fact that he holds the key that opens an entire sex-oriented subculture to his members, a much vaster and more varied scene than could be offered by any single outfit. He also runs what may be America's most knowledgeable introduction service—frequently bringing partners together first, then sending them on to a round of those activities they couldn't enter partnerless.

Steele operates from a Hollywood house that provides both his office and his residence. He employs three secretaries for general business, and one male receptionist who concentrates on homosexuals. His waiting room, usually crowded, could belong to an exceptionally hip dentist. There's a tastefully carnal print on the wall, and the choice of available magazines runs from *Time* to *Screw*, with slightly forlorn copies of the evangelizing Fundamentalist monthly *Plain Truth* thrown in for contrast.

The SFA head is fair, florid and youthful, with a rosy complexion, long hair and a pleasantly pitched speaking voice that occasionally reveals the remnants of a southern accent.

"I was born in Virginia and raised in Mississippi," Steele explained. "Right in the heart of the rural Bible Belt. But my Trappist abbey was in Iowa. I was in there—as a postulant and then as a novice—for almost two years. And prior to that I was in prepseminary with the Benedictines for another two years. So, yes, you might say that I have an—er—religious background."

He lit another of the nonfilter cigarettes he smokes almost uninterruptedly. "But then I, well, began to have problems with the Church. And at twenty-eight I decided to leave. When *that*—which was the underpinning of my entire thinking—had gone, what did that mean in terms of the rest of my life style?" He smiled serenely and marked two distant points on his desk with his fingers. "And that was how we got from there . . . to here."

"What did you do after you left the monastery?" I asked.

"Went back to school, studying accountancy. I was still working as an accountant when I started the SFA. Part-time at first, in the evenings. Then—in 1970—I quit my last job and began to work in my office here."

Steele's work consists largely of interviewing prospective members, although "interviewing" is not really the right term. It is a gauging process of the client's libidinous tastes and qualifications, during which Steele decides where to send the applicant and who with.

He deals with three categories—straight males, straight females, and male homosexuals—each of which fills out a different questionnaire.

"No, we don't enroll lesbians," he said. "First of all, because few of them swing. They prefer to stick to one girl friend. But then also because—well, because I've found that gay men are not hostile toward women, but most lesbians are hostile toward men. And hostility I don't need."

Steele charges fifteen dollars per introduction, one hundred and twenty-five dollars for a year's membership with unlimited introductions. This is apart from whatever his clients have to pay at the various functions he sends them to. The real luxury affairs—he calls them "Disneylands"—run as high as fifteen dollars per couple. "But they have everything—light plays and artificial caves and pools, buffets, and fantastic gadgets," he explained. "The average are much cheaper, around five dollars a couple."

He leaned forward, fixing me with intense, bright-blue eyes. "You see, that's why we don't arrange parties of our own. If we did, we'd be just one more competition scene. As it is now, I can send my members to six—ten—sometimes more functions during any week. Nearly every swingers party in the area registers with us here. And because we send them up to 50 percent of their participants we have a certain amount of control over their arrangements. If I get complaints about the way they run things, I strike them off our list."

"Have you had any trouble with the police?"

"Oh, we've been shopped," Steele said casually. "They've sent plainclothesmen to check us out. But no trouble. All they wanted to see was if we're connected with any form of prostitution—which we aren't."

I brought up the major plus point of the SFA's reputation: "How do you manage your sex balance? Most of the movements are always short of female members."

Steele blew an elliptical smoke ring and stubbed out his cigarette before answering. "Various ways. Our actual membership is only about 25 percent female. They pay lower rates. If they're—uh—specially qualified, nothing at all. But that's only a small part of it." He lit a fresh cigarette, settled back.

"We also get numbers of married women—without their husbands. I have a Mexican lady, for instance, who's a regular. No, her husband doesn't mind at all. So we don't depend on single girls. Nor do we depend on members. Our members have girl friends. And the girl friends have girl friends. So it spreads out." He described a widening circle with his hands. "It's mainly a word-of-mouth process, based on our—well, reputation. The actual ads we run bring in only a small proportion. The rest are attracted by this word-of-mouth publicity. They may never actually *join* the SFA, but they'll date our male members. So once I've determined what type of partner a member wants, I may put in two or three days of telephoning—from one contact to the next—until I get him the right person. Within reason, of course.

"Much of it depends on the man's *purpose*," said Steele. "Whether he wants somebody to go to parties with or a real affair. We have girls on our lists who'll attend parties with almost *any* of our members. Just so they're a couple and can get in. And then there are those who answer specific ads."

"How do they answer—by mail?"

"No, they usually phone. Then they'll come and see someone here at the office. If I'm in, they'll see me."

"You, rather than one of your secretaries?"

"Yes. I do a better job interviewing women than anyone else here. It's a matter of approach." He said it without boastfulness, merely as a statement of fact.

The SFA ads come out in a large number of publications, and with practice you learn to spot them by style alone. They possess a particular trenchant brevity that conveys maximum relevance in minimum space. Their phrasing appears edited by a professional—but not their spelling. The one that sticks indelibly in my mind ran:

Girl would like to exchange sex for Afgahn [*sic*] puppy.

After covering this cross-section of the sexual freedom movements now under way, I was left with a couple of nagging questions: Why are they all run by men? And why do they all find it difficult to attract female adherents?

The truism about women's sexual indoctrination is only a partial answer at best. Millions of women throughout the country have shaken off umpteen other kinds of indoctrination. Against abortion. Against contraception. Against the wearing of trousers. Against drinking, smoking, political violence, motorcycle riding, swearing, drug taking, short hair, and what-have-you. Why, then, are those millions not flocking to the banners of sexual freedom?

The explanation may be that a woman's idea of sexual freedom differs basically from a man's. Whereas to the man it means a widening of his choice of partners, the woman may see it rather as a widening of her role with *a* particular partner. This, too, could be a result of historical conditioning, of course. But if so, it has sunk in considerably deeper than any of the above proscriptions.

What made me reach this tentative conclusion was a curious pattern discernible in the interviews I had with the more enthusiastic movement members. The males enthused about the large variety of girls they met through their organization. The females spoke glowingly about some specific fellow they had encountered through it. Although both parties were praising the same concept, they were actually referring to quite different benefits.

I also talked to a disillusioned New York lady, who had left her movement after three years of membership. "The men," she commented, "think they're onto something new and revolutionary because they get this plethora of sexual opportunities. But, hell, any reasonably attractive gal lives with this plethora from the time she's sixteen. She just can't utilize it because of what *men* may think of her. And those Freedom guys aren't going to change that."

Her words somehow reminded me of an old Arabian fable. The ox, the donkey, and the pig appeared in audience before Haroun-al-Raschid, the mighty Caliph of Baghdad. They complained that whenever humans got mad at each other they didn't call each other "you man," but ox, donkey or pig. It was, they argued, patently unfair and humiliating, as well as illogical.

The Caliph stroked his beard. "By Allah," he finally said, "you are right. Injustice has been done to you. I proclaim that henceforth none of the faithful in my realm shall call others by the names of animals. This I command!"

The trio thanked him profusely and left the palace. When they were outside the ox said to the pig: "And now that old donkey back there thinks his command has helped us."

fourteen

CONS AND KILLERS

The surprising part about the mating trade is not that it attracts sharks, but that it hasn't been swallowed up by them. Considering the vulnerability of the participants, the crime rate seems almost modest—the number of capital offenses definitely so.

Although the field offers a ready-made hunting ground for thieves, confidence tricksters and assorted amateur chiselers, most of them operate on petty-larceny levels. In terms of physical peril it is vastly more dangerous to enter a New York subway station alone at night than to join the most disreputable of dating clubs. Even the ratio of sexual assaults is no higher than in certain grade schools, despite immeasurably better opportunities.

The unique aspect involved is the sex balance of the criminal element. For organized mating is the only venture on record in which as many felonies are committed by women as by men. According to some police authorities, female crooks in the game may actually outnumber males. The superior sense of security with which men generally conduct their quest is therefore quite false. If anything, they have *more* to worry about than the ladies.

To date, America has experienced two sets of multiple lonely-hearts murders, though neither of them matched the baroque melo-drama of the French Landru case.[1] In both instances the killers were women and the majority of victims men.

Belle Brynhilde Poulsatter Sorenson Gunness may have been the first slayer in history to attract prey by means of matrimonial ad-vertising. She certainly had no physical attractions with which to lure them. Photographs show her as a barrel-shaped, heavy-browed matron, weighing perhaps two hundred pounds, with broad, doughy features and the expression of someone who has just drunk vinegar. The farmers who were her neighbors during the seven years of her murder career remembered her as unusually taciturn and aloof. As one of them later testified: "She weren't gabby, that's for sure."

Belle was born in Selbe, Norway, and came to the United States as a child. Very little is known about the early part of her life. When she arrived at La Porte, Indiana, in 1901, she was already the widow Sorenson, aged about forty, with two children and sufficient funds to buy a forty-eight-acre farm a mile out of town. She kept pigs there, which she slaughtered herself.

Apart from her silence, Belle's most remarkable attribute was physical strength. She could hoist a flour sack on her shoulders like a mill hand and lift both her children together with one arm.

Within a year she had married again—a fellow Norwegian named Peter Gunness, who suddenly turned up on her farm one day. The Gunness couple also took in a foster child, Jennie, and for seven months seemed to live in quiet harmony. But just before Christmas 1902, Mr. Gunness was killed when an iron sausage grinder fell on his head from a kitchen shelf.

That, at least, was what Belle told the La Porte coroner, who duly entered a verdict of "accidental death." The widow Gunness collected her late husband's four-thousand-dollar life insurance. In 1903, she gave birth to his son, Philip, which increased her brood to four.

[1] Henri Desiré Landru, the "Bluebeard of Gambais," was guillotined in 1922 for the slaying of ten women, most of whom he met via matrimonials ads. His famous Assyrian spade beard, incidentally, was not "blue" but ginger. Charlie Chaplin based the plot of his murder comedy *Monsieur Verdoux* on his career.

From then on, with monotonous regularity, a certain ad appeared in the pages of several Midwestern matrimonial journals:

> Buxom, comely widow with family, hard-working and affectionate, desires kind and honest husband of Scandinavian birth, preferably Norwegian, to help her lift mortgage on well-stocked 50-acre farm. Sincere men only. Triflers need not apply.

There is a peculiar Grimm's-fairy-tale flavor about the way in which one sturdy Norseman after another knocked at the gate of Belle's castle, was duly admitted, lavishly feasted for a few days or weeks—and never again seen alive. They brought their savings with them, these kind and honest men, a few hundred or a few thousand dollars, but somehow the mortgage on the farm was never lifted. It still kept appearing in the ads, although the money had long gone into Belle's substantial bank account.

While corresponding with her suitors, Mrs. Gunness was nowhere near as dour as in person. One of the letters she wrote to a certain Andrew Helgelein of South Dakota has been preserved as a sample of her style:

"Think how we will enjoy each other's company. You, the sweetest man in the whole world. We will be all alone with each other. Can you conceive of anything nicer? I think of you constantly. When I hear your name mentioned, when one of my dear children speaks of you, I hear myself humming it with the words of an old love song—it is beautiful music to my ears.

"My heart beats in wild rapture for you. My Andrew, I love you. Come prepared to stay forever."

Which, in due course, Mr. Helgelein did.

Out of this cavalcade of nine to a dozen suitors—the exact number was undeterminable—only one returned to the outer world. He was George Anderson from Missouri, and he probably owed his life to the fact that he scared easily. He was served a fabulous Old Country welcoming meal by his hostess, then put to bed in the guest room. Two years later he testified:

"I woke up with a start in the middle of the night. I saw Belle standing over me in her long nightgown with the lamp in her hand. She was peering down and there was a look on her face—I've never seen an expression like that on the face of nobody. It made me kind of cold all over, put me in a cold sweat. I let out a yell and she ran out of the room. I just grabbed my clothes and got out of the place, fast as I could . . ."

Unfortunately, Mr. Anderson didn't relate his experience to anyone until it was too late. In La Porte, Belle explained his departure as she explained the disappearance of all the others: "I don't know what's the matter. Men won't stay with me. They come, and then they pack up and go. I'm not lucky with men."

Suitors were not the only people who vanished from the farm. In 1906, Belle's adopted daughter Jennie likewise evaporated. She had, the widow informed neighbors, "gone West with relatives." Mrs. Gunness had a—possibly unconscious—way with *double-entendres*.

In April 1908, Belle suddenly called on a La Porte attorney with a peculiar request. She said that she was in fear of her life and therefore wished to make her will "in case something happens to me." The menace, she claimed, came from an erstwhile hired man she had dismissed and who was now threatening to burn her house down. The attorney offered to call the police, but Belle wouldn't hear of it. All she wanted was her testament.

The man in question was a husky but dim-witted French Canadian named Ray Lamphere. He had worked on Belle's farm for years, until she ran him off the property. He claimed that she still owed him wages and went around the neighborhood muttering strange things about the widow—though nobody had heard him *threaten* her.

But on the morning after Belle's visit to the attorney, her farm went up in flames. By the time rescuers arrived, there was nothing left but smoldering ruins. In the cellar, the fire fighters found four charred corpses. Three of them were easily identified as the Gunness children. The fourth was the body of a woman with the head missing. She was assumed to be Belle.

Lamphere was immediately arrested and charged with murder. But when the doctors got around to examining the headless corpse, they decided that the dead woman had been at least four inches shorter and some thirty pounds lighter than Mrs. Gunness. Whoever she might have been, she was *not* Belle.

Searching for the missing head, deputies began to dig up the enclosed yard of the farm. Instead of a head they found bodies—stuffed into sacks, shrouded in wrapping paper or blankets. One by one they unearthed the remains of seven men, a girl and two children. They also found bones and scattered limbs belonging to other bodies . . . more bodies . . . perhaps thirteen in all. Together with the four in the burned cellar, it amounted to the biggest charnel house in the annals of American crime.

But who was the headless woman? And where was Belle? Neither of these questions has been answered to this day.

Ray Lamphere was acquitted of murder, but sent to prison for arson. He told several different and garbled versions of his activities on the farm. In one he admitted having helped Mrs. Gunness bury a few of her victims, though he maintained that she did all the killing. She killed her suitors for the money they carried, some visitors because they had become suspicious of what was going on. She slaughtered them the way she did her hogs—smashing them over the head with a cleaver, then cutting their throats. He did not reveal why she hadn't killed *him*. Chances are that Lamphere was the widow's lover for a time, possibly her accomplice. But the murders had begun long before he entered her services and continued after he had left.

No trace of Belle Gunness has ever been discovered. Nor do we know what caused her to murder her own children and flee, although nobody had voiced suspicions against her. She may have lived to a ripe old age somewhere in obscurity.

There is a distinctly old-fashioned, nineteenth-century air about the La Porte horror. The setting was rural, the scene static, the motive straightforward financial gain. In what might be called *modern* multicides the background is usually urban, the operations mobile and the motivations—while ostensibly monetary—tend to have pathologically warped and twisted sexual undercurrents. The second set of America's matrimonial murders—those for which the newspapers actually coined the label "Lonely Hearts Killings"—were textbook examples of the latter genre.

There are people for whom the term *folie à deux* has a chemically explosive meaning, who resemble substances like saltpeter and sulphur, which—harmless while apart—become destructive when mixed. Thoroughly a strange alchemy of personalities each compounds and magnifies the latent evil in the other. If they don't meet, the world rarely gets to know of their existence. But when they do, the result is apt to make headlines of the most gruesome kind. The best-known pair in that category were Loeb and Leopold. And the only reason why Martha Beck and Raymond Fernandez consumed somewhat less newsprint acreage was because neither of them happened to have millionaire parents.

Raymond Fernandez was born in Hawaii of Spanish parentage and made a fair living by swindling elderly women whose matrimonial ads he answered. He looked like a smudged carbon copy of Charles Boyer, wore a toupee to cover both his baldness and a scar on his skull, and dabbled in voodoo practices which—he believed—gave him hypnotic powers of seduction.

Voodoo, however, had less to do with his conquests than his choice of victims. They were, without exception, aging, unattractive and profoundly silly—the kind who would melt at his rococo-sugared flatteries that gave more robust-minded women the giggles. He had an infallible nose for spotting females hungering for attention and the trappings of romance. And it was precisely this talent that guided him like a radio beacon to his fate.

Her name was Martha Beck. She lived in Pensacola, Florida, worked as a nurse in a home for crippled children, and had recently joined "Mother Dinene's Friendly Club for Lonely Hearts." Only some uncanny instinct could have made Fernandez write to her, because, at twenty-six, she was nowhere near the seniority bracket he customarily picked. Martha was monstrously bloated and overweight from a pituitary-ovarian deficiency, racked with loneliness, and ceaselessly tortured by overpowering sex urges caused by her glandular condition. Her psyche was rubbed raw from constant taunts about her size, she had two children from a brief, desolate marriage to a bus driver, and when she received Fernandez's letter—the only response she'd had—she was on the verge of suicide.

On December 28, 1947, Raymond came to visit her in Florida. For Martha it meant the turning point of her life. She was an intensely—almost obsessively—romantic creature who spent most of her spare time devouring *True Confessions* and her nights dreaming about them. Here, at long last, was her Prince Charming, a man who called her "divinely feminine" and who assured her that they had found each other through "psychic destiny." She didn't so much fall in love with Fernandez as become manic about him.

It took Raymond two days to discover that Martha had no money worth taking. He thereupon returned to New York, quite unaware of what he had unleashed. He got an inkling of it when Martha turned up on his doorstep, with her children, determined to move in with him. He ordered her away—she went and came back. He objected to the children—she promptly handed them over to the Welfare Department. He fled to a different address. Martha tracked him down and threatened to kill herself in front of his door if he didn't let her in. She was, she told him, ready to do *anything* except let him go.

Raymond became frightened. The last thing he could afford was to draw attention to himself. He made a final desperate effort to get rid of his succubus. He revealed to Martha how he earned his living, convinced that *this* would cool her ardor. It did nothing of the kind. Martha replied that, since that was his livelihood, she would help him with it. Now Fernandez's resistance collapsed. He was linked to this balloonlike appendage who knew enough about him to put him in jail. It was a link that kept him fastened tight all the way to the electric chair.

One of the eleven women on his correspondence list was a sixty-six-year-old widow in Albany named Janet Fay. Mrs. Fay, a pious Catholic, was enchanted by the religious allusions with which he garnished his letters. She invited him to visit her in Albany and appeared only slightly dismayed when Fernandez brought his "sister" along with him. The charm of the thirty-five-year-old man was sufficient for her to elope with him. After drawing six thousand dollars from her bank account, Mrs. Fay accompanied Ray and

Martha to the apartment they had rented in Long Island. She left behind a cute little note saying, "Surprise!"

What happened there we know only from the couple's court-room confessions, which were probably true in essence if not in detail. Mrs. Fay shared the bedroom with Martha, Fernandez slept on the living-room couch. But during the night the old lady wandered into the living room. Martha followed her and found her "naked, with her arms locked around Ray."

He allegedly called something like, "For God's sake, keep her quiet," and fled to the bathroom. Then, Martha claimed, she blacked out. The next thing she remembered was standing with a heavy ball-peen hammer in her hand and Mrs. Fay lying on the floor with a smashed skull, blood streaming from her forehead.

Fernandez groaned, "What did you do—what did you do?" Martha said, "I don't know. I saw her making up to you and I couldn't stand it."

The man was "shaking and sobbing and dropping things," but under Martha's instructions he got the body wrapped up in a tight bundle. This they buried in the cellar of another place they rented eight days later in Queens.

During the next few weeks Fernandez was flickering with tension, Martha serene and buoyant. She was united with Raymond in a bond that he would never be able to break. For the first time in her life she felt emotionally secure. It was she who persuaded him to follow up another letter he had received via Mother Dinene's friendly service. It came from a cheerful, bespectacled widow named Delphine Downing, who was only forty-one and lived with her small daughter Rainelle in suburban Grand Rapids, Michigan.

Once again Fernandez came a-visiting with his "sister." They stayed at the widow's house for two weeks, Ray and Delphine making marriage plans and sleeping together, Martha—burning with suppressed rage—disturbing them as much as she could.

For what followed we again have to rely on trial confessions, which accounts for the weird unreality of the tale, the impression of dreamlike haphazardness. Martha fed Mrs. Downing sleeping pills in what she believed were lethal quantities. They were not, for when little Rainelle began crying, her mother tried to sit up in bed. Martha, trying to hush the child, began choking her, leaving visible marks on her throat. The mother was struggling out of her daze, and Martha became panicky.

"She'll see the bruises and call the police," she whispered. "Do something."

Raymond picked up the late Mr. Downing's service pistol. Then he shot the widow twice through the head.

Mrs. Downing was buried in the basement of her own home, her killers were left alone with the child. Rainelle cried constantly, at intervals screamed for her mother. Sooner or later neighbors were bound to inquire about the noise. Fernandez's nerves seemed to have reached the breaking point. "Get rid of the kid," he shouted, "smother her—anything—but shut her up."

Martha picked Rainelle up and carried her down to the basement. There, a few feet away from where her mother lay buried, stood a washtub filled with water. Martha held the child's head under water until she stopped struggling. The former children's nurse ("highly competent, patient and gentle") had turned child-killer.

With the same near-irrationality the pair stayed in the house for another two days. Long enough for neighbors to become alarmed at their presence—and the absence of the former occupants. Long enough for the police to arrive. They found two freshly cemented patches in the basement.

Fernandez started confessing within a few hours. He seemed almost relieved to be out of the nightmarish vortex of seduction and murder in which he had spun like a drowning scorpion for a year. Martha was less loquacious, but she backed up everything he said. In March 1949, they were extradited to New York to face trial for the slaying of Mrs. Fay.

To say that the newspapers had a field day with the couple would be an insipid understatement. If ever a future dictator were to seek arguments against freedom of the press, he could cull them out of the New York tabloids of that period. They resembled nothing so much as a circle of demented children prancing around a victim squealing, "Yah, Yah, Yah."

They appeared incapable of mentioning Martha Beck without repeating the fact that she was fat. "Heap of blubber," "233 lbs. of venom," "Blimp Woman," "Cold-eyed Flesh Mountain," "Overweight Monster," "Waddling Virago" and "Flabby Fury," were a few random titulations. You can go through months of press coverage without finding one reference to Martha that didn't include an avoirdupoisal adjective. Sometimes it seemed unclear whether she was being tried for murder or for obesity. And it conveyed a vivid picture of the kind of treatment which—since her childhood—had festered in her soul.

She clung to her naïve romanticism to the end. Her final statement read like the opening of a particularly cloying *True Confessions* piece: "My story is a love story, but only those tortured by love can understand what I mean . . ."

She entered the Sing Sing death chamber twelve minutes after Fernandez. The electric chair had not been designed for her dimensions. She had to wedge herself forcibly between the armrests.

Martha Beck was far from being the "icy killer" of the tabloids, but her type may possibly be the more dangerous. Her scale of values had warped. Human lives counted less than her passion for Raymond; murder for its sake was justified. It is such an unbalanced moral concept rather than innate savagery that characterizes the multicide. To him or her this evaluation is perfectly genuine, not merely a ploy. People whose judgment has become distorted in that way (or been twisted by indoctrination) may view homicide or even genocide as a minor offense compared with, say, disobedience to orders.

About that species an English satirist wrote: "If once a man indulges himself in murder, very soon he comes to think little of robbing, and from robbing he next comes to drinking and Sabbath breaking, and from that to incivility and procrastination."

These are the people who account for the majority of crimes committed in the mating trade—though, fortunately, on less violent levels. Most of them consider the idea of mate-hunting as basically sinful. To them the defrauding of participants is on a par with cheating felons, something that may be done without lowering one's moral self-esteem in the slightest. They always appear vaguely astonished at being called criminals themselves.

A typical example was Mrs. Mimi Kreeger, arrested for mail fraud in 1968. Operating from an Ohio post office box, Mrs. Kreeger wrote sizzling letters to one hundred and fourteen men and three women in distant states, selecting their names from the ad columns of various mating magazines. She promised to visit them for "voluptuous weekends" if they would be kind enough to send her the air fare. At the time of her arrest she had collected nearly four thousand dollars in that fashion. Mrs. Kreeger willingly admitted that she'd harbored no intention of leaving Ohio, her husband and four children. Her explanation was simple and significant: "Well, I never had enough household money, and those people—all they wanted was sex."

This is very much the attitude of the numerous introduction-service swindlers who send out fictitious names and addresses in return for their clients' fees. The fact that these clients "wanted sex" automatically placed them beyond the pale of customers deserving honest treatment. It is, if anything, a supremely *moral* attitude, though the morality doesn't coincide with the law of the land.

The prevalence of women in this particular racket reflects—on a magnified scale—the general rise of female criminality. In 1971, for the first time since its inception, four women figured on the FBI's list of the Ten Most Wanted Fugitives. And the FBI's statistical survey for 1970 showed that since the previous year the number of females arrested for felonies had soared 11 percent, versus only 4 percent of males. Over the last decade, while arrests for all serious crimes were up 73 percent among men, they had risen 202 percent for women.

Within the mating trade they have the decided advantage of dealing with victims who are, to some extent, emotionally involved and therefore highly vulnerable. Many men will disregard even the most elementary precautions when dating a totally strange female. And while they rarely risk their lives that way, they frequently risk their property.

I once met a twenty-five-year-old New York girl who specialized in stealing the cars of her dates. Her method was so primitive and repetitious that one might have assumed she would spend the greater part of her youth in jail. In fact, she'd been caught only once, and let off with a suspended sentence because she was a "first offender" and pretty to boot. Her technique—such as it was—consisted of meeting men at singles functions and letting them drive her home, always giving a phony address. At some point she would ask them to stop and buy her an ice cream to eat on the way. About half of her escorts would climb out, leaving the key in the ignition. Whereupon she simply drove off. She sold the automobiles to various hot-car dealers she knew and changed her pickup grounds by drifting up and down the entire East Coast, scouring singles parties from Manhattan to Savannah, Georgia.

The moral justification she handed me sounded like an echo of Mrs. Kreeger: "Those guys were just after hopping into bed with me." Which, apparently, entitled her to swipe their vehicles.

The mating trade is also a lucrative field for crooks hunting in pairs, since so many swinging events are open to couples only. For them the most common form of knavery is blackmail; either on a petty or on a fairly grandiose scale.

The blackmail business today requires considerably more research than it did just a few years ago. The choice of victims has narrowed to the same degree as public tolerance has broadened and fear of scandal diminished. Whereas the threat of publicizing "indiscreet" photographs was once potent enough to make almost any business or professional man pay up, an increasing number now feel free to paraphrase the Duke of Wellington's famous, "Publish and be damned!"

More than enough people, of course, are still willing to be squeezed rather than face exposure, but their background has to be carefully checked out first. A Los Angeles couple calling themselves John and Frannie Lukas utilized their swingers contacts for that purpose. The Lukases (they were eventually convicted under their real names, neither of which was Lukas) ran ads describing themselves as "unusually attractive" and seeking "high-class couples" for erotic foursomes. Pretending to be ultraselective, they accepted only those partners in which the husband's position rendered him blackmail prone. Since Frannie was a former movie actress who had kept her looks intact, they had plenty of candidates.

The bed in which Frannie cavorted with the husband was covered by a concealed camera, which she could activate by pretending to adjust the bedside lamp. The resultant snaps were sufficiently candid to make a series of husbands pay from five hundred to two thousand dollars rather than have them sent to their employers, board of directors or clients.

The downfall of the pair was due to faulty investigation work. They failed to spot a police sergeant and lady who posed as a funeral-parlor director and wife.

But by far the most popular trick is simply "borrowing" money—popular because it is difficult to prove fraudulent in the legal sense. And here female gullibility outshines the male, sometimes to a degree that makes you doubt the victims' mental faculties.

I know cases of supposely rational women who became engaged to men a few days after meeting them via an ad column. They then handed those gallants what amounted to their life savings "to put down on a house." Which, needless to state, was the last they saw of them.

I know others who met—in the same fashion—"wealthy out-of-town executives," temporarily strapped because they had lost their travelers checks. Could they oblige with a couple of hundred? They could. How did they know these men were either wealthy, executives, or even out-of-towners? Because they'd said so! And they hadn't *looked* like liars!

In one memorable instance I tried to interfere with a stroke of conmanship and promptly got myself thrown out for my audacity. The lady concerned was the aunt of a friend in Florida—a tall, gangling, fiftyish souvenir-store proprietress who dabbled in theosophy and was big on spotting "psychic vibrations." She was smitten with a man who had joined her dating club, a "great, fair, wonderfully positive human being." An Australian, very rich, who owned a huge sheep ranch at Killara in New South Wales, where they would live after marriage.

As tactfully as I could I observed that Killara, New South Wales, was an exclusive residential suburb of Sydney and hadn't a sheep within a hundred-mile radius. Also, that no Australian would call such a property a "ranch." He'd say "station."

Her only reaction was the kind of irritated glance you get for interrupting a good conversation with niggling irrelevancies. What, her expression conveyed, has that to do with the man I'm talking about? I tried again a while later, and this time her response was energetic enough. She informed me that my presence under her roof was no longer desired. "Some people," she announced, "get pleasure out of tearing down others who live on a higher plane."

The end of the affair, as I learned from her nephew, was almost too predictable. The "rancher" didn't lose his travelers checks. Instead, a bank draft from Australia was unaccountably delayed. The vibratory aunt had to help out with several thousand dollars (she never revealed the exact sum). After which her intended vanished. Presumably to a higher plane.

In part the whole depressing pattern of deception is based on people's imagined ability to "know a person." The signs and symptoms on which this knowledge is founded are both numerous and fallacious, ranging from chin structure to the quality of a smile. These are supposedly intelligent businessmen who still boast of gauging character by the way a man shakes their hand and looks them in the eye. Every confidence swindler in the world develops a firm handshake, coupled with the "eye-catch." It's a stock-in-trade they share with politicians.

In the same category is the kindness-to-animals bit, which allegedly denotes a sterling soul. All one can say about that foible is that Heinrich Himmler, Ivan the Terrible and Caligula adored animals and were very kind to them indeed. So, for that matter, was Charles Manson.

The same applies to the even more dangerous fancy that *children can tell.* I've heard this trotted out periodically by doting mommas who assured me with great earnestness that their little ones, somehow, "know good people from bad." I can only hope that their welfare never depended on that ability. The history of crime bulges with evidence to the contrary. Children flocked to the unspeakable Hamilton Fish, who tortured them to death and occasionally ate them.[2] They shied away from the somber-faced Beethoven, who loved them with all his heart.

As far as any kind of facial or behavioral character guidelines are concerned, I can almost vouch for their nonexistence. During my years as a crime reporter I covered around thirty murder trials on three continents, including five for multiple homicide. Not once did I see an accused who *looked* like a killer in the conventional image. Frequently they looked the reverse. Peter Manuel, the Scottish burglar who wiped out two soundly sleeping Glasgow families, had the appearance and manner of an exceptionally bright undergraduate. "Grandma Kroeger," who strangled two crippled oldsters in California, looked and talked exactly like an amiably eccentric grandmother, complete with Rosicrucian pamphlets and rimless specs, which she constantly mislaid. The one feature all of them had in common was an air of unquenchable self-righteousness.

I also discovered that perfectly truthful witnesses are often shifty-eyed, evasive and hesitant, that they may sweat profusely, contradict themselves and lose their tempers. They may also be quite wrong in what they claim to have seen or heard. This does not necessarily indicate that they are lying under oath. Merely that—like most people—they have only hazy recollections of what happened around them at 7:15 P.M. on the night of February 4 a year or two earlier. As one illustrious justice remarked: "God help you if your alibi depends on an honest eyewitness."

The handful of subsequently convicted perjurers I watched in action all gave clear and incisive answers, sat at ease, and never had to be prodded. They'd learned their lessons by heart.

[2] Hamilton Fish was executed for murder and cannibalism in New York in 1936, at the age of sixty-six. He had six children and five grandchildren and had slowly butchered an estimated fifteen children over a period of twelve years.

But this, as I mentioned above, is only part of the deception process, the comprehensible part. There is another aspect to it, touching a barely explored region of the human psyche. We don't even have a scientific term for it, unless we accept the recently coined expression "victimology." Very roughly, this means the subconscious desire of the victim to *be* a victim, to cooperate with his or her victimization, which may range from being lied to to being murdered.

For the most drastic manifestations of this condition the late F. Tennyson Jesse invented the label "murderee." She based this on a phenomenon criminologists have noticed over and over: the macabre way in which certain people seem *drawn* toward their destroyers, the dogged insistence they display in continuing their association with them despite every kind of warning and often in the teeth of their own judgment.

Age, sex and period don't appear to matter. In the 1850s the English medico William Palmer poisoned between twelve and fifteen people, mostly fellow horse players, at a time when the street urchins of his native Rugeley openly called him "Dr. Arsenic." His victims knew his reputation, several loudly voiced their fear of him, yet they continued to let him administer the medicines of which they died in convulsions. (The street urchins, incidentally, were wrong. The Doc's standard poison was strychnine.)

A similar situation came to light in 1966 in Tucson, Arizona, at the trial of Charles Schmid. The twenty-three-year-old "Smitty," an undersized, clownish psychopath, had strangled three teen-age girls and left their bodies in the desert. His last two victims dated him *after* they had heard him boast about his first killing. At the time of his arrest the police estimated that about fifty local teen-agers knew about the murders—including "Smitty's" wife of three weeks, who had married him despite "all the wild things" she had heard about him.

What is this phantom compulsion that links Dr. Palmer's Victorian turf companions with Schmid's teen-agers? The parallel could be stretched as long as criminal history. Around every slayer who continues killing over a period of time we find people who seem almost hypnotically attracted by him or her. And only *certain* people. On the majority the effect of the killer may be decidedly negative—from indifference to repulsion. Only in some does the nearness of potential death trigger an urge for communion that remains as mysterious as it is lethal.

It may be part of a definite suicide syndrome, akin to what makes certain motorists consistently drive beyond safe speeds or play "chicken" on the road. Seeking the proximity of could-be killers may constitute a variation of the toying with near-fatal doses of barbiturates that has claimed so many lives. It might be interpreted as semisuicidal, "giving death a chance" rather than methodically bringing it about.

But this doesn't explain the motive behind the milder forms of "victimology," where the issues are merely fraud or exploitation. For anyone burdened with a sense of responsibility, an encounter with this species becomes a study in frustration. Examples, warnings, even documentary evidence, get you nowhere with them. It is as if you were broadcasting on a wavelength that doesn't reach the particular receiver in their minds. Or—and this can be worse—they may abandon one exploitative relationship and promptly start another . . . of exactly the same type.

Love, infatuation or strong physical attraction play a role, but not always, and never to a degree that would render such blindness explicable. It seems more closely related to Alexander Pope's line: "We first endure, then pity, then embrace." There are women who quite consciously despise the men who leech on them, yet not only permit them to continue but derive a vicarious pleasure from the process. If this is masochism it is certainly the most oblique and sublimated version of that condition. The earmarks are rather those of a form of atonement.

Over several years I had the opportunity to observe a man who seemed to possess a radar antenna for females of that kind. A native of Hungary and originally named Ladislas, he had switched to Leslie—or Lee—after settling in New York. He was the living antithesis of a Casanova type—about sixty, short and rotund, with a fringe of grayish hair around his bald pate that gave him the appearance of a melancholy ostrich. He ranks as one of the most stupendous bores I have encountered. He had two jokes of classical vintage, which he would deliver unfailingly on every occasion. The rest of his conversation consisted entirely of the various misfortunes that had befallen him that particular day.

Yet this gentleman had been more or less kept by women for the greater part of his adult life. He employed a stock euphemism for the process. Mabel had *assisted* him in this, Sarah had *assisted* him in that—and so on through a whole galaxy of *assistants*. What it meant was that the ladies concerned had supplied him with the money for his innumerable business ventures (mostly fly-blown little antique shops and photographic portrait studios with audible death rattles), and when they—invariably—failed, put up more money to save him from fraudulent bankruptcy charges.

Ladislas-Leslie belonged to at least fifteen dating services and matrimonial bureaus, apart from answering mating ads on a free-lance basis. The greater portion of his time, in fact, was spent writing contact letters and attending appropriate functions. To watch him was to marvel. He would peer nearsightedly around the gathering, attune his invisible beacon and—like a guided missile— zero in on his target.

Those targets were by no means always unattractive, though he wasn't fussy in the matter of looks. At various times his *assistants* were indisputably charming, well-groomed widows or divorcées with excellent incomes and twice his personality. But the outcome was always the same. The ladies would either stake him to, or bail him out of, another stillborn enterprise, after which he would politely bid them adieu and depart for fresh pastures. They not only accepted this with good grace, but occasionally took him back for a second round, which ended exactly like the first.

It must be said in Leslie's honor that he never actually *cheated* his amours out of cash. The money they gave him always went for the purpose designated, and its inevitable collapse left him genuinely broke. When he promised them marriage it was always with the proviso, "After I get the business on its feet." And since he never did, he couldn't be accused of breaking his plighted troth.

I once asked Leslie how he managed to wring such sizable sums from ladies who obviously knew how many beans make five. He considered the question gravely for a moment. Then he said with his faint Magyar accent: "Well, sometimes I have to weep. But mostly I appeal to them to save my good name. They can tell I come from distinguished ancestors."

I never really solved the enigma of Leslie's success via consistent failure. I suppose that was the reason he never lost his fascination for me. I only had one occasion to quiz one of his conquests in private. She was a smart, forceful widow in her early fifties, with a shattering laugh and a bundle of General Motors shares.

She appeared quite willing—nay, determined—to discuss our mutual friend. "Poor Lee," she said. "Always trying so hard."

"Trying what?" I asked with curiosity.

"Oh, everything. Maintaining his dignity. Making good. But it's hard for a man with his principles."

I thought perhaps I hadn't heard right. "What principles?"

"Well," she smiled coyly, "like not marrying until he can keep a woman the way she was—well, accustomed to. How many men feel that way nowadays? I know he isn't much good in business—but he doesn't give up."

"No," I admitted, "he doesn't."

"Now, my late husband," she said, "was very good in business. Office supplies. And that's all he ever talked about—nothing to do with me at all. But when poor Lee talks about his business—he's talking about *me*, you understand?"

I was beginning to, slightly.

"Of course, he's hopelessly impractical. And trusting. People are always taking advantage of him. He just wasn't brought up for this money-grubbing scene here. He's—kind of lost in it. You know, I've actually seen him cry with unhappiness. Real tears." She indicated the tears on her cheeks. "That's why he needs somebody like me to—uh—assist him a bit. And that's quite a good feeling. Being needed."

The last time I saw Leslie, he had opened a picture-framing shop on the Lower East Side. Financed by the lady with the GM bundle. They were going to get married after he got the business on its feet.

fifteen

OLD VIEWS AND NEW HORIZONS

The strangest paradox of contemporary mate-matching is the way millions of participants have reverted to one of its most archaic forms. There are probably more modern Americans seeking partners via astrology than the total number of ancient Greeks and Romans that ever did so.

From being primarily augurs, U.S. astrologers are swinging over to becoming the sex counselors of the Aquarian generation. At this moment the market is being inundated with paperbacks, columns, pamphlets and records telling rapt audiences how to find, select, capture and hold their mates by using zodiacal guidelines. Dozens of periodicals are featuring regular planetary advice for lovers—one of the field's hottest sellers is entitled *Astrology and Sexual Compatibility*—and two brochures offer illustrated instructions as to which coitus positions go best with what zodiac sign.

Scientific-minded astrologers may frown on this utilization of the "Royal Art," just as they frown on most of its predictive uses. But the concept has been so widely accepted among the under-thirties that they frequently exchange planetary signs before asking each other's names. Or—to facilitate the process—they may wear them around their necks, in their lapels or as sweater designs.

The theory behind this symbolism is fantastically complex, open to at least as many variables and interpretations as psychoanalysis. Not only does the individual's horoscope have to be considered, but also his or her momentary aspect in conjunction with the other person. Thus two signs may be fundamentally incompatible ("square"), such as Leo and Scorpio. Or they may be intrinsically matable, e.g. Libra and Gemini, but one of them passing through an adverse planetary period that makes romance inadvisable for the moment. It isn't enough merely to know each other's astrological profile; juxtaposition has to be checked constantly as well.

Each of the twelve zodiac signs, or "houses," is supposedly imbued with certain sexual characteristics, which may be diluted or mingled if the subject was born "on the cusp" of a neighboring sign. Sagittarians, for instance, are inclined to be romantically venturesome, but may be restrained by the conservative and inhibiting influence of the adjoining Capricorn. Libra is a passive symbol, the idealistic monogamist, but stands next to Scorpio, the potentially most promiscuous sign of all. Gemini, the Twins, embody both sexes and are therefore the "house" of homosexuals. In an individual, however, this may merely mean that he or she displays the attitudes of both sexes at certain times.

The traditional form of planetary matching was for an astrologer to compare the horoscopes in question, pronounce on their compatibility and decide on an auspicious date for the wedding. The do-it-yourself methods employed by current believers would have struck the ancients as ludicrous quackery.

But since the arrival of computerized horoscoping in 1967, it was only a question of time until matchings likewise would be handled electronically. There are half a dozen outfits in America now doing this. The principle on which they operate, however, differs sharply from that of the computer matchmakers (see Chapter 4). The astrological matchers do not couple partners from a pool of prospects. They merely compare the horoscopes of two—at the most three—persons, whose details are sent to them. A tentative selection, in other words, must already have taken place before the computer is consulted.

"No, it isn't always a question of a girl trying to decide between two boys," said Eugene Brown, director of Zodiactronics. "Often it involves members of the same family. People wanting to know how they're liable to get along with their future in-laws, for instance. But the majority of our clients are straight one–one matches."

Zodiactronics' offices on New York's Fifth Avenue have the same nonoccultist air of streamlined efficiency you would find in any computer company. The only unusual touch is supplied by a sign on the wall saying simply GALILEO.

"Oh, *that*," Brown smiled a little wistfully. "That's to remind me that I'm supposed to write a book about him. But . . . I never got around to it. No time."

With gray-speckled hair, executive glasses and mellifluously persuasive voice, Brown could pass as a marketing specialist or advertising man—both of which he has been at some stage. "I'm not an astrologer myself," he said frankly. "That's the department of my fellow director. But I believe strongly in what we're doing."

What Zodiactronics does is offer clients Compatibility Profiles based on astrological birth data they supply. The information goes into an IBM/360 computer, which then comes up with a report running some eight to ten pages, comparing the charts, analyzing character traits, pointing out special areas of harmony and discord in the partners, adding advice on possible improvements that lie within the powers of the participants. It also keeps a score, from 0 to 100, on each person's rating in a particular field. The final arithmetical summary separates the scores for total compatibility and attraction. The two may differ sharply; lots of people come out with a very high attraction figure and a very low compatibility total. They can draw their own conclusions from this.

The process costs eight dollars per couple, another five dollars for a third profile. What clients get out of it depends as much on their attitudes as on the scores. In the Improvement bracket the computer's advice may be: "The one with both Mars and Venus in negative signs is more passive sexually. You can improve this relationship by increasing the aggressive sexuality of the one who has the balanced Mars and Venus. This creates a more magnetic attraction, regardless of which one of you is male or female."

Whether this analysis is accurate remains a moot point. It may even be irrelevant. For the parties concerned already know that they have at least one area in common: their interest in astrology. Which is more than tens of thousand of other couples can claim.

It is also more than can be established by the very latest of mating techniques, which is rapidly assuming the proportions of a fad. This is the matching of brain waves, particularly of Alpha waves. The human brain produces billions of electronic impulses, which can be recorded and traced on a machine, the electroencephalograph (EEG). They are divided into four distinct wave lengths: Alpha, Beta, Theta and Delta. It is Alpha, which predominates when a person is in a relaxed state, that has captured the public imagination.

At the moment, there are at least two dozen different Alpha-detectors being marketed commercially, ranging from reasonably sensitive machines to outright junk boxes. Several do nothing more than pick up the sound of scalp movements. But a number of entrepreneurs, operating in improvised "laboratories," charge between ten and thirty-five dollars to match these impulse graphs for alleged "sexual and spiritual compatibility." Since there isn't a shred of evidence that Alpha waves are even remotely connected with a person's sexuality, they could just as well be matching their customers' dandruff.

Their clients undoubtedly are of the same kind as those seeking a shortcut of the mating procedure by studying "Psycho-Command Power." This is an extraordinarily handy knack, since it enables the practitioner to "materialize" almost anything—from piles of ready cash to one's ideal mate.

The procedure is vividly explained in a book authored by one Scott Reed, entitled *The Miracle of Psycho-Command Power*. Mr. Reed relates that after years of researching in scientific and occult libraries, he discovered "the supreme command for summoning desires out of thin air." For him, he reveals, it meant a new home, a new car, plus "ten thousand dollars . . . twenty thousand dollars . . . thirty thousand dollars . . . yes, and more!"

For others it can fulfill different purposes. Among his quoted examples: "Bradford D. bemoaned the fact that he lived alone. At thirty-five he was a lonely, miserable bachelor. He began using the SUPREME COMMAND with Psycho-Command Power, to ask for love and companionship. Soon afterward . . .

"The doorbell suddenly rang, and a beautiful tall blonde young woman appeared, who introduced herself as Elizabeth. As in a daze, she followed him . . . and their date was followed by many intimate revelations . . . and many other attractive young ladies who were magnetically attracted to him."

You can mail-order Mr. Reed's recipe for six dollars and ninety-five cents. At this price it may put computer dating out of business.

Although the analogy may seem far-fetched, brain-wave matchings and psycho-commands are equally part and parcel of a cultural scene that demands *instant* everything, from coffee to compatibility. There is even an electrical device advertised as "instant orgasm." The purest expression of this drive for immediate and almost effortless results is the pill-for-every-problem syndrome that manifests itself in the nine hundred or so psychotropic drugs currently on the U.S. market.

Psychotropic means mind-altering. It embraces the entire family of antipsychotics, tranquilizers, aphrodisiacs, analgesics, antidepressants, euphorics, psychedelics and intoxicants—an avalanche of chemically induced bliss. In the Age of Drugs, when mood-conditioning appears just a pill away, almost any scheme of push-button mate selection strikes people as at least feasible. In our own fashion we have grown as naïvely acceptant of miracles as medieval peasants.

But just as many of the nonprescription drugs are placebos, working chiefly by imagination, so most packaged mating games turn out to be exactly that—games. What's more, they are games played according to rules fast becoming obsolete.

The so-called sexual revolution has not yet achieved anything like total victory. The great mass of middle Americans, the proverbial "silent majority," still acts pretty much according to the dicta of the 1950s. But the forces of change already dominate two extremities from which their influence must eventually prove decisive: the opinion-shaping media at one end, and the junior generation at the other. Barring unforeseen upheavals, their ideas seem destined to become the norms of the future.

As yet, however, they have only accomplished a change of people's attitudes rather than their actions. They have made them doubt their old behavior pattern without inspiring them with much confidence in the new. This has resulted in a state of moral confusion which—especially among women—amounts to a form of schizophrenia. Their actions, still governed by traditional mores, are no longer in accord with their newly adopted mental concepts.

It has also created considerable fury among those who knew how to play a winning game in the old setting and feel less sure about the new. Their spokeswoman could well be Anita Roddy-Eden Manville from Atlanta, Georgia, who won a jackpot in the old style. It came in the gnomelike shape of the fabulously wealthy Tommy Manville, who made her his ninth wife in 1952. (Mr. Manville had two more before dying in 1967.)

The dazzling blonde and highly temperamental Mrs. Manville IX saw nothing much wrong with the setup as it was then, but plenty with how it is now. As she recently told a London reporter:

"In my heyday, every girl in America had this dream of marrying a millionaire. But today, what interest do they have in material things? They'd rather find a pad in Greenwich Village. It's sad. In those days marriage was important where today it's unimportant . . .

"Women have always had freedom to get what they want. If you're strong, you can always get what you want. Women's Lib, uh? I'd like to knock that Gloria Steinem on her arse. If we were on a television show together there'd be a fist fight. She deserves it if anyone does."

Regardless of how one feels about Anita Manville's views, they are certainly clear-cut, positive, and devoid of internal conflicts. She called herself "a horrible prude" and seemed as proud of that as she was of capturing a multimillionaire, whom she dubbed as "an idiot" in the course of the interview. The old rules suited her fine. The entire gossip-column-Reno-divorce-alimony-headline atmosphere of twenty years ago was a world she accepted and coped with very efficiently.

The trouble with the champions of the new—still emerging—moral order is that their views aren't equally concrete. While fully aware of what they *don't* want, they are less certain of what they *do* want. This was brought home to me during my conversation with Ms. Jacqueline Michot-Ceballos, president of the New York City chapter of the National Organization for Women (NOW), the largest and most influential of the various women's liberation bodies.

Ms. Ceballos, Louisiana-born and with Creole ancestors, is a dark-eyed brunette of deceptively nonchalant charm. Her *léger* smile vanishes the moment the conversation hits an emotional nerve. Then her whole supple body tenses and a cutting edge creeps into the lilt of her voice. The transformation is instantaneous and startling, and it occurs whenever you mention the very past Mrs. Manville found so blissful. A case of one woman's meat . . . etc.

"I came to New York from Louisiana as a girl, to study music and become an opera singer," she told me. "Sure, I had plenty of dates, but I just hated the routine. Why? Well, look, the boy paid—because the world is so arranged that *he* had the money. So we went where *he* wanted to go. Dinners and movies and night-clubs. When all the time *I* wanted to go to concerts and museums and the opera."

She eventually married a Colombian and was living in Bogotá with her husband and their four children when she read Betty Friedan's *Feminine Mystique*. "It was like a revelation to me," she said. "It changed my life."

Ms. Ceballos' new life is undoubtedly less comfortable than her old. She receives no pay for her job with NOW, which keeps her frantically busy for stretches no office worker would put up with. She earns her living by lecturing to groups all over the New York area. Her two daughters are with her, the sons with their father.

You get the feeling that she would gladly work twice as hard if it meant achieving the aims of her movement.

But what are these aims? What is the ideal social arrangement at the end of NOW's rainbow?

"The ideal state?" She smiled rather pensively. "A place where anyone can ask anyone for a dance, for a date, an affair, marriage, regardless whether it's him or her that does the asking. But this can only be achieved if we get equality of opportunity and of income. This would bring together the divergent aims of the sexes. Now the man is after sex and the woman after a relationship. And why? Because her standard of living depends on the male—so she has no choice in her aims. With equal incomes, *both* could decide just what they wanted, what they *really* wanted, not what is dictated by economic necessity."

"Well, they get equal incomes in Russia," I put in. "Would you call the women there liberated?"

She shook her head vigorously. "I've been to Russia. And to Eastern Europe. The women there all tell you how 'liberated' they are—how they work as doctors and dentists and sea captains and all that. But when I asked them if they'd ask a man to go out with them, they all threw up their hands in horror and chorused, 'No! It is not customary!' What kind of liberated women are these, I ask you!"

She needn't have told me; I had seen the positively Chekhovian dating and mating patterns still in vogue in the U.S.S.R. (Just two years ago student bodies at Moscow University were actually arguing about whether or not it was proper for a boy and girl to kiss on a first date. The majority believed it was not. It smacked, they declared, of "bourgeois frivolity.")

But Ms. Ceballos had illustrated the basic inconsistency of her statements. On the one hand, she and most women's libbers expound the thesis that economic equality would rectify our male-dominated mating system. On the other hand, she admits that in those countries where it exists it has done nothing of the kind. Not even after a period of more than half a century. In fact, the reverse happened. Immediately following Bolshevik Revolution, there was a brief span of genuine egalitarianism, lasting into the early 1920s. From then on, the system steadily regressed into a Victorian morality mold disguised as "proletarian self-respect," more stringently puritanical than Babbit's Midwest. It deprived women even of those surreptitious liberties a small minority had enjoyed in Czarist times.[1]

In 1971, two pretty coeds of the University of California conducted a revealing social experiment. Linda Dankman and Candy Cooley were working on a class paper entitled "A Sociological Study of the Divergence of Sexual Dimorphism." For the sake of research they decided—temporarily—to adopt masculine dating roles.

They would ask a number of boys out for dates, pay all the expenses involved, open doors, light cigarettes and initiate whatever petting was to take place. The results were interesting, if not altogether unexpected.

Some men turned down their date offers saying, "I don't think we know each other well enough," or "A friend of mine just arrived in town." As Linda remarked, "I was just waiting for one boy to tell me he had to wash his hair that night." The eleven dates they actually landed all reacted in a more or less standard fashion.

Staying within what the girls called "traditional American date form," they arranged to hold the men's hands, put their arms around them and kiss them good night.

"Guys thought we were out for a little bit of action, but we didn't really have problems," Linda related. "A couple of guys would get it on and we'd just say, 'Hey, man, what are you doing?' You can't aggress to a certain point and not expect the males to take over."

This, it should be noted, despite the fact that the girls were in the paying—economically dominant—position. Most of the men claimed that they had enjoyed their turnabout rendezvous. None of

[1] It is interesting to note that the Soviets never managed to eradicate that allegedly capitalist evil—prostitution. They merely rendered it uncomfortable and varied the forms of payment. In the famine years of the early 1930s it was food, in the 1950s mainly foreign cosmetics and nylons. Today it's back to cash.

them knew that they were being used as guinea pigs in an experiment. And not a single one called the girls back for another date!

The crux of the problem appears to lie very much deeper than financial inequality. As Soviet Russia proved, even fifty years of egalitarian job opportunities don't affect the peculiar social stance now termed *male chauvinism.*

The stance undoubtedly originated in primeval times and was based simply and brutally on superior physical strength. Man made the rules because he had the muscles to enforce them. He also had the meat he brought back from the hunt as an economic inducement to obedience. Woman's only bargaining point was her sex, and even that to a limited degree, because she could be made to surrender it by force. But as it represented her only means of obtaining some of the good things the Pliocene Period offered, she had to learn to bargain with it, to control it, to indulge in it not so much when she wanted sex but when she wanted something else.[2]

From this perpetual need to control, to utilize sex for non-sexual purposes, grew the—in natural biological terms—anomalous situation we face today. The English authoress Elaine Morgan summarized it in her book *The Descent of Woman:*

> We are not the match for Homo sapiens that we were originally designed to be. We chase after him for love, companionship, excitement, curiosity, security, a home and family, prestige, escape, or the joy of being held in his arms.
> But there still remains a basic imbalance between the urgency of his lust and ours. I believe this imbalance was not in the original primate blueprint. It's a scar of evolution, not man's fault. God knows it isn't woman's, either.

This—one might say *unnatural*—imbalance, plus woman's procreative role, has colored every mating arrangement in human

[2] Contrary to traditionalist legendry, this is not the case in the more highly developed animal species. Among carnivores, particularly the large cats, the female hunts not only for herself but for her young as well. Father Lion does *not* bring home his prey for the family, as the schoolbooks still have it. The human female is also the *only* mammal that ever gets mated against her will.

history. The point that woman's sexuality appeared somewhat more restrained, combined with the fact that only she got pregnant, would have rendered a perfectly equal position difficult in any case. What made it impossible—and deliberately so—was that mankind chose to institutionalize and sanctify this inequality by means of religion.

Every one of humanity's great faiths preaches antifeminism to *some* extent—not so much in original concept as by subsequent interpretations and additions. The founders of these creeds—with the possible exception of Muhammad—were above sexual bias, but their apostles, disciples and successors were steeped in it, sometimes to the point of phobia. They were men who regarded sex and their own fleshly urges with distrust, often disgust, and held woman responsible for arousing them. Not, perhaps, a very logical conclusion, but an understandable one.

At the moment, it is fashionable in America to single out Judaeo-Christianity as the sole exponent of spiritual antifeminism, to see a more equitable balance in non-Western religions. This is as far from reality as the legend of the family-providing he-lion. In Muhammad's own words, spoken in the tenth year of the Hegira: "And treat your women well, for they are with you as captives and prisoners; they have not power over anything as regards themselves. And ye have verily taken them on the security of God, and have made their persons lawful unto you by the words of God." He expressly authorized Muslims to shut their wives up in separate apartments and to "beat them with stripes, yet not severely."

The currently prevailing form of Buddhism teaches men that reincarnation in the form of an animal is preferable to returning as a woman. And Hinduism, despite its numerous female deities, accords earthly women little more than slave status. India's female prime minister is—theologically—as much of a paradox as Israel's.

Judaism and Christianity merely appear more male chauvinistic because they are closer at hand. Jewish girls know that their menfolk recite a daily prayer containing the words: "Blessed art Thou, O Lord . . . for not making me a woman." The Christian world for years has been listening to the endless, convoluted, acrimoniously hair-splitting arguments among church bodies as to whether or not women are fit to be ordained and to preach, and if so, how often, with what authority and on which subject.

St. Paul's distaste for sexuality in any form was so pronounced that he left us with the possibly most grudging affirmation of marriage on record: "If they cannot contain, let them marry: for it is better to marry than to burn." St. Thomas called woman "a male gone awry," risking blasphemy in order to express his antipathy. And St. Ambrose, after explaining that Adam had been deceived by Eve in Paradise, concluded that "it is right that he whom that woman induced to sin should assume the role of guide lest he fall again through female instability."

This attitude became, if anything, more pronounced after the Reformation. Luther declared: "If a woman grows weary and at last dies from childbearing, it matters not. Let her only die from bearing, she is there to do it."

The female's natural body functions, assuredly bestowed upon her by the divine creator all religions claim to serve, were somehow twisted into obscenities. Her menstrual cycle became a recurring period of uncleanliness, the "curse," the "foul flow," the "time of impurity," during which all creeds recommended that man shun her; some even banished her to isolated rooms. The echo of these taboos is still audible in the industry that has grown around menstruation, which manages to produce hygiene advertisements that can cover an entire column with syrupy gush without once mentioning *that* word.

There are three ways in which human beings can respond to this kind of psychic and physical pressure: open rebellion, sullen submission or philosophical acceptance. Women never had even the remotest chance to rebel. You cannot sulk, en masse, over forty or so centuries. Only acceptance remained, palliated by a strange —yet thoroughly human—enthusiasm for the very doctrines that enslaved and humiliated them.

Women showed themselves the most ardent champions of every religious tenet evolved by man, clinging to the most orthodox and oppressive portions of it long after the majority of males were ready to abandon them. Without the unswerving support of their female flock, the more archaic forms of Judaism, Catholicism and Hinduism would probably have disappeared by now.

While this may seem incongruous, it is nevertheless quite consistent with mankind's historical behavior pattern. The mechanisms of colonial administration were based on precisely that formula.

Every modern colonial empire—and several of the ancient ones—was held largely by garrisons of natives, with only the commanding officers belonging to the ruling nation. These native cohorts proved themselves not only loyal, but often fanatically devoted to the cause of their alien masters. For over a hundred years the crack troops of the British and French empires included Sikhs, Hausas, Spahis and Senegalese—drawn from the very people they had subjugated.

Apart from this, apparently universal, trait of devotion to one's overlord, women also had an instinctive adherence to the *status quo*, regardless of its form. Change meant upheaval, which always entailed physical dangers for them and their children. Better an uncomfortable but familiar order than the perils and dubious improvements of turmoil. Thus they fought tooth and nail against the abolition of widow-burning in India, of the veil and the harem in Turkey, of foot-binding in China, of child marriages in Egypt; just as they numbered among the most violent opponents of female suffrage, divorce reform and birth control in Western countries. Which, while undoubtedly irrational, is certainly no more so than a religious dogma that worships a female image as divine, yet calls its earthly prototypes "unclean vessels."

Throughout most of history most women accepted the place men assigned to them—whether it was in purdah, in the harem or in the kitchen. Very few voiced the sentiments of John Stuart Mill's wife, Harriet, who wrote: "We deny the right of any portion of the species to decide for another portion what is and what is not their 'proper sphere.' The proper sphere for all human beings is the largest and highest which they are able to attain to."

Since, for women, the higher spheres were attainable only through marriage, that institution became the lodestar of their lives *in whatever shape they knew it.* Anyone trying to tamper with it—even for their supposed benefit—aroused their deepest suspicion and hostility. This included the English reformers (all men) who battled on behalf of the Married Women's Property Bill, designed to give a wife some measure of control over her own possessions. The Victorian husband of a hundred years ago owned not only everything his wife brought into the marriage, but also whatever she might acquire later, and could deprive her of it any time he thought fit. He was legally entitled to keep a mistress on the earnings of his wife, regardless of whether he was living with his spouse or separated from her!

Before achieving victory, these reformers endured torrents of abuse from church-affiliated ladies, who accused them of "trying to loosen the sacred bonds of matrimony." They were the petticoated parallels of the grizzled Sikh havildar (sergeant) who implored his British colonel to assure him the English would never leave India. "Because if you do," he said, "there will not be a virgin or a rupee remaining between Calcutta and Bombay."

The invention of the pill, a somewhat more equitable moral code and improved economic opportunities cannot change such an atavistically ingrained attitude overnight or even over a few decades. Marriage, a feeling of permanence, will continue as the paramount female mating aims for many years yet. So will the subconscious assumption linked with them—that sex is something women do for men, as a kind of *quid pro quo* for affection, security and status.

The women's liberation movement has so far only affected our social double standard, without altering much of the psychological value system behind it. Most men still regard their nonmarital sex experiences as conquests; most women still vaguely as surrenders. Until these contradictory viewpoints have been reconciled, the mating trade in all its aspects remains a process of buying and selling—frequently with faked coins.

While it is within the powers of organized femininity to break down economic barriers and force entry into every male stronghold, it can't touch the notions of sexual conquest embedded in man's mind. The suggestions advanced by some overwrought extremists—

boycott by means of celibacy or lesbianism—are patently unenforce-
able. It's like trying to improve a city's water supply by advocating
that half the inhabitants drink only orange juice.

It may prove equally difficult to eradicate from the female mind
the conception of sex as a trading commodity, to be bartered for
something else. In her essay *The Liberated Woman,* writer Midge
Decter expressed the traditional feminine view of marriage as a
"transaction"—the male giving up "blind boyhood lust" and assuming the responsibilities of supporting a family in return for a
comfortable home and an available body in his bed. The fact that
this essay was published as part of a book in 1972 shows how
deeply etched this image still is.

But not until *both* parties agree on their aims and are in a position to state them without subterfuges, will the mating game
become a mutual quest for happiness rather than the camouflaged
form of blackjack it is today.

Meanwhile—and it may be a long meanwhile—we have to find
our bearings in the confusing twilight of the moral and sexual
interregnum through which we are passing. The various social
get-together devices aren't much help in that respect. They don't
teach the altered viewpoints needed for the shifting of roles sym-
tomatic of the waning of one era and the birth throes of another.

A few organizations, unconnected with the actual process of
mate-seeking, are attempting to do just that. One of them is the
Institute for Advanced Study of Rational Psychotherapy, whose
motto is a sentence by the Stoic philosopher Epictetus: "Men are
not disturbed by the things that happen to them, but by their
view of these things."

The Institute shares a stately mid-Manhattan town house with
the affiliated Institute for Rational Living. Both are the creations of
Albert Ellis, a Ph.D. in clinical psychology, who achieved nationwide fame with a series of books on sex subjects published in the
1950s.

Ellis, who works a routine fourteen-hour day, looks as if he had
been loosely strung on a frame of high-tension wires. A thin,
angular, carelessly dressed man of fifty-nine, he is one of the rare

individuals who can be dogmatic with his mouth full. He was having a Spartan lunch while talking to me and drove home points with emphatic gestures unhampered by the dry cracker between his fingers. His hawkish profile, topped by a wild shock of graying hair, give him a messianic air in striking contrast with his New Yorkese style of speech. His self-assurance is overwhelming and further reinforced by a flat rapid-fire delivery that machine-guns rather than addresses listeners.

Ellis' rational-emotive psychotherapy is based on the premise that emotional disturbances stem from irrational philosophies, meaning viewpoints. His Institute for Rational Living believes that people can be taught to live sane, self-actualized lives, to re-educate themselves emotionally by discussion, reading, and considerable homework. Together these therapy courses, seminars and workshops —combined with the Living School (a nongraded establishment for children from six to nine)—amount to one of the most comprehensive attempts to reshape value patterns now in process.

I asked Ellis how he tackled the divergence of aims that poisons the entire mating scene.

"By preparing people for it. I tell my women clients that the men out there are going to be after their ass. But what's so awful about that? Why shouldn't they be? Why *should* they relate first and screw second? The sting—the trauma—is the horseshit around it. The shock of rejection. 'All he wanted me for was a lay, therefore I'm no good.' So I tell them to stop defaming themselves because all the man wanted was a lay. That's his nature—it has nothing to do with *them.*"

He pointed a bony finger at me. "What's more, I tell them that the males who're *out* after love first are almost invariably schnooks —losers. A self-respecting man *is* out after a lay! What I specifically do is what I do with all my clients, men and women. I take their basic philosophy, which is 'It's Awful!', and I get them to change it to 'Tough Shit.' That's the way it is—now how do I go about being happy under these difficult circumstances which I didn't create—which I don't want—but which I'd better use."

"In other words, you take the sting out of the situation."

"I get them to stop the *awfulizing* about a situation that is merely inconvenient for them. And then"—he gave a busy grin— "I get them to do very well in most cases."

"But have you noticed any change in the general desire of women for permanence—meaning marriage?"

"Yes, some. I've found an increasing number of bright, educated women's lib girls who—first of all—don't want children, and secondly, don't want marriage. They want a relationship. So there is *some* change. But it's a small minority and they're not typical women. Typical women's lib, maybe, but not typical women. Most women —I might say unfortunately—aren't in women's lib."

Ellis' creed is rationalistic and existential almost to the point of hedonism. Yet it has an undertone of illusion-shattering harshness some people may find more difficult to bear than any number of psychic traumas. As Ellis told another interviewer:

"The reason you're here is because you're here, and you don't ask asinine questions like, 'What is my identity?' That's a nutty question if there ever was one. You say 'What am I going to do to enjoy myself now that I'm here?'—that's the purpose. I mean there is no cosmic purpose, no gods, no devils of any kind; that's all horseshit. Man has this biological propensity to believe in magic. He won't accept the reality that he's only got seventy-five years . . ."

This may be the true voice of the interregnum. It can't be the voice of permanence, because humanity won't function with its feet planted, so to speak, in midair. Stop the quest for the cosmic purpose and you stop every other quest as well.

But Ellis' tenet of acceptance—of recognizing a situation in its true proportions and mentally adjusting to it—could well be the recipe for our time of transition. The ancient Stoics and Epicureans held similar concepts, though they expressed them rather more elegantly.

Acceptance in this sense, however, is not confined to any particular *status quo*. It means, above all, acceptance of change. The parts men and women play in the nuclear age cannot be the same as they were in an agricultural and early industrial society; no matter how well this might suit some of them. Trying to keep them anchored in that phase is like stopping one hand of a clock while the other marches on. This can only result in broken clockwork.

The reshaping and relearning of relationships now gradually taking place on the marital and family scene must eventually transform the mating market as well. But progress there should not be measured in mechanical terms if it is to be worthy of the name. It isn't a matter of more efficient computerizing or better-organized singles gatherings or even some future form of practicable brain-wave matching. This merely means spinning faster while remaining stationary.

A genuine advance can only be accomplished through mutual recognition of needs and desires and the equally mutual will to respect them. Progress of that kind would do more than ease the competitive pressures of the mating trade. It may even render it obsolete.